Microsoft® Excel™ 2003

Top 100

2nd Edition

Simplified®

TIPS & TRICKS

by David Peal

Visual

WILEY

Microsoft® Excel™ 2003: Top 100 Simplified® Tips & Tricks, 2nd Edition

Published by
Wiley Publishing, Inc.
111 River Street
Hoboken, NJ 07030-5774

Published simultaneously in Canada

Copyright © 2005 by Wiley Publishing, Inc., Indianapolis, Indiana

Library of Congress Control Number:

ISBN: 0-7645-9761-2

Manufactured in the United States of America

10 9 8 7 6 5 4 3 2

2K/QW/QU/QV/IN

Contact Us

For general information on our other products and services contact our Customer Care Department within the U.S. at 800-762-2974, outside the U.S. at 317-572-3993 or fax 317-572-4002.

For technical support please visit www.wiley.com/techsupport.

WILEY

Wiley Publishing, Inc.

U.S. Sales

Contact Wiley at
(800) 762-2974 or
fax (317) 572-4002.

PRAISE FOR VISUAL BOOKS

"I have to praise you and your company on the fine products you turn out. I have twelve Visual books in my house. They were instrumental in helping me pass a difficult computer course. Thank you for creating books that are easy to follow. Keep turning out those quality books."

Gordon Justin (Brielle, NJ)

"What fantastic teaching books you have produced! Congratulations to you and your staff. You deserve the Nobel prize in Education. Thanks for helping me understand computers."

Bruno Tonon (Melbourne, Australia)

"A Picture Is Worth A Thousand Words! If your learning method is by observing or hands-on training, this is the book for you!"

Lorri Pegan-Durastante (Wickliffe, OH)

"Over time, I have bought a number of your 'Read Less - Learn More' books. For me, they are THE way to learn anything easily. I learn easiest using your method of teaching."

José A. Mazón (Cuba, NY)

"You've got a fan for life!! Thanks so much!!"

Kevin P. Quinn (Oakland, CA)

"I have several books from the Visual series and have always found them to be valuable resources."

Stephen P. Miller (Ballston Spa, NY)

"I have several of your Visual books and they are the best I have ever used."

Stanley Clark (Crawfordville, FL)

"Like a lot of other people, I understand things best when I see them visually. Your books really make learning easy and life more fun."

John T. Frey (Cadillac, MI)

"I have quite a few of your Visual books and have been very pleased with all of them. I love the way the lessons are presented!"

Mary Jane Newman (Yorba Linda, CA)

"Thank you, thank you, thank you...for making it so easy for me to break into this high-tech world."

Gay O'Donnell (Calgary, Alberta, Canada)

"I write to extend my thanks and appreciation for your books. They are clear, easy to follow, and straight to the point. Keep up the good work! I bought several of your books and they are just right! No regrets! I will always buy your books because they are the best."

Seward Kollie (Dakar, Senegal)

"I would like to take this time to thank you and your company for producing great and easy-to-learn products. I bought two of your books from a local bookstore, and it was the best investment I've ever made! Thank you for thinking of us ordinary people."

Jeff Eastman (West Des Moines, IA)

"Compliments to the chef!! Your books are extraordinary! Or, simply put, extra-ordinary, meaning way above the rest! THANKYOU THANKYOU THANKYOU! I buy them for friends, family, and colleagues."

Christine J. Manfrin (Castle Rock, CO)

CREDITS

Project Editors
Dana Lesh
Jade Williams

Acquisitions Editor
Jody Lefevere

Product Development Manager
Lindsay Sandman

Copy Editors
Dana Lesh
Jill Mazurczyk

Technical Editor
Allen Wyatt

Editorial Manager
Robyn Siesky

Editorial Assistant
Adrienne Porter

Manufacturing
Allan Conley
Linda Cook
Paul Gilchrist
Jennifer Guynn

Screen Artists
Elizabeth Cardenas-Nelson
Jill Proll

Book Design
Kathie S. Rickard

Production Coordinator
Maridee Ennis

Layout
Jennifer Heleine
Amanda Spagnuolo

Illustrator
Ronda David-Burroughs

Cover Design
Anthony Bunyan

Proofreader
Linda Quigley

Quality Control
Brian H. Walls

Indexer
Sherry Massey

**Vice President and Executive
Group Publisher**
Richard Swadley

Vice President and Publisher
Barry Pruett

Composition Director
Debbie Stailey

AUTHOR'S ACKNOWLEDGMENTS

This book was fun to write, and I hope you find it useful to read. Many people made it possible. At Wiley Publishing, special thanks to publishers Barry Pruett and Richard Swadley; to Media Development Supervisor Rich Graves for his continued support; to Acquisitions Editor Jody Lefevere for giving me the chance to write this book; to master juggler and product manager Jade Williams for her wise guidance; to Technical Editor Allen Wyatt for sharing his technical expertise; to copy editors Jill Mazurczyk and Dana Lesh. This is also the place to express my more private gratitude to my wife Carol and my two budding Office adepts, Gabriel and Ella.

HOW TO USE THIS BOOK

Excel 2003: Top 100 Simplified® Tips & Tricks includes 100 tasks that reveal cool secrets, teach timesaving tricks, and explain great tips guaranteed to make you more productive with Excel 2003. The easy-to-use layout lets you work through all the tasks from beginning to end or jump in at random.

Who Is This Book For?

You already know Excel 2003 basics. Now you'd like to go beyond, with shortcuts, tricks and tips that let you work smarter and faster. And because you learn more easily when someone *shows* you how, this is the book for you.

Conventions Used In This Book

① Steps

This book uses step-by-step instructions to guide you easily through each task. Numbered callouts on every screen shot show you exactly how to perform each task, step by step.

② Tips

Practical tips provide insights to save you time and trouble, caution you about hazards to avoid, and reveal how to do things in Excel 2003 that you never thought possible!

③ Task Numbers

Task numbers from 1 to 100 indicate which lesson you are working on.

④ Difficulty Levels

For quick reference, the symbols below mark the difficulty level of each task.

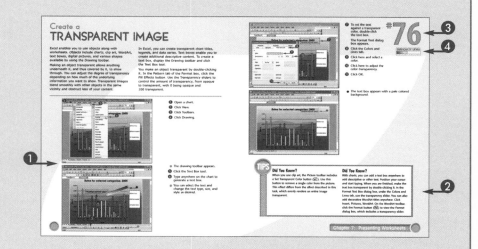

DIFFICULTY LEVEL	
DIFFICULTY LEVEL	Demonstrates a new spin on a common task
DIFFICULTY LEVEL	Introduces a new skill or a new task
DIFFICULTY LEVEL	Combines multiple skills requiring in-depth knowledge
DIFFICULTY LEVEL	Requires extensive skill and may involve other technologies

Table of Contents

1 Working with Data

2 Working with Formulas and Functions

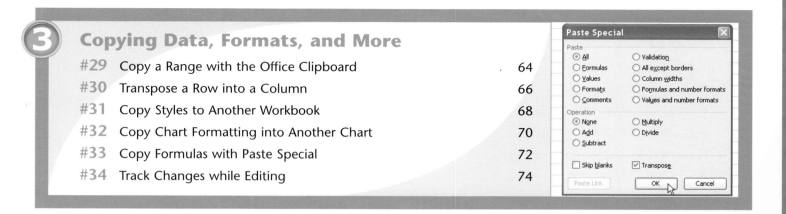

③ Copying Data, Formats, and More

④ Using Excel Lists

Table of Contents

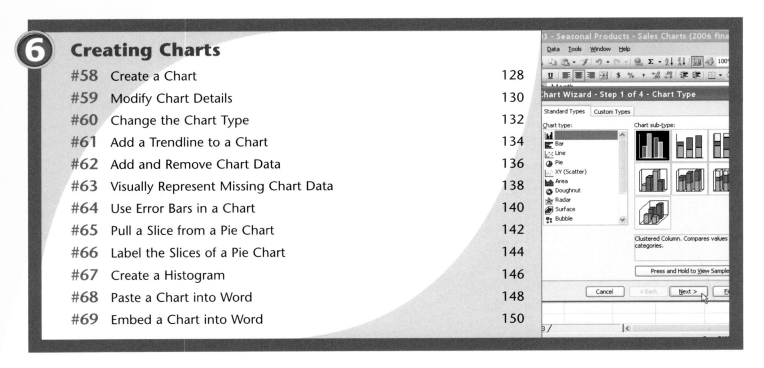

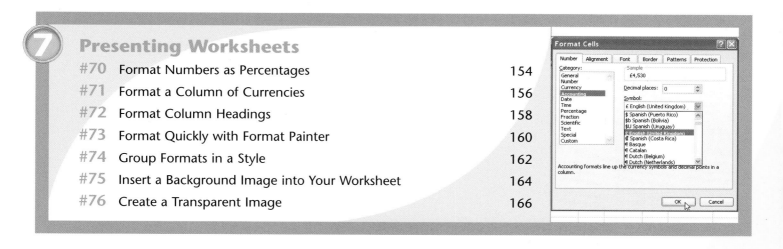

Table of Contents

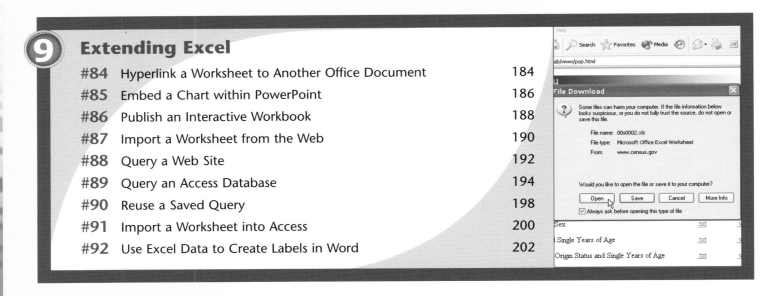
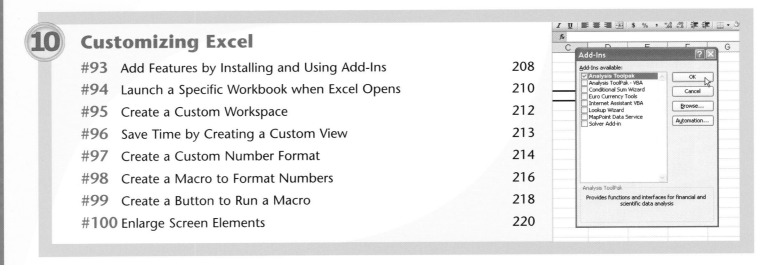

Working with Data

When you use Excel, you are primarily working with *numbers*. Wherever you use numbers in your life — doing taxes, running a small business, planning a vacation, analyzing investments, maintaining a budget, keeping track of a coin collection, or something else — Excel can probably help make your work easier, quicker, and more accurate. With Excel, you can also explore new ways of entering, presenting, and analyzing your information.

To get the most from Excel 2003, you need to be able to enter and work with whole numbers, decimals, fractions, dates, and times. This chapter shows you how to make data entry more efficient. Using a *pick list* narrowly restricts data entry to a set of numbers and other values that you define, thus minimizing error. The Excel AutoFill feature lets you fill a row or column with a series of numbers, dates,

or times automatically generated from one or more values. This chapter also shows you how to incorporate symbols and special characters in your worksheets.

Two techniques for viewing your information allow you to compare different parts of your worksheet: freezing panes and outlining. Both temporarily hide part of your worksheet to make comparisons easier.

Two data-entry tasks can be indispensable for people with disabilities, and for anyone who wants an occasional alternative way of entering data: by keyboard instead of mouse, and by voice. Finding and replacing data is a useful technique regardless of how you enter data. Finally, you learn in this chapter about InfoPath, which makes it easier to generate a wide variety of complex business worksheets.

Top 100

Enter
NUMBERS AND FRACTIONS

With Excel, you can type all kinds of numbers. The simplest kind of number is the whole number, such as seven (7). Excel is a spreadsheet program that greatly simplifies the structured and sometimes finicky process of entering and manipulating numbers. Excel can hold other kinds of information, but number processing defines what Excel does best.

A document in Excel is called a *workbook.* New workbook documents consist of three worksheets. With Excel, you can add more worksheets at any time. Each worksheet is a grid of rows and columns. The columns are indicated by letters, and the rows by numbers. A *cell* is the unit of every worksheet where you enter numbers. Each cell has a unique address, defined by a row and column, such as D5.

You can also enter fractions and have them appear in either decimal form (.75) or as fractions (¾). All numbers you type in Excel appear both in the cell and in the formula bar above the worksheet.

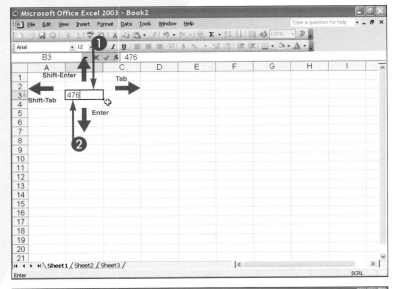

ENTER A WHOLE NUMBER

① Click a cell.

② Type the number.

③ Press Enter to move down one cell.

To move one cell to the right, press Tab.

The number moves to the right side of the cell in which it is entered.

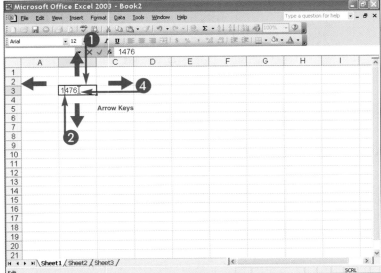

EDIT A NUMBER

① Double-click its cell.

② Press the arrow keys to position the cursor before the number to change.

③ To delete numbers, press Delete.

④ To insert numbers, type the numbers in a cell.

⑤ Press Enter, or Tab, or click another cell to go on to the next task.

4

ENTER A FRACTION

① Click a cell.

② Type a whole number followed by a space and the fraction.

③ Press Enter, or Tab, or click another cell to go on to the next task.

The fraction appears in the cell.

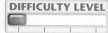

DIFFICULTY LEVEL

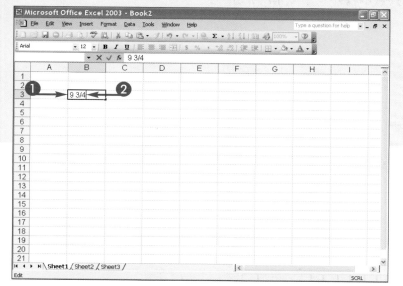

CONVERT A FRACTION INTO A DECIMAL

① Click a cell.

② Type an equal sign (=).

③ Type the whole number followed by a space and the fraction.

④ Press Enter.

● The decimal appears in the cell, while the equal sign is still visible in the formula bar.

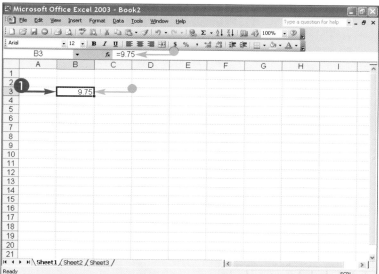

TIPS

Apply It!

To change a fraction into a decimal, you can also enter it into a cell and reformat it. Click the cell, and then click Format and Cell. The Format Cells dialog box appears. Under the Number tab, click Number in the category list. In the Decimal Places box, indicate how many places to the right of the decimal point you want to display. For example, if you format .75 with three decimal points in the Format Cells box, 750 will appear in the cell when you close the box.

Customize It!

After entering a number, you can move the cursor one cell up, down, right, or left. To set this option, click Tools and Options. In the Options dialog box, click the Edit tab. Under Settings, select the Move selection after Enter check box. Then click the Direction down arrow and select a setting. Press OK.

Enter
DATES AND TIMES

With Excel you can enter the current date by simply selecting the cell where you want the date to appear and pressing the Ctrl and semicolon (;) keys simultaneously.

For past and future dates, you have many ways to enter dates, including: Aug 1, 1914; August 1, 1914; 1 Aug 1914; 08-01-1914; 8-1-1914; 08/01/1914; and 8/1/1914.

Each date format has at least one non-numeric character such as a forward slash (/), comma (,) hyphen (-), or text as in a month's name or abbreviation. For years between 1930 and 2029,

you can enter a year as two digits (31). For the sake of formatting consistency across worksheets, however, it is a good idea to use four digits to represent years, for example, 1931.

Times are simpler to enter. Enter the current time by pressing Ctrl+Shift and pressing the semicolon key (;) simultaneously. For other times, hours and minutes each consist of one or two digits, separated by a colon, such as 11:11 AM. A leading zero is not necessary, as in 3:00. Excel assumes that a time is AM unless you indicate otherwise by typing PM.

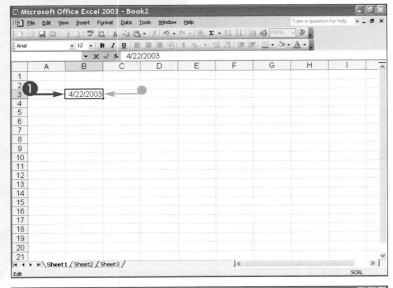

ENTER CURRENT DATE

1 Click the cell where the date is to appear.

2 Press Ctrl.

3 Type a semicolon (;).

4 Press Enter.

● The current date appears in the cell.

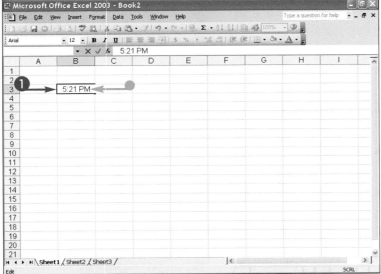

ENTER CURRENT TIME

1 Click the cell where the date is to appear.

2 Press Ctrl+Shift.

3 Type a semicolon (;).

4 Press Enter.

● The current time appears in the cell.

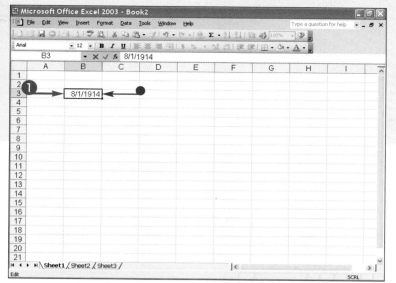

Enter a Date

1 Click the cell where the date is to appear.

2 Type a date.

3 Press Enter.

● The date appears in the cell, formatted according to the current settings for that cell.

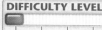
DIFFICULTY LEVEL

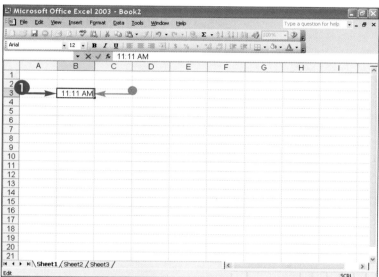

Enter a Time

1 Click the cell where the time is to appear.

2 Type a time.

3 Press Enter.

● The time appears in the cell, formatted according to the current settings for that cell.

TIPS

Did You Know?

To change the way a date or time appears in a cell, click its cell. Click Format and then Cells. In the Format Cells dialog box, in the Number tab, click Date in the Category list on the left. Click a format from the Type list on the right. Note that each format has an example showing the format. Click OK. Use this technique for applying the same format to all the dates or times by selecting more than one cell before clicking Format and then Cells.

Did You Know?

Countries differ in their standards for representing times and dates, as well as currencies and numbers. To change the default standards for your computer, open the Regional and Language Options control panel. Under the Regional Options tab, select a different country. Click OK.

Name
CELLS AND RANGES

Excel allows you to name individual cells and groups of cells, called *ranges*. A cell named NY_Sales_Tax or a range named State_Populations is easier to remember than the corresponding cell addresses. You can use named cells and ranges directly in formulas to refer to the values contained in the cells. When you move a range to a new location, any formulas referring to the range are adjusted automatically. The cell addresses for a range change automatically if values are inserted into or removed from it.

To name a cell or range of cells, click the cell or click and drag to select the range. Open the Define Name dialog box. Enter a name in the first field and click OK.

Use short, memorable names when possible. Excel range names must be fewer than 255 characters. The first character must be a letter. Spaces and symbols are not allowed, except the period and underscore. To use a name, see Task #18.

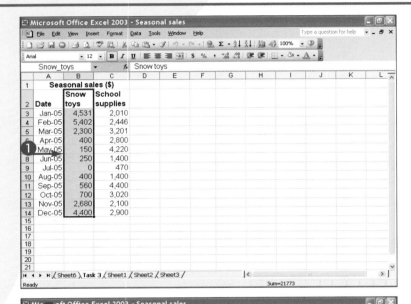

NAME A RANGE OF CELLS

① Click and drag to select the cells you want to include in the range.

You can alternatively click a cell with a value to create a named cell.

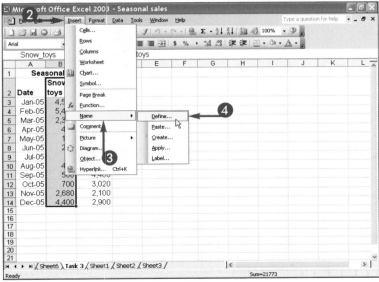

② Click Insert.

③ Click Name.

④ Click Define.

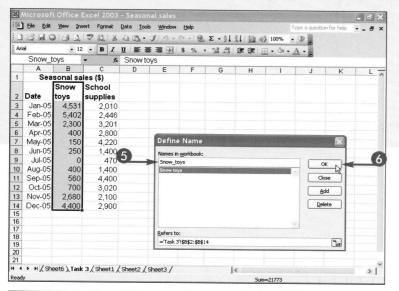

The Define Name dialog box appears.

5 Type a name for the range.

6 Click OK.

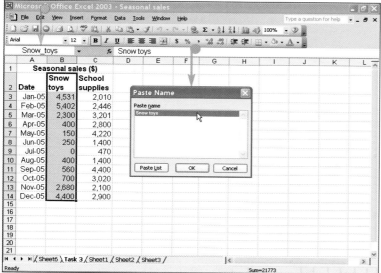

● The defined name is now available from the Names box.

● It is also available in the Paste Name box (click Insert, Define, and Paste).

TIPS

Did You Know?

To copy a range anywhere, highlight the range, right-click and select Copy. Then click the first cell of the new location, right-click and select Paste. To move a range, select Cut instead of Copy.

Did You Know?

To name several cells or ranges, click the first cell or range you want to name and then click Insert, Name, and Define. In the dialog box, name the range in the first field and then click Add. To select the next cell or range to name, type its name into the Names in the workbook field. Click the button to the right of Refers to, and then click the cell to name. Click Add. Repeat for each cell or range name you want to add. When you are finished, click OK.

Validate data entry using a
PICK LIST

Excel enables you to restrict the values you can enter into certain cells. By restricting values, you ensure that your worksheet entries are valid, increasing the likelihood that calculations based on them are also valid. Remember that inaccurate sales data can result in incorrect reports and faulty planning.

Creating a *pick list* restricts the entries that you can enter into a cell. During data entry, a pick list forces you or someone using your workbook to click a value from a drop-down menu rather than typing it — and potentially typing it wrong. Pick lists save time and reduce errors.

Another type of validation does not restrict entries to specific values but instead ensures that information has the correct format, whole number or decimal, or falls within a range of values that you define as acceptable. For this type of validation, you can provide instructions to users about what to type; the instructions appear when the cell is selected. Similarly, you can create an error message that appears after a value has been entered.

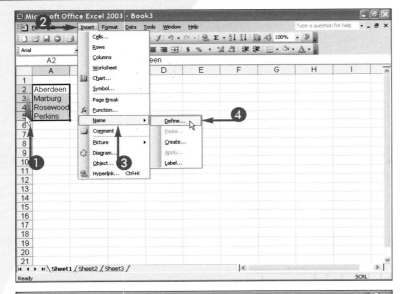

CREATE A PICK LIST

Before creating a pick list, type the values you want in the pick list into adjacent cells in a column.

① Click and drag to select the list.

② Click Insert.

③ Click Name.

④ Click Define.

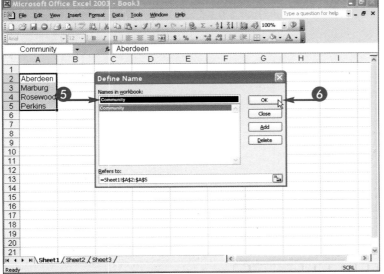

The Define Name dialog box appears.

⑤ Type a name for the list.

⑥ Click OK.

Repeat steps **1** to **5** for each pick list.

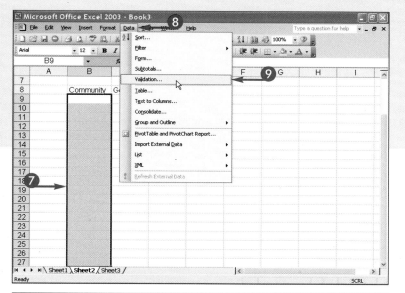

7 Click the empty cells requiring the pick list.

8 Click Data.

9 Click Validation.

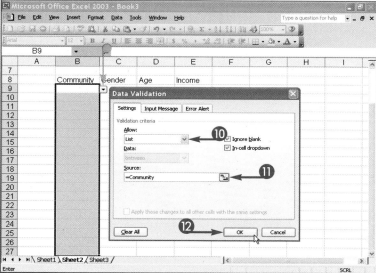

The Data Validation dialog box opens.

10 Click List.

11 Type = and the name defined in step **5**.

12 Click OK.

● A drop-down list appears to the right of each cell selected in step **7**.

To enter data in a cell, click the drop-down menu and click a value.

Did You Know?

You can use the same pick list with different columns in a worksheet. You can also create different pick lists within a column. You can even create input messages without pick lists, to provide tips for data entry without constraining the user's choices.

Did You Know?

Pick lists need not consist of numbers. You can create a pick list consisting of the names of regions, employees, products, and so on.

Did You Know?

To remove the validation drop-down list, click any cell with the settings to remove, then click Edit and Go To. In the Go To dialog box, click the Special button. In the Go To Special dialog box, select Validation and then Same below it. Click OK. From the menu, click Data and then Validation. In the Data Validation dialog box, click Clear All and OK.

Extend a series of dates with
AUTOFILL

Autofill gives you a way of ensuring accurate data entry when a particular data series has an intrinsic order: days of the week, a data series with increments of .2, and so on.

Using AutoFill requires that you first type one or more values from which to generate other values. First, click the cell you want to extend. Selecting two or more cells determines the step size, or increment, by which you want to jump in each cell. With the cell selected, click the Fill handle in the lower-right corner. With the handle selected, your cursor appears like a cross. When several cells are selected, the fill

handle appears in the lower right of the last cell in the range. Drag the Fill handle to extend the series.

When you release the mouse button, Excel fills in the cell values. If it is unclear how to extend the series, Excel provides a menu icon, which you click to select fill series, fill weekdays, or whatever is appropriate in your case. A context menu pops up to let you select whether to copy the values, fill the series one day at a time, or extend it by weekdays, months, or years. You can copy or extend your data with or without formatting.

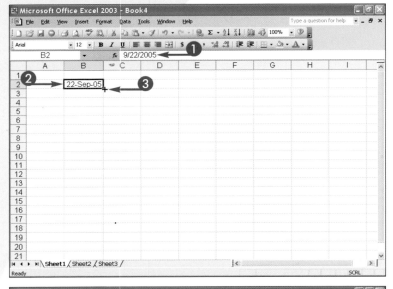

EXTEND A DATE

① Type a date.

   Note: To enter a date, see Task #2.

② Right-click the cell.

   You can also left-click.

③ Click the Fill handle
   (⇧ changes to ✛).

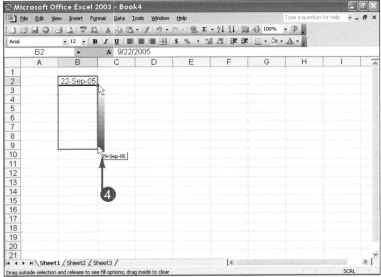

④ Drag the cell to include your desired number of cells.

⑤ Release the mouse button.

A menu appears.

⑥ Click your menu choice.

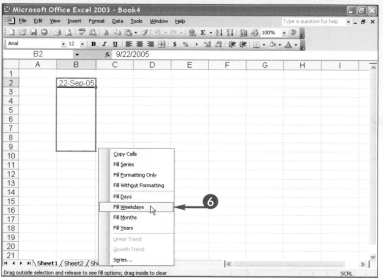

● The extended series reflects the choice.

To format an extended date series, click the cells, right-click, click Format Cells, click Date, and apply a format. Click OK.

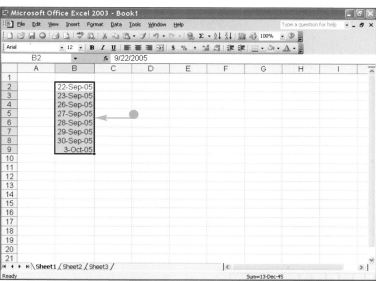

Did You Know?

When you right-click to extend a time, you can click Series to increment the series an hour at a time. To extend a series by a custom interval, type any number in the Step value of the Series dialog box. Then click OK.

Did You Know?

When you are making text entries, Excel attempts to guess, or *autocomplete*, the values of subsequent entries in adjacent cells in the same row or column. If you type **Brushes** in one cell (B2) and **Combs** in the cell immediately below (B3), typing letter C into cell B4 prompts Excel to complete the entry by filling in the letters **omb.** If more than one entry begins with the same letter — Brushes and Bibs — Excel autocompletes the entry when you have finished typing the letters that the multiple entries share.

Add a
SYMBOL OR SPECIAL CHARACTER

In Excel, you are not restricted to the standard numerals, letters, and punctuation marks on your keyboard. You can also select from hundreds of *special characters* such as foreign letters, and currency characters such as the Euro (€). Each font has a different set of special characters. A smaller set of standard characters, called *symbols,* is always available as well, including dashes, hyphens, and quotation marks.

Symbols and special characters serve many uses in Excel. Many financial applications, for example, call for currency symbols. Symbols and special characters are useful in column and row heads, as part of the text describing column and row content, for example, Net sales in €.

Using symbols and special characters in the same cell with a value like number, date, and time usually prevents the value from being used in a formula. You cannot, for example, add €100 and €100. However, including *(in €)* in the row or column head makes it unnecessary to include the currency symbol with a particular value.

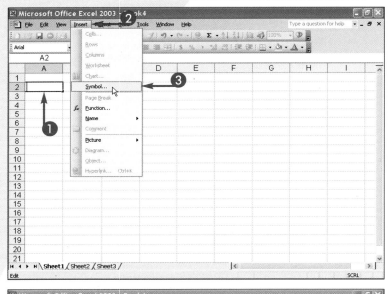

ADD A SYMBOL

1. Click the cell in which you want to insert a character.

2. Click Insert.

3. Click Symbol.

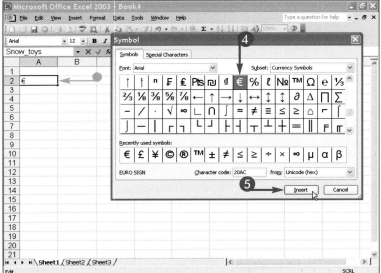

The Symbol dialog box appears.

4. To insert a symbol, locate the character and click it.

5. Click Insert.

● The character appears in the cell.

14

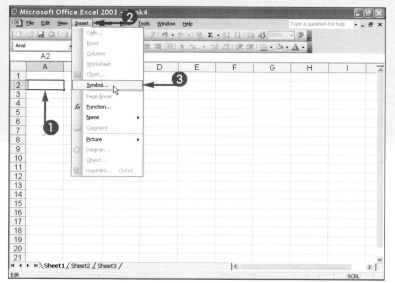

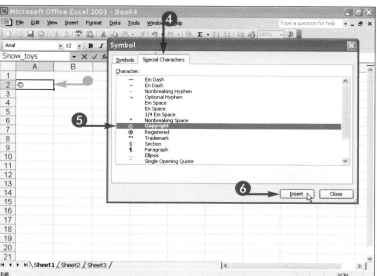

1 Click the cell in which you want to insert a character.

2 Click Insert.

3 Click Symbol.

The Symbol dialog box appears.

4 Click the Special Characters tab.

5 Locate the character and click it.

6 Click Insert.

● The character appears in the cell.

Did You Know?

In Excel, numbers, dates, and times are by default right-aligned. Ordinary letters and special characters are left-aligned. Only right-aligned values can be used in numeric calculations. Left-aligned values are treated as blanks — zeroes — in calculations. To have a currency symbol appear with a value, as in $400, such that the cell value can be used in a calculation, click Format and Cells and then apply the currency or accounting format to the cells. For more about formatting currencies, see Task #71.

Did You Know?

Excel fonts are based on *Unicode*, a set of 40,000 characters enabling the display of unique characters from approximately 80 languages, including right-to-left alphabets like Hebrew. To use a language other than English and set up an appropriate keyboard, click the Windows Start Menu, click Control Panel, and click Regional and Language Options. Use the Regional tab to choose another language and the Languages tab to set up the keyboard. Some Asian languages require that you download special fonts.

Compare multiple spreadsheets using
FREEZE PANES

When your rows or columns get long, it becomes difficult to see all entries without scrolling the worksheet. Excel enables you to *freeze* one of two rows or columns that cannot display in the same screen for comparing. You can then drag the second window next to it, enabling you to compare the two.

The simplest way of doing this is to select the column or row with the data you want to compare and freeze it by clicking Window, Freeze Pane. A black line represents the border between the frozen and

non-frozen parts. To compare the frozen row with another row, you drag the other border of the row toward the black line. To drag a border, click the line separating one row number and another and drag it.

Excel offers an alternative way of comparing parts of a screen that does not involve freezing. By clicking and dragging the Split box at the top of the right-hand scroll bar, you can divide a worksheet into two halves, each of which you can scroll separately.

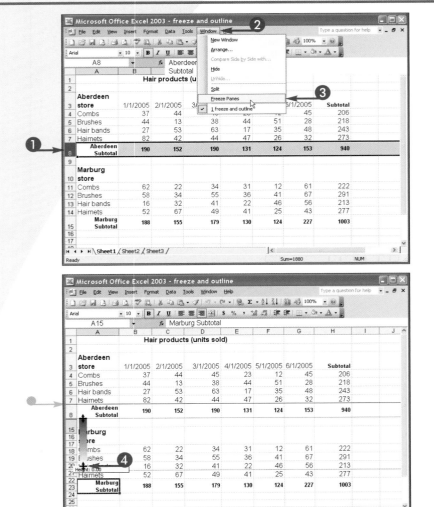

FREEZE A ROW

① Click the number of the row on the far left to highlight the row for freezing.

You can also select a row by clicking a cell and pressing Shift+Spacebar.

② Click Window.

③ Click Freeze Panes.

Alternatively, you can click and drag the Split box to divide the worksheet into two separately scrollable parts. For more information on splitting, see Task #100.

● A black line defines the border between the frozen pane and the rest of the worksheet.

④ To drag a row to the black line, click the border between two row numbers on the far left and drag the border toward the black line.

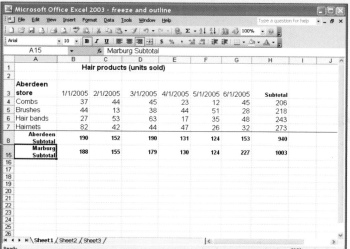

You can now compare the rows.

- Notice the gap in row numbering. Several rows are temporarily hidden.

  Rows on either side of the line can be dragged to the line and compared there.

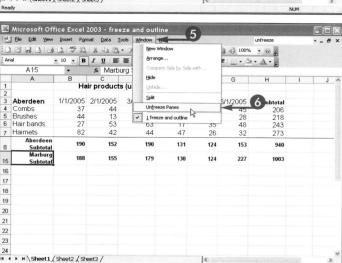

⑤ To remove the black line and unfreeze the panes, click Window.

⑥ Click Unfreeze Panes.

TIPS

Did You Know?

You can hide an entire worksheet by clicking Window and then Hide.

Did You Know?

Unfreezing a worksheet does not always restore the previous view of your spreadsheet. To redisplay rows, click Window and then Unfreeze. Select the entire worksheet by clicking Ctrl+A or clicking in the cell to the left of the A at the very top of the worksheet. Carefully click and drag one of the row's borders, for example, separating 1 and 2 in the column on the far right. All rows assume the height of the row whose border you dragged.

Did You Know?

Outlining provides another way to compare non-adjacent parts of a worksheet, as shown in Task #8. Both work especially well with lists, a type of worksheet discussed in Chapter 4. Sorting a list allows you to display rows in subgroups that share an attribute, for example, all rows for people who live within a certain community. With lists, you can perform a calculation for a subgroup and then compare subgroups using freezing and outlining.

Hide rows to compare data with
OUTLINING

You can use the Excel Outline feature to temporarily hide a set of rows. For example, you can hide the details relating to weekly sales in order to compare monthly sales. With outlining, you can hide several sets of rows, and compare more than two rows. You can apply outlining to columns as well as rows, but hiding rows is more common.

Outlining a set of rows creates a clickable button on the far left of the worksheet. The button displays either a Minus sign or a Plus sign, depending on what is displayed in the worksheet. You can click the Minus

sign to hide rows or columns and the Plus sign to display them again. Adjacent to the button is a solid vertical line that indicates, by its length, the scope of the hidden details and the approximate number of rows or columns hidden.

Outlining was designed for use with structured information called lists, but can be used with any worksheet. When you outline a PivotTable, outlining has the same effect as in an ordinary worksheet, as shown in Task #54.

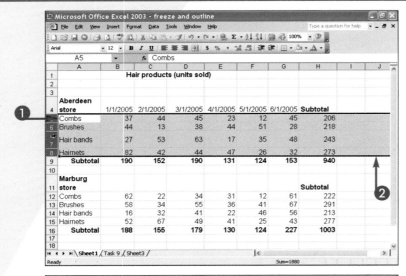

① Position 🔓 on the first row of the set of rows to hide.

② Click and drag to select the other rows to hide.

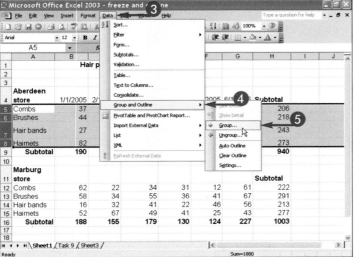

③ Click Data.

④ Click Group and Outline.

⑤ Click Group.

You can also select the rows and press Shift+Alt+Right Arrow.

You can repeat steps **1** to **4** to hide other rows or columns.

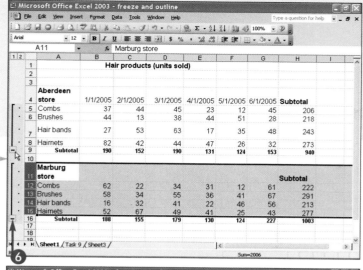

- Excel creates a new left margin with a Minus sign that you click to hide the rows.

⑥ To hide the rows, click the Minus sign.

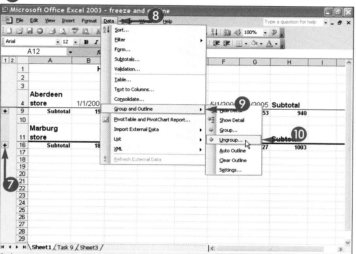

The rows disappear and the Plus sign replaces the Minus sign.

- To display the rows again, click the Plus sign.

⑦ To remove an outline, display it by clicking the Plus sign.

⑧ Click Data.

⑨ Click Group and Outline.

⑩ Click Ungroup.

TIPS

Did You Know?

You can *nest* outlines with one group of outlined rows contained within another. You can outline each product, and then hide certain rows to compare the others. Or, you could hide all of the products and just compare the product subtotals.

Did You Know?

You can compare data by freezing panes. This method provides a quick way to compare different parts of a worksheet but is more cumbersome to remove. For more about freezing panes, see Task #7.

Access Excel by
KEYBOARD

If you have a visual impairment, it can be difficult to see the mouse cursor and view the visual feedback that results from mouse clicks. Fortunately, you can interact with Excel in many ways, not just by a mouse. You can use keyboard alternatives to perform common mouse actions. Everyone potentially benefits from accessibility options. Even non-impaired users find keyboard alternatives faster than using the mouse.

Keyboard alternatives apply to the basic actions of moving the cursor, making menu choices, and

entering data. In addition, you can accomplish many specific tasks by keyboard. For example, to generate a chart based on a worksheet where the cursor arrow is positioned, press F11. To outline rows, select the rows and press Shift+Alt+Right Arrow.

To find out more about Office accessibility features, press F1 and type **accessibility** in the Search field of the task pane. For another accessibility technique, speech recognition, see Task #10.

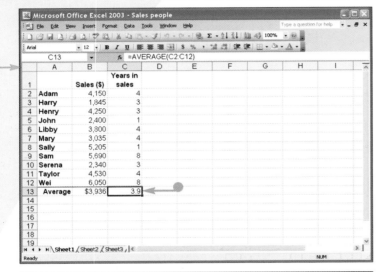

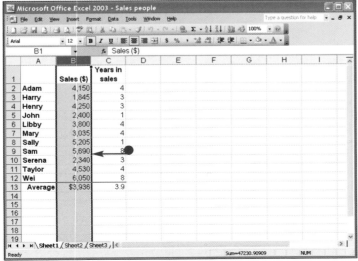

SELECT CELLS

To select an entire worksheet, press Ctrl+A.

● To highlight the worksheet using the mouse, click the cell in the uppermost left corner.

● To select a cell, use the arrow keys to move to it.

To select a row, use the arrow keys to move to the first cell in the row and press Ctrl+Shift and the right arrow several times.

● To select a column, use the arrow keys to move to a cell in the row and press Ctrl+Shift and the down arrow several times.

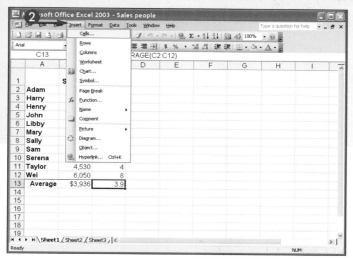

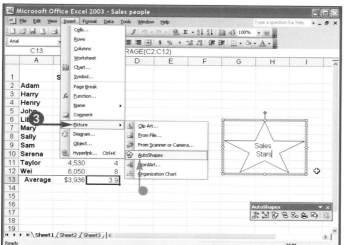

SELECT FROM MENU

1 Press Alt.

2 Press the underscored letter of the menu.

The menu appears.

3 Press the underscored letter of the menu option you want.

● If there is a submenu, press the underscored letter of the option you want.

TIP

Useful Keyboard Shortcuts	
Shortcut	*Function*
Alt+Underscored letter of menu name	Select a menu from an Excel menu
Underscored letter of menu command	Select the menu command
Alt+Enter	Display the choices in a drop-down menu
Up- and Down-arrow keys	Select an item in a drop-down menu
Tab	Move to the next item in a dialog box
Shift+Tab	Move to the previous item
Ctrl+PageDown or PageUp	Move to the next or previous worksheet in a workbook
PageUp or PageDown	Go up or down a screen within a worksheet
Home	Jump to first cell in a row
Ctrl+Home	Jump to first cell in a sheet
End	Jump to last cell in a row
Ctrl+End	Jump to last cell in a sheet

Access Excel by voice with
SPEECH RECOGNITION

Speech recognition allows visually impaired users to communicate with a computer by speaking rather than by typing at the keyboard or clicking mouse buttons. The non-impaired may prefer speech recognition because of its convenience and increasing reliability. When using speech recognition, you can also type and use the mouse at any time.

To use speech recognition, you must plug a computer microphone into the USB or audio jack in your PC. To use the microphone for data entry, you must then install speech recognition for Microsoft Office applications. For instructions, click F1, search for speech recognition, and read the article called *Install and train speech recognition*.

To train Office to recognize your voice, click the Windows Start menu, select Control Panels, and double-click Speech. In the Speech Properties box, click Configure Microphone. Read and follow the instructions. When you are finished, return to the Speech Properties box. Click Training Profile, and follow the instructions for teaching Speech Recognition to learn about your voice. You may need to read multiple passages for the software to recognize your voice. It takes considerable training and use for the software to become adept at recognizing your voice.

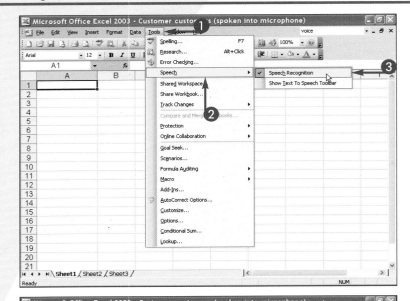

ENTER DATA WITH SPEECH RECOGNITION

1. Click Tools.

2. Click Speech.

3. Click Speech Recognition.

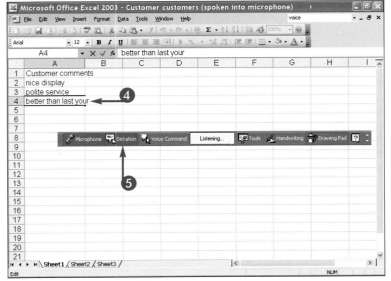

The Language toolbar appears.

4. Click the first cell for data entry.

5. Say **dictation** or click the Dictation button.

6. Speak the numbers or words into the microphone.

Say **Enter**.

Repeat steps **4** to **6** for other values you want to enter.

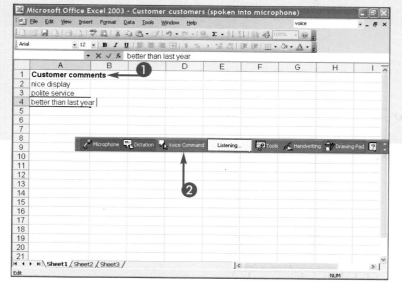

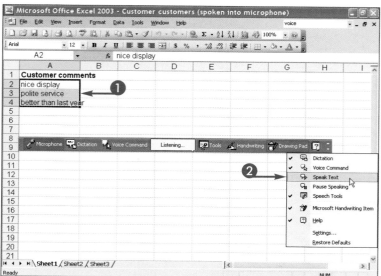

EDIT SPOKEN DATA

1. To bold text, click the cell or say its address.

2. Click or say Voice Command.

3. Say **bold**.

4. To correct an error in a cell, repeat steps **1** to **2**, then in step **3**, say **Delete**.

5. Speak the numbers or words again, or type them in.

CONVERT DATA INTO SPEECH

1. To have Excel read back the values you have entered, click and drag to select them.

2. Click the Speak Text button and select Speak Text.

TIPS

Did You Know?

Speech recognition has two modes, Dictation and Voice Command. Use *Dictation* to enter data or other values and *Voice Command* to use menus, menu commands, and dialog boxes. To switch between modes, you can use the Language bar, an unusual floating toolbar that becomes available when you select Tools, Speech, and then Speech Recognition. This toolbar, when minimized, appears at the bottom of your screen. To restore it, right-click it and select Restore Language Bar.

Caution!

To improve the accuracy of your spoken data entry, spend extra time training the Office speech recognition tool. Using the Speech control panel, click Train Profile, read one of the passages provided, and repeat for several passages. Speak at a normal volume and consistent rate. Hold the microphone at the same distance from your mouth throughout.

FIND AND REPLACE DATA

Cells can contain numbers, text, comments, formats, and formulas. With Excel, you can search for any of these elements to view them, replace them, or perform some other action. You may, for example, find and replace values to correct mistakes, or perhaps you need to return to a value to add a comment or apply formatting.

The Excel Find and Replace dialog box is available in two ways: by clicking Edit and Find, or by pressing the Ctrl+F keys on your keyboard. The Find feature is part of Find and Replace, which is available to you by clicking Edit, Replace or pressing Ctrl+H.

To find and replace values, you need to specify which characters you are seeking and their replacement. Click the Options button to specify additional details. Use the Within drop-down menu to indicate where to search: the current worksheet or current workbook. Use the Look in drop-down menu to indicate whether to search within a formula or within the displayed cell content. Click the Formatting button to restrict your search to characters formatted in a certain way, such as bold or percentages.

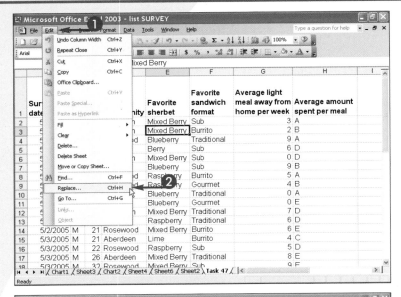

REPLACE A VALUE

① Click Edit.

② Click Replace.

You can alternatively press Ctrl+F to open the Find and Replace dialog box.

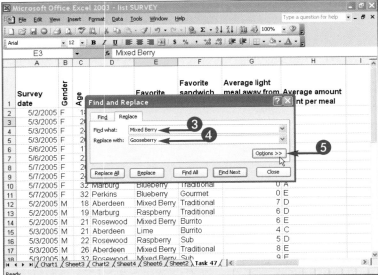

The Find and Replace dialog box appears.

③ Type the characters you want to change.

④ Type the replacement characters.

⑤ Click Options for more details.

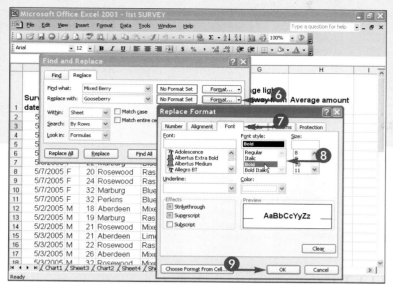

The expanded Find and Replace dialog box appears.

⑥ To search for characters formatted in a certain way, click Format.

The Replace Format dialog box appears.

⑦ Click a tab.

⑧ Select your options as appropriate.

⑨ Click OK.

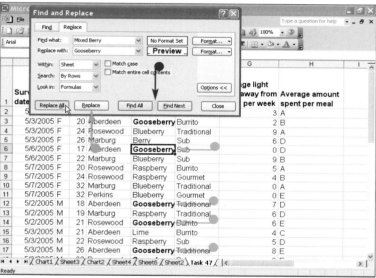

● The replacements are made.

● You can click Replace to make one change at a time.

● If you do not want to replace values, click Find All or Find Next to highlight cells in the worksheet but not replace values.

Did You Know?

To find a value, formula, or comment in another workbook, click the Open folder on the toolbar. In the Open dialog box, click the Tools menu in the upper-right corner, and click Search. In the Search for drop-down menu, type your search text. In the Search in drop-down menu, specify which disk to search. In the Results should be drop-down menu, click the Excel check box. Click Search.

Did You Know?

The Format button has a drop-down menu that gives you the option of defining a format based on an existing cell. From the submenu, click Choose Format from Another Cell. Use the eyedropper symbol to click a cell whose format you want to apply to the cell you are seeking.

Generate a worksheet with
INFOPATH

You can use InfoPath to quickly generate complex Excel worksheets. InfoPath and OneNote are new to the Office suite. Both were designed to extend the capabilities of individual Office applications such as Excel. For more about OneNote, which enables you to jot down virtually limitless notes about one or more documents, see Task #16.

InfoPath is a separate Office program. It allows designers to create and export forms to the Web or to Excel, where they automatically generate a new worksheet. InfoPath also includes numerous ready-made forms for immediate use in specific business tasks, such as expense reports, purchase orders, and sales reports. When you choose a form, you find a simple interface consisting of data entry fields, pre-filled menus, check boxes, and buttons. You fill out information one record at a time.

Values entered into InfoPath can then be exported into Excel for analysis and charting. Additional data can be supplied through the InfoPath form or within Excel, using automatically created forms. To create your own InfoPath forms, start with InfoPath Help by pressing F1.

Generate a Worksheet with Infopath

① Double-click the InfoPath icon.

The InfoPath application appears.

② To start a new form, click More Forms.

The Forms window appears, with the first item selected.

③ Double-click a form to open it.

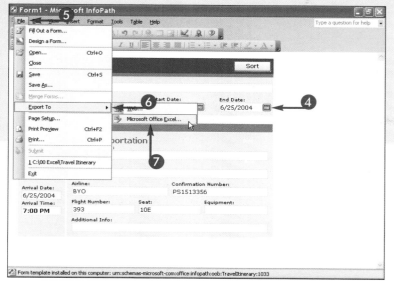

The specific form appears with blank fields.

④ Type your values.

To select a date, click the Calendar icon and navigate to the appropriate date.

⑤ Click File.

⑥ Click Export To.

⑦ Click Microsoft Office Excel.

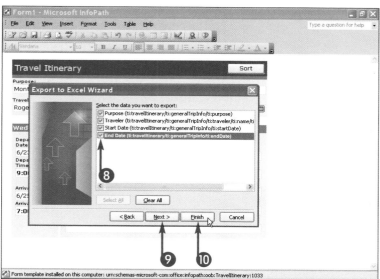

The Export to Excel Wizard appears.

⑧ Click to select the data you want to export.

⑨ Click Next to continue through the screen options.

⑩ Click Finish when you are done.

Excel displays a worksheet based on the form.

You will need to edit the column heads to remove the references to the InfoPath source data.

TIPS

Did You Know?
Fields and values imported from InfoPath into Excel form the basis of an Excel list. To use Excel for data entry, place your cursor in the list, click Data and then Form. For more about Excel lists, see Chapter 4.

Did You Know?
InfoPath field names appear as Excel column heads, and values entered in InfoPath appear in columns. Edit columns so that only key words appear.

Did You Know?
InfoPath simplifies date entry. In date fields, you click the Calendar button, and then click the appropriate month and day, using the Greater Than and Less Than buttons to cycle through months.

Working with Formulas and Functions

Excel provides you with tools for storing numbers and other kinds of information. Its real power comes from manipulating all this information. The more than 300 functions built into Excel enable you to perform tasks of every kind, from adding numbers to calculating the internal rate of return for an investment.

You can think of a function as a black box. You put your information into the box, and out comes the results that you want. You do not need to know any obscure algorithms to use these functions.

Each bit of information that you provide is called an *argument*. Excel's Function Wizard provides guidance for every argument for every function. A *formula* consists of an equal sign; one or more functions; their arguments; operators, such as the division and multiplication symbols; and any other values required to get your results.

Many Excel functions do special-purpose financial, statistical, engineering, and mathematical calculations. The Function Wizard arranges functions in categories for easy access. The Payment function in the Financial category, for example, enables you to determine an optimal loan payment given principal, interest rate, and length of the loan.

This chapter introduces useful techniques for making formulas and functions even easier, including the Function Wizard and the Excel calculator. You can also find tips for working more efficiently with functions by naming cells, creating constants, and documenting your work. Finally, you can find tips for using generally both useful functions such as IF and special-purpose functions such as Payment and IRR.

Top 100

ADD VALUES
in different ways

In Excel, you can carry out calculations, such as simple addition, in three ways. One method is to use the familiar plus sign (+). In a cell, type an equal sign and the values to be added, each separated by the addition operator, for example, **=457 + 231**. Press Enter and Excel does the math and displays the answer in the same cell.

A second method involves the Sum function, Sum(). Functions perform calculations on your information and then make the results available to you. To use the Sum() function, you type an equal sign and sum() directly in the cell where you want the result to appear. Place the numbers you want to add inside the parentheses, separating them with commas. If the numbers are on the worksheet, click the cells. Excel adds the value in those cells.

A third method is to use Excel's AutoSum feature, which offers a point-and-click interface for several functions, including Sum(), Average(), and Count(). Enter the numbers to add in a worksheet. From a blank cell, click the AutoSum button, or click Sum and then click and drag the cells containing the numbers.

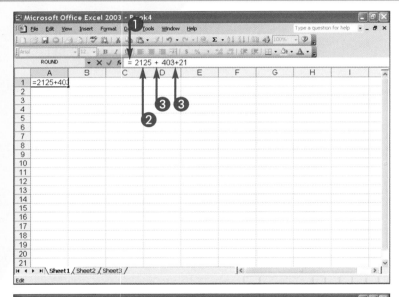

ADD NUMBERS USING AN OPERATOR

❶ Type = in the formula bar.

❷ Type the first number to be added.

❸ Type +.

❹ Type the next number to be added.

❺ Repeat steps **3** and **4** for other numbers to add.

❻ Press Enter.

The result appears in the cell.

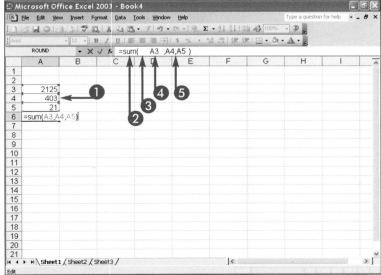

ADD WITH A FUNCTION AND CELL ADDRESSES

❶ Type the numbers to add into adjacent cells.

❷ In another cell, type = followed by **sum()**.

❸ Click inside the parentheses.

❹ Click to select the first number you want to add.

❺ Drag to select additional numbers you want to add.

❻ Press Enter.

The result appears in the cell.

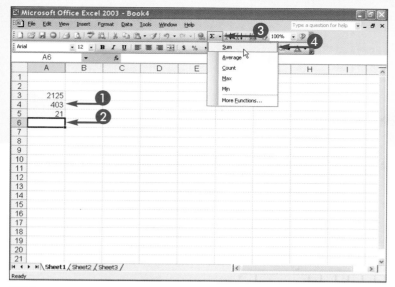

ADD NUMBERS USING AUTOSUM

1 In adjacent cells, type the numbers to add.

2 Click the cell where you want the result.

3 Click the AutoSum button.

4 Click Sum.

DIFFICULTY LEVEL

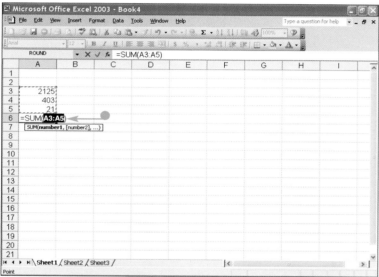

● Excel places **=sum()** in the cell, with the cursor between the parentheses, with adjacent cell addresses ready to be added.

5 To accept the cell addresses chosen by Excel, press Enter.

6 To select other addresses, click and drag them.

The result appears in the cell selected in step **2**.

Did You Know?

When typing an Excel formula manually, instead of using the Function Wizard, you must precede the function by an equal sign (=). If more than one function is used in a formula, only the first function needs the equal sign. Use the formula bar to simplify data entry.

Did You Know?

When you click to select more than one value in multiple cells, Excel automatically places the sum of the values in the status bar, at the bottom of the screen.

Put It Together!

You can type a function using the Function Wizard; see Task #14. With Excel, you can also sum values that meet certain conditions; see Task #23.

Make magic with the
FUNCTION WIZARD

Excel's Function Wizard simplifies the use of functions and can thus reduce error. You can take advantage of the Wizard for every one of Excel's functions, from Sum() to the most complex statistical, mathematical, financial, and engineering function. One simple but useful function, Round(), rounds off values to a number of decimals of your choice.

You can access the Wizard in several ways. The first involves selecting a cell where the result is to appear and then clicking the Insert Function button and using the Insert Function dialog box to select a function. A second way, which is a bit quicker, makes sense when you know the name and spelling of your function. Start by selecting a cell for the result. Type an equal sign, the name of the function, and parentheses and then click the Insert Function button.

Both methods bring up the Function Arguments box, where you type the values, or click the cells containing the values, that you want in your calculation. Excel takes care of the details, returning your results.

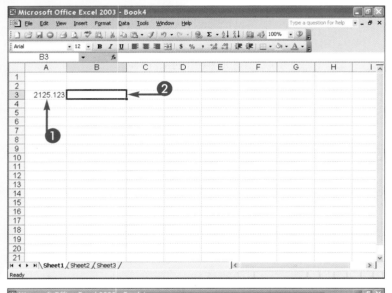

① Type your data into the worksheet.

*Note: This example shows the **Round()** function, which takes two arguments, one indicating the number to be rounded and the other indicating the number of digits to which it is to be rounded.*

② Click the cell in which the result is to appear.

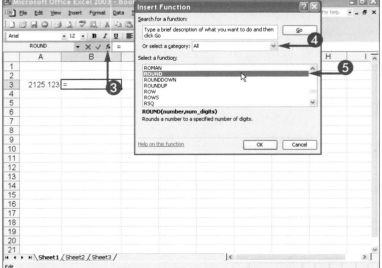

③ Click the Insert Function button.

The Insert Function dialog box appears.

④ Click here and select All to list all the functions.

⑤ Double-click the function that you want to use.

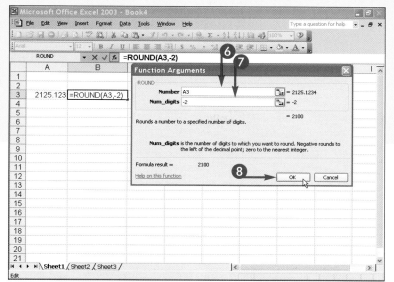

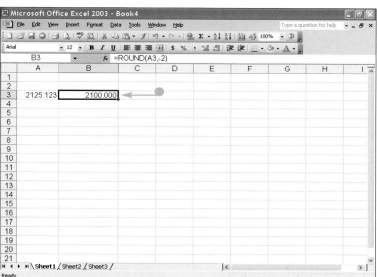

The Function Arguments dialog box appears.

6 Click the cell(s) containing the value(s) that you entered in step **1**.

7 Click or type in other arguments.

Note: *In this example, you type in the number of decimal places to which you want to round. A negative number refers to decimal places to the left of the decimal point.*

8 Click OK.

● The result appears in the cell. 2,100.000 preserves the number of digits of the original number, but rounds two decimal places to the left of the decimal point.

Did You Know?

If you do not know which function you want to use, type a question in the Search for a Function field in the Insert Function dialog box. For help with the function itself, click Help on This Function in the Function Argument dialog box for that function.

Caution!

Do not confuse `Round()` with number formatting. `Round()` works by evaluating a number in an argument and rounding it to the number of digits that you specify in the second field of the Function Arguments dialog box. When you format numbers, you simplify the appearance of the number in the worksheet, making it easier to read. The underlying number is not shortened. To find out more about formatting, see Chapter 7.

Document formulas with
COMMENTS

A *comment* is a bit of descriptive text that enables you to document your assumptions when you create a formula. If someone else maintains your worksheet or uses it in a workgroup, your comments can help the user by providing useful background information. You can enter comments in the cells containing any formulas that you want to document or otherwise annotate.

Like comments in Microsoft Word, comments in Excel do not appear until you choose to view them. Excel associates comments with individual cells and

indicates their presence with a tiny red triangle in the cell's upper-right corner. You can view an individual comment by clicking, or passing your mouse cursor over, the cell. You view all comments in a worksheet by clicking View and then Comments.

When you track your edits, a comment is automatically generated every time that you copy or change a cell. The comment records what was changed in the cell, who made the change, and at what time and date. For more information, see Task #34.

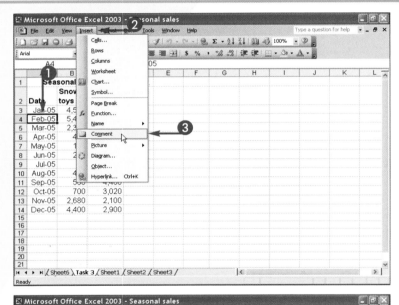

ADD A COMMENT

① Click in the cell where you want to add a comment.

② Click Insert.

③ Click Comment.

A comment box with a yellow background appears.

④ Type your comments.

Note: To apply bold and other formatting effects as you type, select the text, right-click, click Format Comment, and then make changes as appropriate.

⑤ Click outside the cell when you are done.

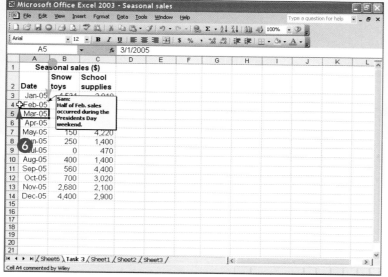

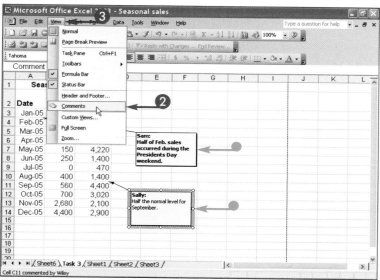

- A tiny red triangle appears in the upper-right corner of the cell.

6 Move ⊡ over the cell to display your comment.

Note: To edit the comment, right-click the cell and click Edit Comment from the pop-up menu. Change or add text as appropriate. Click outside the cell when you are done.

DISPLAY ALL THE COMMENTS

1 Click View.

2 Click Comments.

- You can now see all the comments in the worksheet.

Note: To close the comment boxes, click View and then Comments.

Did You Know?

Excel automatically includes the name of the person who enters a comment. If you are using someone else's computer and do not want your comments to appear under that person's name or want your comments to be anonymous, you can remove or change the name. Select it and backspace over it or type another name.

Did You Know?

When a comment gets in the way of another comment or blocks data, you can move it. Position your cursor over the border until the arrow turns into a double arrow. Click and drag the comment to a better location and then release the mouse button. Your comments will remain in this position until you display all comments again.

Document worksheets with
ONENOTE

Microsoft OneNote is a new application that enables you to write, speak, and even draw freeform notes for use in planning and documenting all your work in Excel, including your formulas. Using OneNote documents, called *notes*, you can capture information about the data sources involved in creating your worksheets. You can use notes for keeping minutes, writing to-do lists, developing outlines, maintaining schedules, and so on.

All of your notes are kept in a file called My Notebook. My Notebook contains several sections, each represented by a clickable tab. Each section in turn

has one or more pages. At any time, you can add sections and pages to organize your notes. By simply clicking and dragging, you can move notes from one page to another. A section can contain a virtually limitless number of notes.

OneNote is an independent application. Whereas comments are part of a single worksheet, you can run OneNote at the same time with any application. That means you can use OneNotes to coordinate projects involving several applications, such as Project, Access, and Excel.

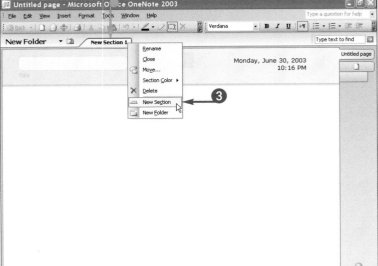

OPEN ONENOTE

1 From your Desktop, double-click the OneNote application icon.

● You can also open OneNote by clicking the OneNote icon in the Quick Launch area of the taskbar.

CREATE A NEW SECTION

OneNote opens.

● The current section, or folder tab, appears in bold.

2 Right-click a tab.

3 Click New Section.

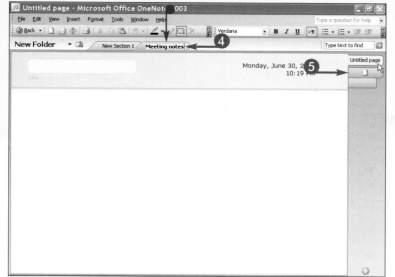

- A new section appears as the foremost tab.

  Note: Sections consist of one or more pages.

④ Label the tab by clicking inside it and typing a name.

  Note: When naming the tab, keep it simple and short.

⑤ To add a page to the section, click the page icon.

16

DIFFICULTY LEVEL

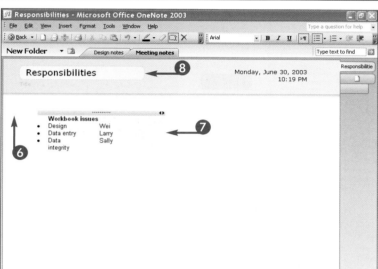

ADD A NOTE

⑥ Click anywhere within the page.

⑦ Type your text.

  Note: You can click anywhere within the page to type a new note.

  Note: As you type, you can use the Format menu to add text effects and bullets.

⑧ Click and type a name or title for the page.

  The note saves automatically.

TIPS

Did You Know?

You can create notes in many ways. With a keyboard, you have all the standard word-processing formatting effects. With a Tablet PC, you can draft notes and draw sketches by hand using the tablet's stylus. On a network, OneNote displays these drawings even for people without tablets. PC users can simulate markers with the drawing tools and create their own notes and sketches.

Did You Know?

As you add notes to a page, you can move and resize them. To move a note, click and drag its title bar. To resize a note, click and drag the double arrow in the upper-right corner.

Did You Know?

To retrieve specific notes from My Notebook, press Ctrl+F and then type a word or two to indicate what you want to find.

Define a
CONSTANT

You use a constant whenever you want to apply the same value in different contexts. Constants make it possible to refer to that value, whether it is simple or consists of many digits, by simply using the constant's name.

You can find constants in many applications. For example, sales tax is a familiar constant that, when multiplied by the subtotal on an invoice, results in a price. Likewise, income tax rates are the constants used to calculate tax liabilities. Although the various

tax rates change from time to time, they tend to remain constant within a tax period.

To create a constant in Excel, you need to type its value in a cell. With the value selected, you define its name using the Define Name box, the same box that you use to name ranges and formulas in Excel, as shown in Task #3. To use the constant in any formula in the same workbook, simply use the name that you defined.

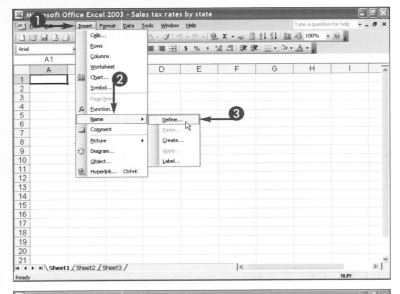

DEFINE A CONSTANT

① Click **Insert**.

② Click **Name**.

③ Click **Define**.

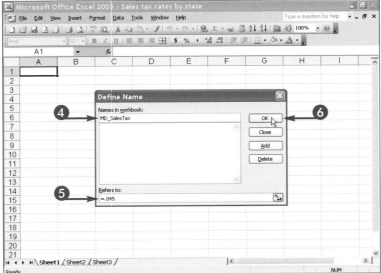

The Define Name dialog box appears.

④ Type a name for the constant.

⑤ Type an equal sign (=) followed by the constant's value.

⑥ Click OK.

You can now use the constant in any worksheet in the current workbook.

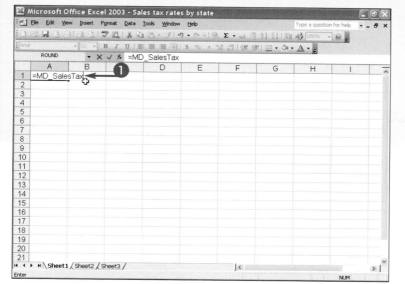

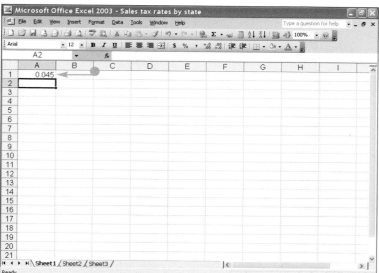

1 Click a cell and type an equal sign, followed by the name of the constant.

Note: If you do not know the constant's name, click Insert, Name, and then Paste. In the Paste Name dialog box, click the name.

2 Press Enter.

DIFFICULTY LEVEL

● The constant's value appears in the cell.

Note: To use named constants and ranges in formulas, see Task #18.

TIPS

Did You Know?

To edit a constant's name, click Insert, Names, and then Define. In the Define Name dialog box, select the name. Make the changes that you want in the Names in Workbook field, and click OK. To delete a constant, select it in the same box and click Delete. These editing features come in handy when you use text constants, which store any string of characters verbatim.

Apply It!

Many mathematical and statistical functions use constants. The best known is pi (3.14159 . . .), used in geometry. The actual number pi has an infinite number of digits to the right of the decimal place. Excel `Pi()` function only has 15 digits of precision with no arguments. Because one of those digits is the 3 to the left of the decimal, Excel's rendition of pi only goes out to 14 decimal places. When entering it by itself into a cell, precede it with an equal sign.

Apply
NAMES IN FUNCTIONS

Constructing formulas can seem complicated, especially when you need several functions in the same formula or when multiple arguments are required in a single function. An *argument*, remember, is information that you provide for the function to do its work.

Using named constants and ranges can make the task simpler by enabling you to use familiar terms of your choosing. A *named constant* is a name

that refers to a single, frequently used value. A *named range* is a name that you assign to a group of related cells. All names apply only to the worksheets in the workbook in which you defined them.

To insert a name into the function, use it in a formula or as a function's argument. You can access all names for a workbook by either typing them in or using the Paste Name dialog box.

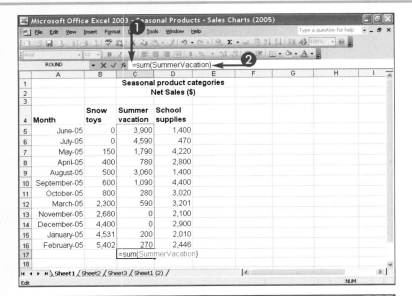

USE A RANGE NAME IN A FORMULA

① Click to place the cursor in the formula.

② Type the name of the range.

In this example, SummerVacation is the range of values in the Summer Vacation column.

You may complete the formula if necessary.

③ Press Enter.

● The cell displays the result.

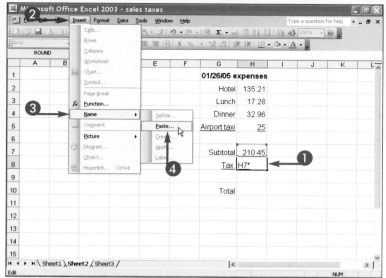

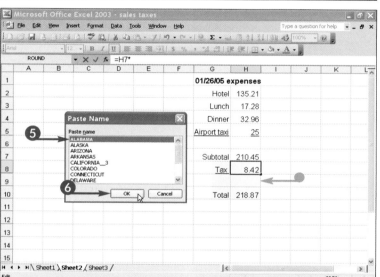

Note: *Use this technique if you forget the name of a constant or range.*

① Click to place the cursor in the formula.

② Click Insert.

③ Click Name.

④ Click Paste.

Note: *To have a constant appear by itself in a cell, type = and the constant's name, then press Enter.*

The Paste Name dialog box opens.

⑤ Click the constant to use.

⑥ Click OK.

If necessary, continue typing the formula and press Enter when you are done.

● The selected constant is fed into the formula, which then displays a result based on it.

TIPS

Did You Know?
Naming a custom formula enables you to reuse it by merely using its name. To create a named function, click its cell. Click Insert, Name, and then Define to use the Define Name dialog box. Then type a name for the function in the Names in Workbook field and press Enter.

Did You Know?
To create several named constants at the same time, create two adjacent columns, one listing names and the other listing values — for example, state names and state sales tax rates. To have the state name stand for the tax rate, the constant, select both columns. Click Insert, Name, and then Create. In the Create Name dialog box, click a check box to indicate which column to use for the name. In most cases, you want Left Column. Click OK.

Figure out the
BEST LOAN TERMS

You can use Excel's Payment function, PMT(), when buying a house or car or taking out a home equity loan. This function enables you to compare loan terms and make an objective decision based on factors such as the amount of the monthly payment.

You can calculate loan payments in many ways using Excel, but using the PMT() function is perhaps the simplest because you merely enter the arguments into the Function Wizard. To make your job even easier, you should enter this information into your worksheet before launching the Wizard. By merely clicking a cell, you can then enter the value of the cell into the Wizard.

PMT() takes three required arguments. For Rate, you enter an interest rate such as 5 percent, typing .05 divided by 12, to calculate the monthly rate. For Nper, number of periods, enter the number of loan periods for the loan you are seeking. For PV, present value, enter the amount of the loan — the present value of future payments. The monthly payment appears in the cell where you typed the function, formatted in dollars, and surrounded by parentheses, which signify that the number is negative, which is a cash outflow.

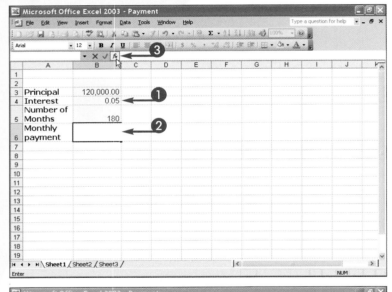

1 Type the principal (the present value or PV) number of periods and interest rate.

2 Click the cell where you want the result to appear.

3 Click the Insert Function button.

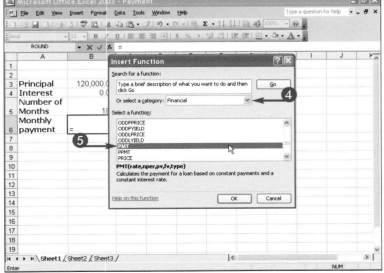

The Insert Function dialog box opens.

4 Click here and select Financial.

5 Double-click PMT.

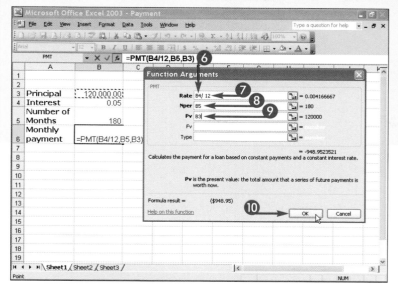

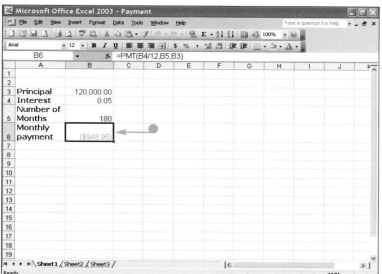

The PMT Function Arguments dialog box appears.

⑥ Click the cell with the interest rate.

⑦ Divide the interest rate by the number of periods per year, for example, type **12**.

⑧ Click the cell with the number of periods.

⑨ Click the cell with the principal.

⑩ Click OK.

DIFFICULTY LEVEL

● The result appears in the cell.

Note: The result shows the amount of a single loan payment.

Note: You can repeat steps 1 to 10 for other combinations of the three variables.

TIPS

Did You Know?

In a worksheet, you can create a loan calculator showing all the values at once. Place the labels *Principal*, *Interest*, and *Number of months* of a loan period in a column. Type their respective values into adjacent cells to the right. Use references to those cells in PMT()'s Function Arguments dialog box.

Did You Know?

Excel's Goal Seeking feature enables you to calculate payments. With Goal Seeking, you can set up a problem so that you can specify a goal, such as payments less than $1,100 per month, and have Excel vary a single value to reach the goal. The limitation is that you can vary only one value at a time. See Task #56 for more information.

Determine the
INTERNAL RATE OF RETURN

Business plans usually include an estimate of how long it will take for an investment to pay off, which can be roughly defined as the point when cash inflows, revenues, exceed cash outflows. Excel's internal rate of return (IRR) function performs this calculation for you, so all you have to do is estimate and enter your projected cash flows. The IRR function shows you the percentage return, or percentage loss, on the initial investment after the length of time that you specify in the function.

To use IRR(), you provide a series of values representing regular cash flows, with at least one positive and one negative value. Optionally, you can provide, as the second argument, your best estimate *guess* about the rate of return. The default value, if you leave out this number, is .1, representing a 10% rate of return. Your guess merely gives Excel a starting point to calculate the IRR.

The function displays an error if the IRR cannot be calculated. For important business decisions, the results of this function should be corroborated by other measures or an accountant's analysis.

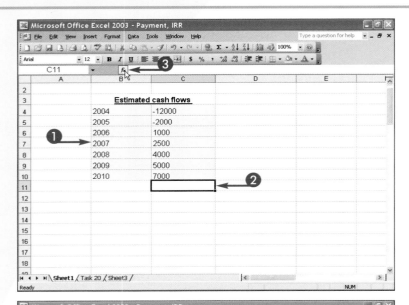

① Type a series of projected cash flows into the worksheet.

Note: At least one cash flow must be negative and one positive.

② Click the cell where the result is to appear.

③ Click the Insert Function button.

The Insert Function dialog box opens.

④ Click here and select Financial.

⑤ Double-click IRR.

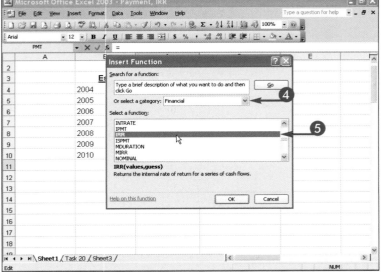

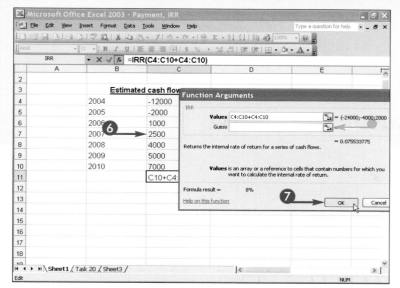

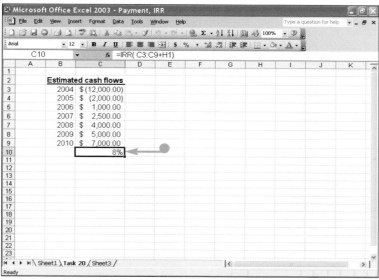

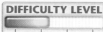
The IRR Function Arguments dialog box appears.

⑥ Click and drag the cash-flow values entered in step **1**.

Only the field appears when the cells are being clicked and dragged.

● Optionally, you can provide an estimated rate of return just to get Excel started.

⑦ Click OK.

● The cell with the formula displays the results of the calculations performed by the function.

Repeat steps **1** to **7** for each set of anticipated future cash flows.

TIPS

Did You Know?

The `IRR` function is similar to the Net Present Value function, `NPV()`, which calculates the present value of future cash flows, enabling you to compare total future cash flows to an initial investment. Whereas `IRR()` returns a percentage — the rate of return on the initial investment, `NPV()` returns the amount by which future cash flows exceed or fall below the investment. Another related function, `FV()`, analyzes the future value of an investment.

Caution!

Excel's `IRR` function has strict assumptions. Cash flows must be regularly timed and take place at the same point within the payment period. `IRR()` may perform less reliably for inconsistent payments, a mix of positive and negative flows, and variable interest rates. For irregular payment periods, use `XIRR()`.

Determine the
NTH LARGEST VALUE

Sometimes you want to identify and characterize the top values in any series, such as the RBIs of the top three hitters in the Major Leagues or the average purchases, in a given period, of your five largest customers.

The `Large` function evaluates a series of numbers and determines the highest value, second highest, or Nth largest in the series, with N being a value's rank order. `Large()` takes two arguments: the range of cells you want to evaluate and the rank order of the

value you are seeking, with 1 being the highest, 2 the next highest, and so on. The result of `Large()` is the value you requested.

Another way to determine the first, second, or following number in a series is to sort the numbers from biggest to smallest and then simply to read the results, as shown in Chapter 4. This technique is less useful when you have a long list or when you want to use the result in another function, such as summing the top five values.

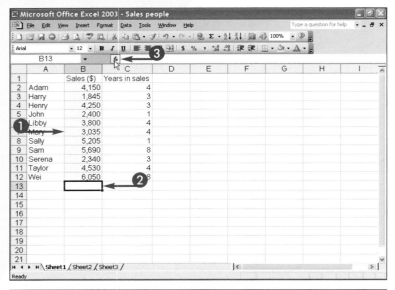

① Type the values from which you want to identify the highest number, or second highest, or other value.

② Click the cell where the result is to appear.

③ Click the Insert Function button.

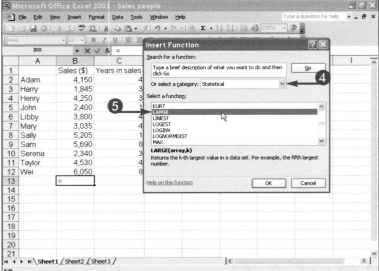

The Insert Function dialog box opens.

④ Click here and select Statistical.

⑤ Double-click LARGE.

The Function Arguments dialog box opens for the `Large` function.

6 Click and drag to select the cells that you want to evaluate.

7 Type a number indicating what you are seeking (1 for highest, 3 for third highest, and so on).

8 Click OK.

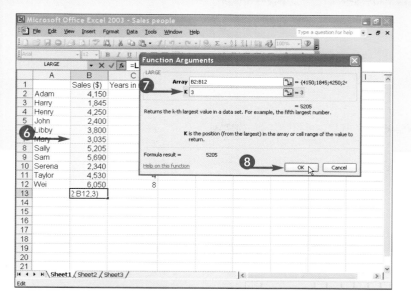

● The cell displays the value that you requested.

If K in step **7** is greater than the number of cells, a `#NUM` error appears in the cell instead.

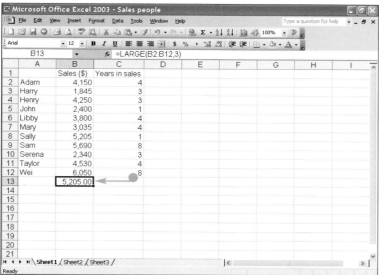

DIFFICULTY LEVEL

TIPS

Apply It!

To add the three or other highest values in a series, you can use `Large()` three times in a formula: `=Large(Sales,3) + Large(Sales,2) + Large (Sales,1)`, with `Sales` being the named range of sales values. Or, you can create a function in which `Large()` calculates all three numbers and stores the results in an *array,* or collection of numbers. `Sum()` then adds up the numbers: `=Sum(Large(Sales,{1,2,3}))`. Note the curly braces!

Did You Know?

Other useful functions work in a similar manner. `Small()` starts with a range of values and a number, for example, 1 for lowest, 2 for next lowest, and so on. It returns the value you requested. The `Min()` and `Max()` functions return the lowest and largest value in a series, respectively. They have one argument: a range of cell values.

Create a
CONDITIONAL FORMULA

With a conditional formula, you can perform calculations on only those numbers that meet a certain condition. For example, you can sum the sales of only those employees with three or more years of experience. The length of time, for example years in sales, is the condition. Only the values for salespeople meeting the condition are summed.

A conditional formula uses at least two functions: The first function, If(), defines the condition, or test, such as *salespeople with more than three years of experience*. To create the condition, you use

comparison operators, such as greater than (>), greater than or equal to (>=), less than (<), and equal to (=).

The second function in a conditional formula performs a calculation on numbers that meet the condition. Excel carries out the IF function first. Sum() adds the values that meet the condition defined in the IF function. Because two functions are involved, when you use the Function Wizard, one function (If) is an argument of another (Sum).

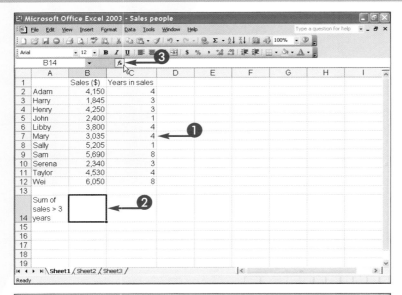

① Type the data into the worksheet before creating the formula.

② Click the cell where you want the result to appear.

③ Click the Insert Function button.

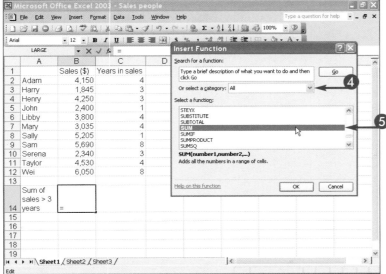

The Insert Function dialog box appears.

④ Click here and select All.

⑤ Double-click SUM.

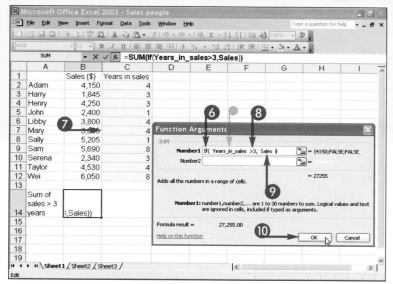

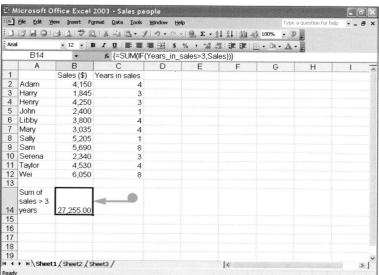

The Function Arguments dialog box appears.

⑥ Type **If()**.

⑦ Click and drag the range of addresses.

● Optionally, you can type a range, for example, Years_in_sales.

⑧ Type a comparison operator, the condition, and then a comma.

⑨ Type the series of values defining the series.

● Optionally, you can use a named range, for example Sales.

⑩ Click OK.

● The result appears in the cell.

TIPS

Did You Know?

`If()` is an array function. It compares every number in a series to a condition and keeps track of the numbers meeting the condition. To run an array function, you press Ctrl+Shift+Enter instead of the Enter key. You must surround the arrays by curly braces ({ }). The braces are entered automatically when you press Ctrl+Shift+Enter but not when you press Enter.

Did You Know?

`If()` has an optional third argument. Use the third argument when you want to specify what happens when the condition is not met. For example, you can use `If()` to test whether any sales values exceed 9,000 and then display `True` if such values exist and `False` if they do not. In advanced functions, such results are used as arguments.

Calculate a
CONDITIONAL SUM

You can use conditional sums to identify and sum investments whose growth exceeds a certain rate, or the amount purchased by certain customers each month, or other useful quantities. The Sumif() function combines the Sum and IF functions into one easy-to-use function.

Sumif() is simple, relative to a formula that uses both Sum() and If(). See Task #22 for a formula that uses both functions. Sumif() enables you to avoid complicated nesting and to use the Function Wizard without making one function an argument of the other. However, using two

functions (Sum and IF) gives you more flexibility. For example, you can use IF to create multiple complex conditions.

Sumif() has two required arguments: a range of numbers and the condition being applied to the numbers. Values that meet the condition are added together. An optional third argument enables you to sum a range of numbers different from the range to which the condition is applied. For example, if a salesperson reaches a certain level in a month, you could add a number in another column to the monthly salary as a bonus.

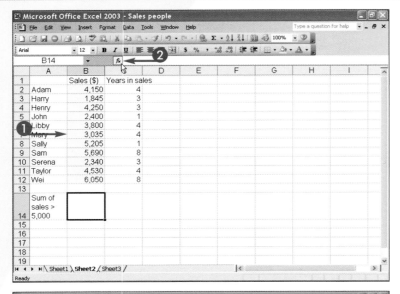

① Create a list of values to sum conditionally.

Note: Each value in the list is tested to see whether it meets a condition. If it does, it is added to other values meeting the condition.

② Click the Insert Function button.

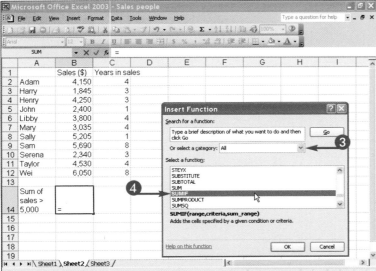

The Insert Function dialog box opens.

③ Click here and select All.

④ Double-click SUMIF.

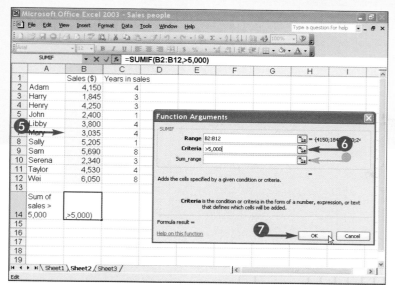

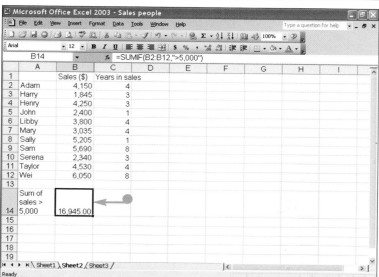

The Function Arguments dialog box appears.

5 Click and drag the range of addresses.

The selected range appears in the field.

6 Type a comparison operator and a condition.

● Optionally, you can enter the cell addresses of other values to be summed if the condition is met.

7 Click OK.

● The result appears in the cell with the formula.

TIPS

Did You Know?

The Countif function works like Sumif(). It combines two functions (Count and IF) and takes two arguments: a series of values and the condition by which the values are tested. Whereas Sumif() creates a new value, Countif() merely returns the number of items that passed the test.

Did You Know?

You can use the Conditional Sum Wizard, an Excel add-in. To install this add-in, see Task #93. Select a cell for the result and click Tools and then Conditional Sum. The Conditional Sum Wizard has four self-explanatory steps. The last step diverges from the Sumif() Function Wizard in that it enables you to have the condition as well as the result appear on your worksheet. You can thus display conditions and results side by side to compare them.

Discover your inner
CALCULATOR

Often, you will want to do quick calculations without using a function. In Excel, you can place a calculator on your toolbar so that it is always available. The Excel calculator is one of dozens of commands that you can add to your toolbar.

You can use the calculator as you would any electronic calculator. You click a number, choose an operator, such as the plus key to do addition, and then click another number. Click the Equals key to

get a result. Use MC to remember a value, MR to recall it, and MS to clear memory.

Statistical and mathematical functions are available in the calculator's scientific view by clicking View and then Scientific. In this view, you can cube a number, find its square root, compute its log, and more. In both standard and scientific views, you can transfer a value from the calculator to Excel by displaying it, copying it, and pasting it into a cell.

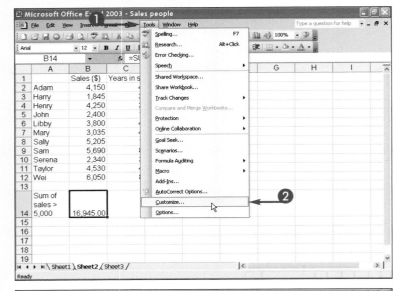

ADD THE CALCULATOR TO THE TOOLBAR

1 Click **Tools**.

2 Click **Customize**.

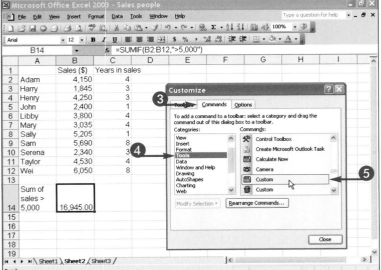

The Customize dialog box appears.

3 Click the Commands tab.

4 In the list of categories, click Tools.

5 In the list of commands, click Custom.

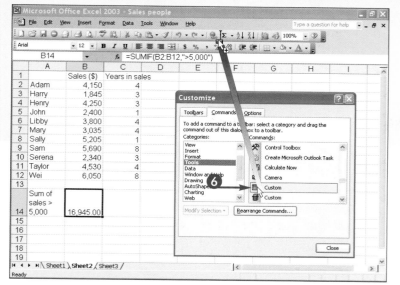

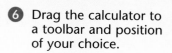

6 Drag the calculator to a toolbar and position of your choice.

The Calculator icon appears on the toolbar, ready for use.

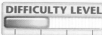
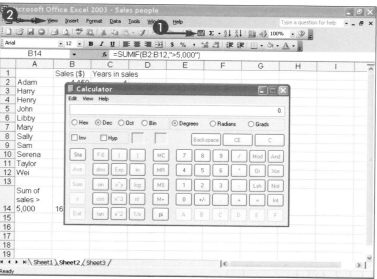

USE THE SCIENTIFIC MODE

1 Click the Calculator button.

2 Click View.

3 Click Scientific.

Note: The Help menu provides information on all the functions. It includes a list of keyboard equivalents of most calculator tasks.

TIPS

Apply It!

To calculate an average, switch to the scientific view and enter the first number to be averaged. Click the Sta button to bring up the Statistics box. Back in the calculator, click another value to average and click Dat. Keep entering data and clicking Dat until all values are entered. Click Ave to find the average.

Did You Know?

To remove the calculator from the toolbar, click the drop-down menu on the far right of the toolbar containing the calculator. Click Add or Remove buttons and then Customize. In the Customize dialog box, click the Toolbars tab. Click to select the toolbar with the calculator, and click Reset.

Find
PRODUCTS AND SQUARE ROOTS

Many Excel users are familiar with the basic operations available by clicking the AutoSum button: addition, subtraction, minimum, maximum, and count. Fewer are familiar with two other basic operations available by directly using the underlying mathematical functions. Using the Product function, you can multiply two or more numbers, and using the Sqrt function, you can find the square root of a number.

Excel can calculate the square roots of positive numbers only. If a negative number is the argument, as in Sqrt(-1), Excel, returns #NUM in the cell.

You use Product() or Sqrt() by entering the values to be used in the function into the worksheet. If you do not want the values to appear in the worksheet, start by clicking the cell where the result is to appear and typing an equal sign, the function name (Product or Sqrt), and parentheses. Click the Insert Function button (*fx*) to enter your values for the formula.

Related to Product() and Sqrt() is Power(). To find the power of any number, such as 3 to the 9th power, try this easy-to-use function.

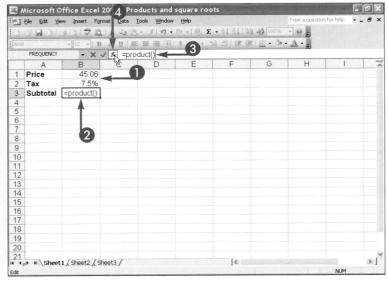

CALCULATE A PRODUCT

① Type the values you want to multiply.

② Click the cell where you want the result.

③ Type =**product()** in the formula bar.

Note: Typing the function directly into the formula bar, directly preceded by an equal sign, is an alternative to choosing it from the Function Wizard.

④ Click the Insert Function button.

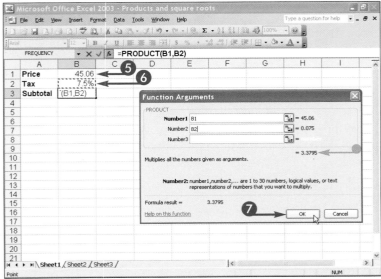

The Function Arguments dialog box appears.

⑤ Click the first value you want to multiply.

⑥ Click the second value you want to multiply.

● Notice how the Insert Function dialog box displays the interim answer.

⑦ Click OK.

The product appears.

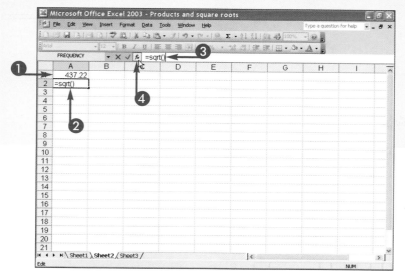

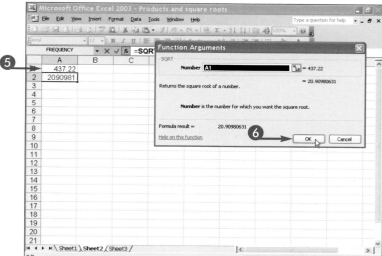

CALCULATE A SQUARE ROOT

1 Type the number for which you want the square root.

Note: If you do not want this value to appear on the worksheet, start with step **2**.

2 Click the cell where you want the square root.

3 Type **=sqrt()** in the formula bar.

4 Click the Insert Function button.

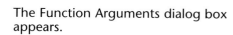

The Function Arguments dialog box appears.

5 Click the cell containing the value entered in step **1**.

Optionally, you can type into the parentheses the number for which you want a square root.

6 Click OK.

The square root appears in the cell.

TIPS

Did You Know?

`Product()` can take logical arguments, such as `TRUE` and `FALSE`, as well as numbers. In a formula, `TRUE` is considered the same as 1 and `FALSE` 0. You use logical values in complex condition formulas using `If()`.

Apply It!

Students can make use of `Product()` and `Sqrt()` in math and trigonometry to create reference tables of products and square roots.

Did You Know?

Each argument in `Product()` can have more than one value, for example, 1, 2, and 3. These values can be represented as an array, a series of numbers enclosed in curly braces: $\{1,2,3\}$. Each value in the array is multiplied by every other value, so that the product of $\{1,2,3\}$ is 6. Arrays can be multiplied by each other, but each value in the array has to be a number.

CALCULATE THE DURATION
between two times

Using Excel functions, you can perform calculations with dates and times. You can, for example, find the number of hours worked between two times or the number of days between two dates. These functions convert every date and time into a *serial value,* which can be added and subtracted and then converted back into a recognizable time or date.

Excel calculates a date's serial value as the number of days after January 1, 1900, so each date can be represented by a whole number. Excel calculates a time's serial value in units of 1/60th of a second. Every time can be represented as a serial value

between 0 and 1. A time-and-date, such as January 1, 2000 at noon, consists of the date to the left of the decimal and a time to the right.

Take the example of 5:46 PM on August 25, 2005. The time's serial value is .740277778, about three-quarters through the day; the date's serial value is 38589, 38,589 days after January 1, 1900. Subtracting one date from another involves subtracting one serial value from another and then converting the result back into a date or time. Often, you must change the format of the result to get a usable result.

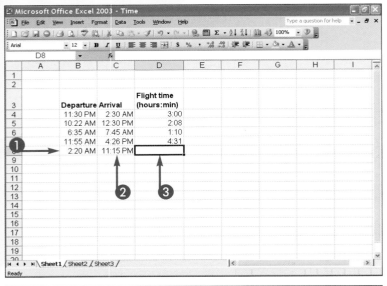

FIND THE DIFFERENCE BETWEEN TWO TIMES

1. Type the time in a cell.

   Note: If you do not include AM or PM, Excel defaults to a.m. If you want p.m., you must type in PM.

2. Type the second time in a cell.

3. Click the cell where you want the result.

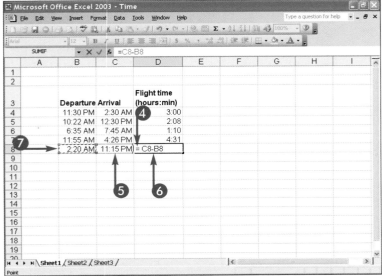

4. Type an equal sign.

5. Click the cell with the later time.

   The cell address appears next to the equal sign.

6. Type a minus sign (-) after the cell number.

7. Click the cell with the earlier time.

   The cell address appears.

8. Press Enter.

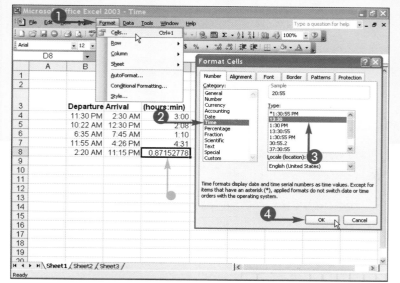

- The result appears as a serial value in the cell.

CONVERT SERIAL VALUE TO A TIME

1 Click Format and Cells.

The Format Cells dialog box appears.

2 Click Time.

3 Click a specific format.

4 Click OK.

- The cell displays the number of hours and minutes between the two times.

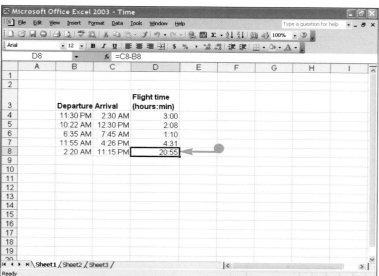

Did You Know?

In subtracting times that cross midnight, 11 p.m. to 2 a.m., you need a programming function called modulus, or `MOD()`. The formula is `=MOD(later time - earlier time, 1)`. Thanks to John Walkenbach's *Excel Bible*, Wiley Publishing, for this tip.

Did You Know?

If subtracting times or date yields a negative time or date, this error is reflected by a series of pound signs (######).

Did You Know?

Showing a time/date in the General format displays its serial value. Formatting a serial value in the Time or Date displays it as a recognizable time or date. To display a time in hour:minute format, right-click it, click Format Cell, click Time, and click the 13:30 format.

CALCULATE DAYS
between two dates

One special-purpose function enables you to find the number of workdays between two dates. Like other Excel functions, date and time functions make use of the Function Wizard. As usual, the Wizard works best when the information that it requires is already entered into your worksheet.

To calculate the number of workdays between two dates, you use the Networkday function. The function's arguments — the information that you must supply — include a start date, an end date, and any intervening holidays that automatically reduce

the number of workdays between the two dates. Excel automatically deducts the number of weekend dates, too. The formula displays the serial value of the number of workdays.

The complementary Workday function calculates the end date given a start date and a number of workdays — or, the start date given an end date and number of days. The resulting serial value must be converted to a date. Right-click the cell, click Format Cells, click Date, click an appropriate format, and click OK.

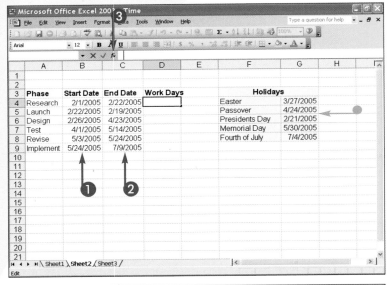

FIND NUMBER OF DAYS BETWEEN TWO DATES

❶ Type the start date.

❷ Type the end date.

● If you want the calculation to consider holidays, type the dates of holidays between the start and end dates.

❸ Click the Insert Function button.

The Insert Function dialog box opens.

❹ Click here and select Date & Time.

❺ Double-click NETWORKDAYS.

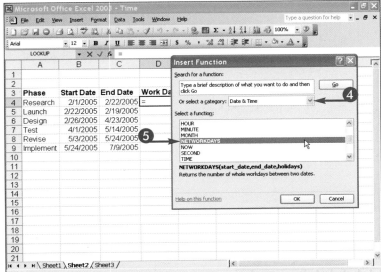

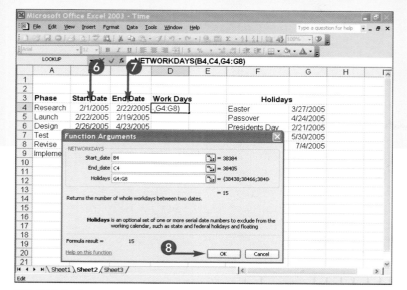

The Function Arguments dialog box opens.

⑥ Click the cell containing the start date.

⑦ Click the cell containing the end date.

Optionally, click and drag the range of dates of holidays.

⑧ Click OK.

DIFFICULTY LEVEL

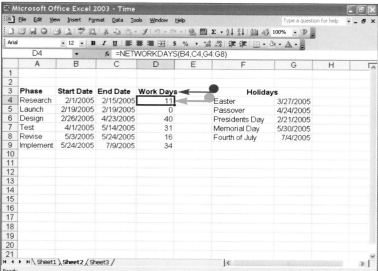

● The cell with the formula displays the net workdays between the two dates.

● Optionally, you can create a text label describing this result.

TIPS

Did You Know?

Excel can perform date arithmetic involving any date since January 1, 1900. You can type in dates before then, but Excel treats them as text and thus cannot perform calculations on them.

Cross-Platform!

Excel for the Macintosh calculates dates from 1904. If you plan to share a worksheet with someone using a Macintosh, you must change the year format. Click Tools and then Options. On the Calculation tab, click the 1904 Date System button.

Did You Know?

The Date function can simplify date calculations. Date() takes three arguments: year, month, and date. By entering these values in different columns, you generate serial values. The day, month, and year must be entered as numbers, for example, 03 instead of March, and so on. By entering these values in different columns, you generate serial values.

Change
TEXT TO NUMBERS

Formulas give you the ability to perform complex calculations quickly and accurately on numbers, dates, or times. Sometimes, however, your numbers *look* like numbers but are, in fact, text — mere characters. A sure sign that a number is merely text is that it is left-aligned in a cell; true numbers, by default, are right-aligned.

In Excel, text and numbers are different *data types*. You can use numbers, but not text, in formulas and functions. Including text in a complex calculation results in an error.

You can address this problem in several ways. Merely reformatting the text cells as numbers does not always work, especially in earlier versions of Excel. You reformat using the Format Cells dialog box. More reliable is the technique of multiplying each numeral by a 1 to convert the data type from text to number.

The numbers-as-text problem often occurs when you import data from an external database such as Excel or other application. Chapter 9 covers importing data in more detail.

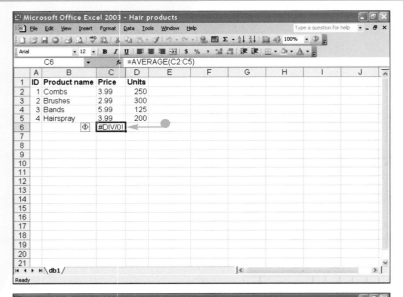

Note: In this example, the price values were imported from Microsoft Access, so they are text and cannot be added.

Note: The numbers are aligned along the left side of the cell, whereas in Excel the default position for numbers is on the right.

● You cannot calculate the average because Excel calculates the divisor as a zero.

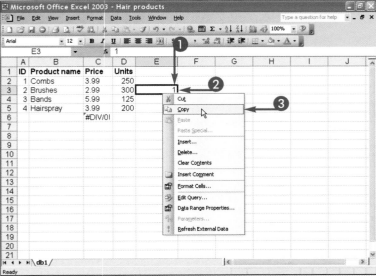

① Type **1** into any neighboring cell.

② Right-click that cell.

A context menu appears.

③ Click Copy.

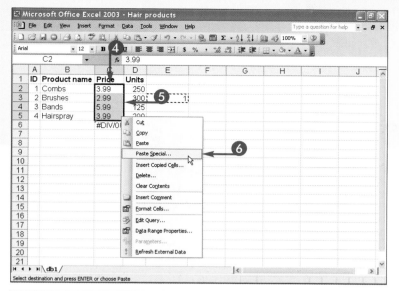

 **28**

④ Click and drag to select the cells you want to convert.

⑤ Right-click the selected cells.

⑥ Click Paste Special.

The Paste Special dialog box appears.

⑦ Click Multiply (○ changes to ⊙).

⑧ Click OK.

● The numbers now appear on the right side of their cells and are usable in operations.

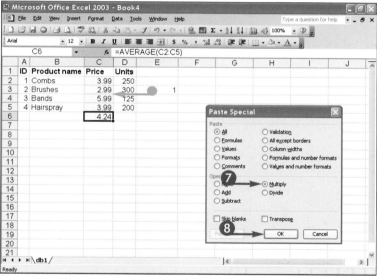

 TIPS

Did You Know?

Excel can convert text-based numbers to actual numbers, but the method does not always work. Click Tools and then Options. On the Error Checking tab, place a check by Number Stored as Text and press Enter. Excel flags cells containing text, placing a green flag in the upper-left corner. Click the menu button appearing alongside any cells with this error. Click Convert to Number. If this works, the number will appear right-aligned in its cell.

Did You Know?

`Datevalue()` and `Timevalue()` convert text dates and times into serial values for use in calculations. As arguments, both take date or time *in quotes* — for example: `=Datevalue("1/5/2005")`. The function returns a serial value, which you can use in a calculation, for example, click Format, Cells, and then click the Date category and choose (left) and appropriate format (right).

Chapter 3

Copying Data, Formats, and More

If you have used Word, you know that copying text for use in another document or application enables you to reuse material and minimize retyping and errors. Copying a value in Excel is similar: Select it and click the Copy button on the toolbar. In the new location, click the cell where you want the value and click the Paste button.

Copying can get more involved in Excel, and it is a lot more powerful because so many elements can occupy a cell: values, functions, formulas, formats, styles, and more. You can copy any of these elements between cells, worksheets, workbooks, and even applications. You can copy one value at a time, such as a specific number or specific bit of text, or many consecutively arranged values at the same time, such as a range.

Excel makes use of the copy features built into Windows as well as those built into Office 2003. New in Office 2003 is the capability of storing as many as 24 different items on the Office Clipboard for pasting into Excel and other Office applications.

In this chapter, you learn to use the Office Clipboard. You also learn to transpose a row into a column, to copy styles from one worksheet to another, to apply formats from one chart to another, and to copy formulas from one cell to another. If you work in a networked environment, you may want to use the tip on keeping track of the changes that result from copying.

Top 100

Copy a Range with the
OFFICE CLIPBOARD

With Office 2003, you can copy content into a storage area called the *Clipboard* and paste it into Excel or another Office application. To use the Clipboard, click the cell or cells containing the content and click the Copy button on the toolbar. You will not be aware of the Clipboard until you attempt to paste the copied information somewhere else. To paste, find a location for the content, click where you want the copied item to appear, and double-click the item on the Office Clipboard. The Office Clipboard task pane appears when you click Edit and then Office Clipboard from any Office program.

In Office, copying one item does not replace an existing stored item, up to a limit of 24 items. You can even select a range of cells, copy it, and paste it elsewhere. The Office Clipboard pastes the entire range, with all values, but if any cell includes a formula, it will not be copied. To copy formulas, see Task #33. Copied items stay on the Clipboard until you close all Office applications.

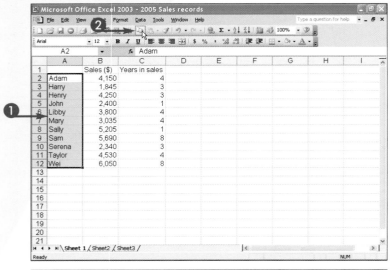

① Click and drag to select the content you want to copy.

② Click the Copy button.

Excel places a copy of the information in the Office Clipboard.

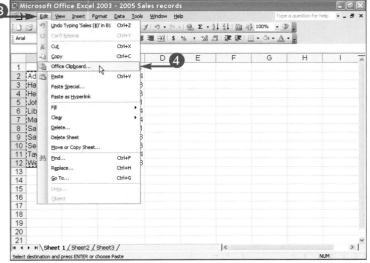

③ Click Edit.

④ Click Office Clipboard.

Alternatively, you can hold down the Ctrl key and press C twice to open the Clipboard task pane.

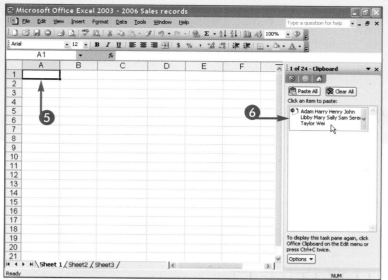

The Clipboard task pane appears.

⑤ Click the destination cell.

⑥ In the Clipboard task pane, double-click the item that you want to copy.

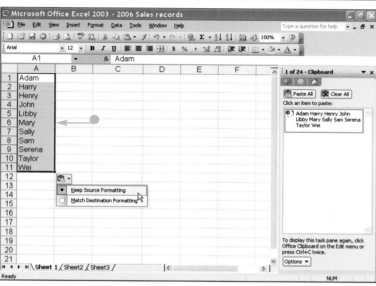

● The content is pasted into the new location.

Note: The Paste Options menu gives you the option of keeping the formatting of the copied item or changing it to match the formatting of the new location. The default is to match the formatting of the new cell. Press Esc to accept the default and remove the menu.

TIPS

Did You Know?

The Office Clipboard holds graphical objects, enabling you to bring digital pictures, WordArt, and clip art from other programs into Excel.

Did You Know?

To copy a cell range within or between worksheets, click and drag to select a series of cells and then click the Copy button. To paste the range, navigate to the worksheet to which you want to copy the range, click the cell where you want the range to start, and click Paste.

Did You Know?

To keep the Clipboard task pane from unexpectedly appearing while you are copying, open the pane, click the Options button on the lower left, and click Collect without Showing Office Clipboard.

TRANSPOSE A ROW
into a column

When you create a worksheet, Excel gives you flexibility in working with rows and columns. At any time, you can insert new rows or columns, delete rows or columns, and move entire rows or columns while retaining most of their properties. Sometimes, however, you may want to transpose a row into a column — or vice versa.

Transposing comes in handy when you have too many columns for the number of rows or when you need to create a *list,* a special kind of worksheet discussed in Chapter 4. A list might consist of rows describing products with each column describing

a feature of the product — its ID, price, the number in inventory, and so on. Lists typically have many rows and fewer columns.

With Excel, you can copy, or *transpose,* a row into a column and vice versa. To do so, copy the row, click the cell where the new column is to start, and instead of pasting, use the Paste Special option. In the Paste Special dialog box, you click Transpose and click OK. To make room for the new worksheet data, you can transpose columns or rows in a different worksheet or workbook.

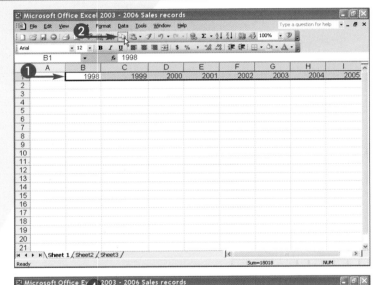

① Click the cells you want to transpose into a column.

Alternatively, you can select a column to transpose into a row.

Note: *Make sure that a series of blank cells is available to accommodate the copied data.*

② Click the Copy button.

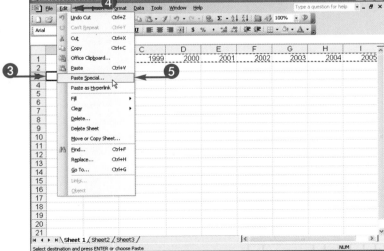

Note: *The moving marquee dots around the selection indicate the cells have been copied to the Clipboard.*

③ Click to select the first cell of the new column or row.

Existing data will be copied over and lost.

④ Click Edit.

⑤ Click Paste Special.

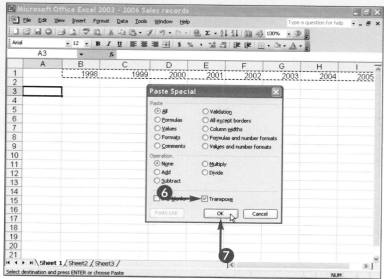

The Paste Special dialog box appears.

⑥ Click Transpose (☐ changes to ☑).

⑦ Click OK.

DIFFICULTY LEVEL

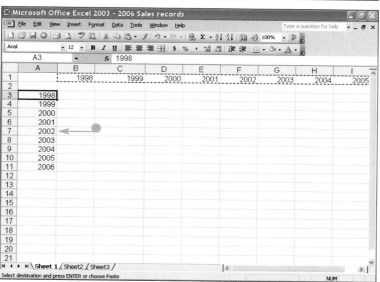

● The data appears in its new position.

TIPS

Did You Know?

The Transpose function goes further than the Paste Special option. It enables you to transpose entire cell grids. Suppose that you have a grid with 3 rows and 13 columns. However, you need a grid of 3 columns and 13 rows. In another part of the worksheet, or another worksheet, select a grid of blank cells measuring 3 columns by 13 rows. In the Formula bar, type **=transpose()** and click the Insert Function button. In the Function Arguments window, select the cells you want to transpose. Press Ctrl+Shift+Enter because Transpose is an array function. For more information, see Task #22.

Did You Know?

You can avoid rearranging worksheets by designing them carefully. Long lists of people, things, transactions, and so on should be arranged vertically, with descriptive column heads. For more about lists, see Task #35.

COPY STYLES
to another workbook

A *style* is a collection of formats that you use within a workbook. With styles, you maintain consistency in the way numbers, dates, times, borders, and text features appear in cells. You can create a style based on any combination of formats available directly in the Format Cells dialog box, which you can access by clicking Format and then Cells. One workbook can contain many styles.

Styles simplify your work and reduce the time required to format worksheets. With styles, you can change many cells by making a single change to the style and applying it to those cells. Likewise, by using styles in other workbooks, you can change many cells by simply changing the style on which they are all based. Copying a style into other workbook is also called *merging*.

To copy styles, you need to open both the workbook from which you will copy the style and the workbook to which you want to apply it.

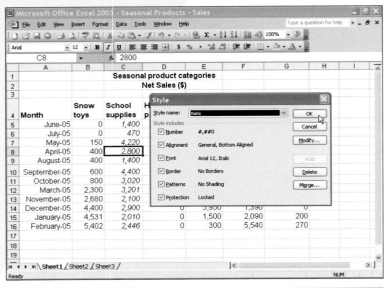

① Create a style in a worksheet.

Note: *In this example, the style calls for numbers in italic.*

Note: *For more on creating a style, Task #75.*

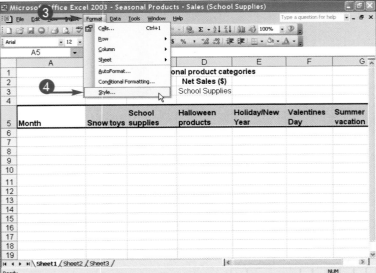

② Open the workbook where you want to copy or merge the styles.

③ Click Format.

④ Click Style.

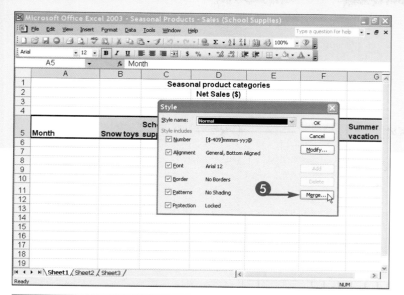

The Style dialog box opens.

⑤ Click **Merge**.

The Merge Styles dialog box opens.

⑥ Select the workbook whose styles you want to use.

⑦ Click **OK**.

The copied styles are now available in the new workbook.

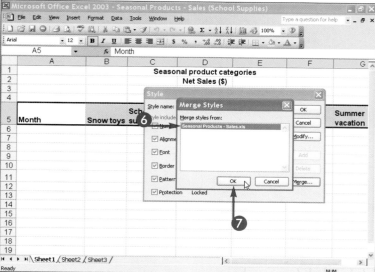

Did You Know?

Each style in a workbook must have a unique name. If you try to copy a style into a workbook containing a style with the same name, when you click OK in the Merge Styles dialog box, a warning box appears. If you want the imported style to take the place of the existing style, click OK. Otherwise, click No or Cancel.

Apply It!

Using a style copied into a workbook is no different from using a style created within the workbook. To use it, you first select the cell or range of cells to be styled. Click Insert and then Format. In the Style dialog box, select a style from the Style Name drop-down menu. Click OK.

COPY CHART FORMATTING
into another chart

Charting a worksheet shows your data in a way that clarifies your information and makes it easier to share it with others. Chart elements include chart type, data series, legend location, and axis units and styling. You can format each element. If you have several charts to format, you can avoid re-creating formats by copying the formatting from one chart and using it for another.

Excel enables you to quickly copy several chart formatting properties from one chart to another. The benefits of copying a chart's formatting include

helping you to achieve consistency across your charts and saving you time in chart preparation. Similarly, formatted charts are also easier to compare, as long as they represent similar data.

Copying formatting from a chart requires that you create and display two charts — one that is formatted and one that is not but is to receive the copied formatting. The charts can appear in different worksheets or workbooks.

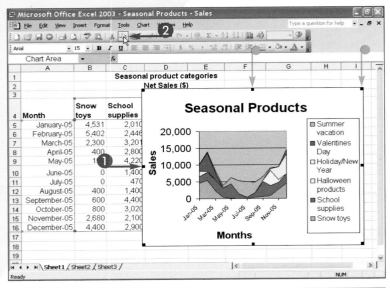

① Select the chart with the formatting that you want to copy.

● The black border and handles indicate the selection.

② Click the Copy button.

③ Generate the chart where you want to copy the formatting.

④ Click the chart.

⑤ Click the Paste button.

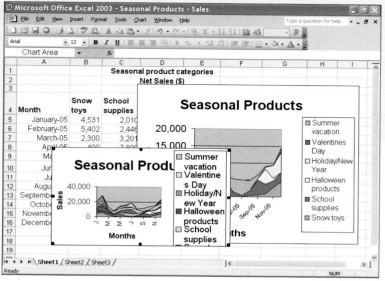

The chart takes on the formatting of the first chart, including its chart type.

 # 32

DIFFICULTY LEVEL

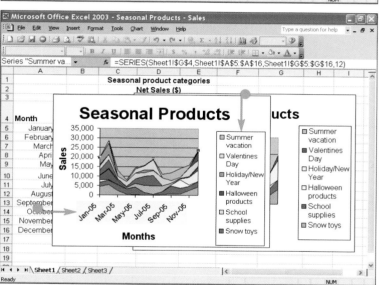

● Individual chart elements on the new chart may appear formatted.

Note: For more about creating charts, see Task #58.

TIPS

Did You Know?

After you have copied formatting to a chart, you can format the chart's elements such as the axes, legend, data series, and chart background. To do so, first right-click the particular element. Then, from the pop-up menu, click Format Data Series, Format Legend, or other element. See Task #59 for more about editing charts.

Did You Know?

You can use the Format Painter to quickly apply formatting from one element, or object, to another. For more information, see Task #74.

Did You Know?

You can copy content, formatting, or anything else only if the Copy button is active on the Excel toolbar.

COPY FORMULAS
with paste special

You can easily copy a formula to an adjacent cell. Click the cell to select it and then move the mouse cursor over the lower-right corner until the cursor turns into a cross. Left-click and drag to the adjacent cell and release. The new cell has a drop-down menu from which you choose Copy Formatting. You can also right-click and again use Copy Formatting. This technique automatically changes any cell addresses in the formula so that they are relative to the new cell.

To copy a formula to a non-adjacent cell or another worksheet or workbook, however, you need to use Paste Special. Paste Special is similar to simple copy

and paste in that you select the cell with the formula you want to copy and click the Copy button. Then you use the Paste Special dialog box.

When you copy the formula to the new cell, any cell addresses in the formula change relative to the cell address of formula's cell. Using the Paste Special dialog box, you can also paste other cell elements such as formats and comments.

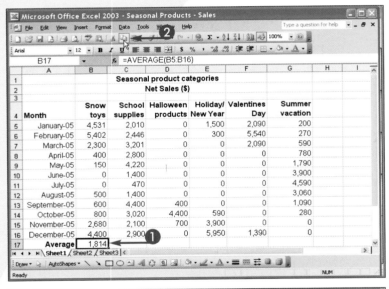

① Select the cell or cells containing a formula you want to copy.

② Click the Copy button.

③ Click the cells where you want to apply the formula.

④ Click the Paste menu button.

⑤ Click Paste Special.

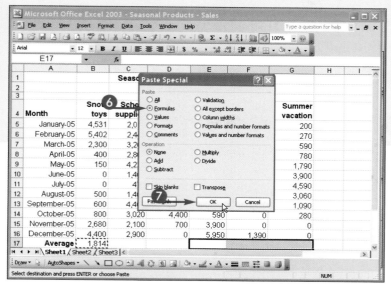

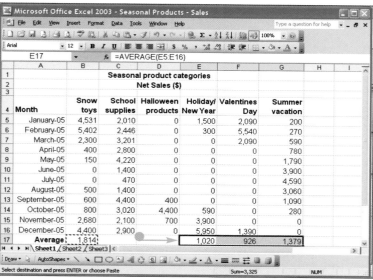

● The formula copies to the new cells and the results appear.

Note: *To copy a formula, you could also right-click and drag the cell selected in step 1 to the adjacent cell.*

TIPS

Did You Know?

To copy a cell element such as value, formatting, or comments, click the appropriate radio button in the Paste Special dialog box.

Did You Know?

At the opposite extreme from copying a formula, value, or comment is copying an entire worksheet. To do so, click the worksheet tab in the lower-right corner to select it. To select more than one worksheet, Shift+click, then right-click, and click Select All Sheets. Click Edit and then Move or Copy Sheet. In the Move or Copy dialog box, select the workbook where you want to move the sheets, indicate where to place the sheets in the workbook, and check the box if you want to copy instead of move. Click OK.

TRACK CHANGES
while editing

If you work in a networked environment and several people work on the same worksheet, you may need to account for who makes what change, in which cells, and when. To do so, you can use the Track Changes feature, formerly referred to as *revision marks.*

In the Highlight Changes dialog box, you can choose from the When, Who, and Where options. Use When to define the time after which edits are tracked, for example, after a specific date. Use Who to identify

the group whose edits you want to track, for example, everyone in the workgroup or everyone but you. Use Where to specify the rows and columns whose data you want to monitor. Changes are indicated by small purple triangles in the upper-left corner of the changed cell. Change details are recorded on automatically generated cell comments. You can view these comments by moving your cursor over the cell.

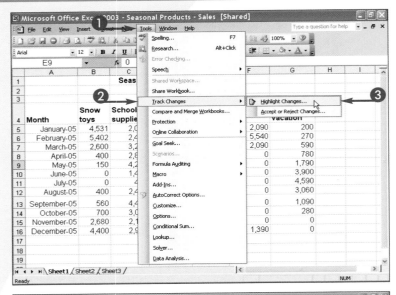

① Click Tools.

② Click Track Changes.

Note: If the menu option is not visible, click the double arrow at the bottom of the Tools menu.

③ Click Highlight Changes.

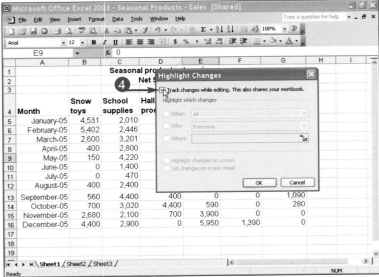

The Highlight Changes dialog box opens.

④ Click Track changes while editing to turn tracking on (☐ changes to ☑).

The optional When, Who, and Where fields become available to click.

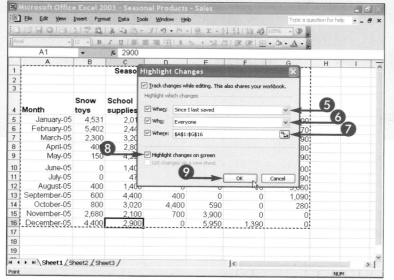

5 Click here and select when to track changes from the drop-down list.

6 Click here and select whose changes to track from the drop-down list.

7 Click and drag to select the cells you want to monitor, or you can enter the cell range.

8 Click Highlight changes on screen to insert a purple flag into edited cells (☐ changes to ☑).

9 Click OK.

A message informs you that the workbook is now saved.

● Purple flags appear in edited cells.

● To view a cell's comment, move over the cell.

Note: others can now edit the workbook. To remove sharing, click Tools and Share Workbook, and then uncheck the check box.

Note: For more about comments, see Task #15.

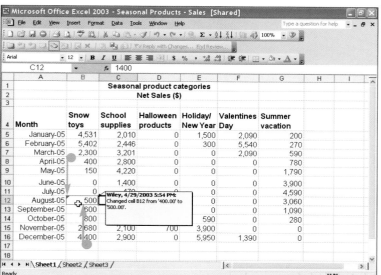

TIPS

Did You Know?

To view all worksheet changes after edits have been made, open the Highlight Changes dialog box and click the List Changes on a New Sheet option. For the Who field, click All. Click to uncheck the When and Where fields. Click OK. Excel creates a new worksheet called History showing, for each change, the type of change, the values changed, the person who made the change, and so on. The worksheet can be sorted and filtered. For more information, see Task #38.

Did You Know?

You can review every change made to a worksheet and either accept or reject the change. Click Tools, Track Changes, and then Accept or Reject Changes. The available options let you restrict your review to changes by certain people and at certain times.

Using Excel Lists

A list is an Excel worksheet with a difference. You create a list as you would any worksheet, but your information must be structured in columns, each with its own text heading. By merely entering worksheet information in this way, you can then tap database-like capabilities that go beyond what is possible with a simple worksheet.

This chapter shows different ways to create lists and enter data into them. Much of the chapter focuses on sorting and filtering. *Sorting* means to arrange list values in order, either alphabetically or numerically. You can sort and re-sort lists as necessary and even sort within a sort. *Filtering* means to display only the list information that meets certain criteria, temporarily hiding the rest. Advanced filtering gives you tools for filtering out duplicate records and applying multiple complex filters to your data.

With data formatted as a list, you can count, average, and subtotal only those parts of your list that meet certain criteria. In a customer survey, for example, you can count the number of senior citizens who prefer a certain sport or compare the time spent online among different age groups in different communities. You carry out calculations by using menu commands or database functions; Chapter 2 shows how to use all Excel functions.

When you organize your data as a list, you have access to *lookups*, a special way of searching for data. You might use a lookup to retrieve a stock price by typing in a stock symbol. Lists also enable you to create a powerful analytical tool called a *PivotTable*, discussed in Chapter 5.

Top 100

GENERATE A LIST
automatically

A *list* is an Excel worksheet with characteristics that enable you to use it as a simple database. You can enter only one list on a worksheet, although non-list information can also appear on the worksheet — such as calculations pertaining to the list.

You organize the information in columns and provide each column with a column head describing what is in the column. You should avoid blank cells and blank spaces at the beginning of a cell because they make sorting difficult.

Lists are quite simple to create on your own. However, if you prefer, you can convert an existing worksheet into a list automatically. Before starting, you should make sure that the data is arranged in columns, each with a descriptive column head. The generated list includes drop-down menus for each column, which you use for filtering columns in different ways.

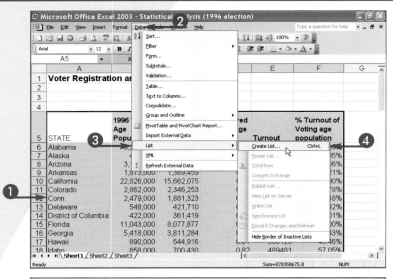

1. Click and drag to select the worksheet, including the column heads but not the worksheet title.

2. Click Data.

3. Click List.

4. Click Create List.

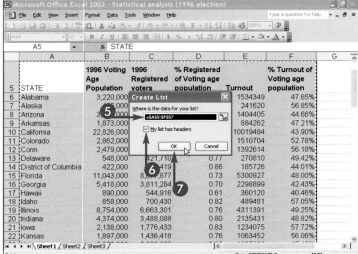

The Create List dialog box appears.

5. Confirm that the cells listed match the cells in your worksheet.

6. Click here to confirm that the list has headers (☐ changes to ☑).

7. Click OK.

You may see a warning about query tables in the worksheet. Click Yes.

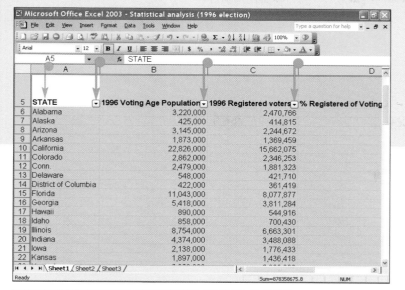

The list appears, surrounded by a border.

- Each column has a column head, in bold.

- Each column has a drop-down column filter.

Note: *For more information about filters, see Task #38.*

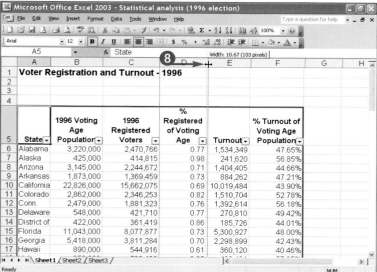

Note: *If you want to add a title, you can insert rows by clicking the top row to select it. Then click Insert and Row.*

8 Click and drag to widen column heads so that numbers fit.

You can reformat column heads as necessary by clicking Format and then Cell.

Did You Know?

Excel has tools enabling you to open and search external databases on the same PC or on a network. Such searches require Microsoft Query, an Office component. You can save and reuse retrieved data in reports and charts. For more information, see Task #92.

Did You Know?

An Excel list is primitive when compared with the data management capabilities of Access or server-based databases. You can create worksheets in Excel and then export them into Access where you can maintain and incorporate the sheets into a set of data tables. For more information, see Task #93.

ENTER LIST DATA
using a form

You can create a list from scratch instead of automatically generating one. Creating a list takes two steps: First, you create the structure for your data. The structure consists of a series of text labels, one per cell, each describing the content of a column. You then enter the actual data. Excel enables you to generate a form to greatly simplify data entry.

A form is an alternative to a pick list. A pick list ensures that the numbers you enter are both

accurate and valid. A form simplifies and speeds up data entry by providing you with a blank field for each column in the list. You type into the fields and tab to move from field to field. When you are done, you enter the set of fields into a row in your list and start entering a new set of fields.

The list form doubles as a search box, which you can use to retrieve values in a worksheet. Filtering your list is another way of pinpointing cells containing specific data.

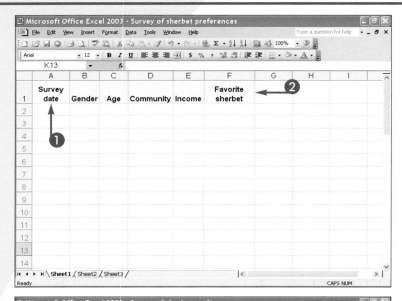

① Type a column head name for the first column.

② Repeat step **1** to continue adding column heads to adjacent cells.

Note: For ease of use, you can click all the column heads and apply the same formatting, such as bold or centering.

③ Click the cell in which you want to begin entering data.

④ Click Data.

⑤ Click Form.

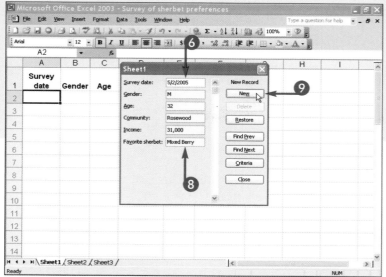

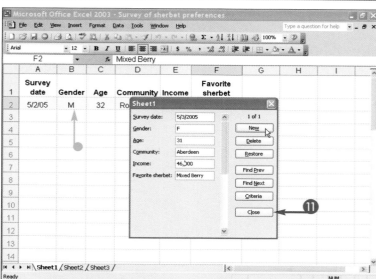

The data form appears, consisting of one field for each column head created in steps **1** and **2**.

6 Type the requested data in the field.

7 Press Tab to move to the next field.

8 Repeat steps **6** to **7** to complete the remaining fields.

9 After completing the first set of fields, click New to enter the data and start a new record.

● The data fills the worksheet, and the form fields clear, ready for another record.

10 Repeat steps **6** to **9** for each new record.

11 Click Close after entering data.

A listing of your data records appears in the spreadsheet

TIPS

Did You Know?

You can let Excel generate a list for you, based on a worksheet. For more information, see Task #35.

Did You Know?

With the data entered, you can use the data form to search for and edit your data. With the list and form displayed, click the form's Criteria button. In the blank fields, type an operator, such as **=** or **>**, and a value in one or more fields. For example, to find all records for *Sally*, you would type **=Sally** in the Name field and press Enter. If several records are available, click the Find Prev (Previous) and Find Next buttons as appropriate.

IMPORT A WORD LIST
into Excel

If you create a table or other collection of structured information in Microsoft Word, you can import that information into Excel and take advantage of list features. It is not more efficient to start a list in Word; however, sometimes you start creating a table in Word that becomes long and elaborate. At that point, maintaining the information in Excel may make more sense than maintaining it in Word.

In Excel, you can perform calculations on the data, use functions, and apply filters, all of which would be time-consuming and inefficient in Word.

When you copy a table from Word and paste it into an Excel worksheet, you may lose some formatting, and some of the data may transfer as text instead of as numbers. For information on converting text to numbers, see Task #28. After you import the table into Excel, you can proceed to add data to the list using a form as explained in Task #36.

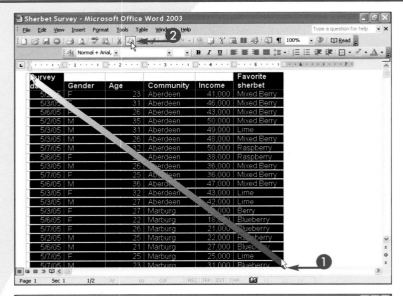

IMPORT A WORD LIST

1 In Word, click and drag to select the cells you want to copy.

2 Click the Copy button.

The table copies to the Windows Clipboard.

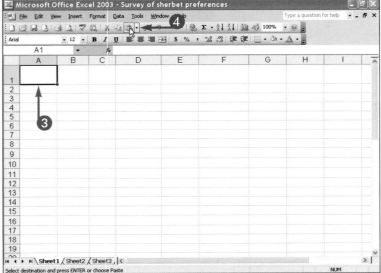

3 In Excel, click a cell in the upper left of the worksheet, making sure there are enough cells below and to the right to accommodate the Word table.

4 Click the Paste button to insert the empty worksheet.

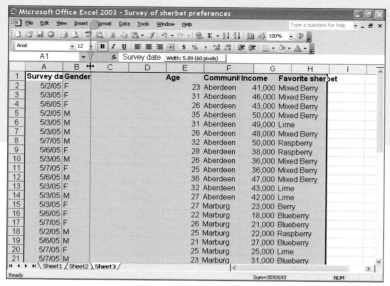

The cells are copied into Word.

● You can click and drag columns to adjust them to the imported data.

 # 37

DIFFICULTY LEVEL

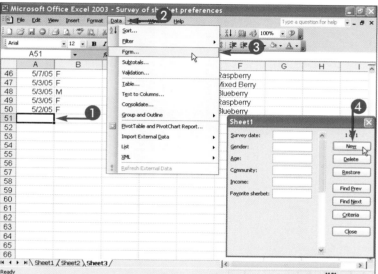

USE THE LIST IN EXCEL

① To add more records, click the first cell of a new row.

② Click Data.

③ Click Form.

④ In the form, click New to start a new record.

Note: Use the data-entry form as explained in Task #36.

TIPS

Did You Know?
The Data menu at the top of the screen appears only when you click inside a list.

Did You Know?
You can import Word data that consists of text separated by commas, tabs, semicolons, or other delimiters. After posting the data into Excel, click Data and then Text to Columns. Use the Wizard to arrange the Word data into Excel cells.

Customize It!
When you transfer data into Excel, or within Excel, the Paste Options menu appears. To prevent unwanted Word formatting from accompanying the imported content, click the menu and click Match Destination Formatting. The Paste Options menu remains visible until you begin another Excel task.

SORT AND FILTER
a list

Sorting and filtering your lists offers you different views of your data; neither view changes the underlying data.

When you sort, you rearrange all of your data in *ascending* or *descending* order. The meaning of these terms depends on the kind of data you have. With customer data arranged by the date the information was entered, ascending order shows the earliest record first, and descending order shows the latest record first. When you sort by customer name, customer names appear in ascending (A-Z) or descending (Z-A) order. When you sort customer

ID numbers in ascending order, they range from the lowest number to the highest. When you sort customer ID numbers in descending order, they range from the highest number to the lowest. When you arrange a list in a familiar order, it is easier to find data, group data, and present it meaningfully to others.

Filtering works like a sieve through which you pass your list data, displaying only data that meets your criteria. In a customer survey, for example, you can choose to view only customers who live in a certain state or city, or of a certain age or gender.

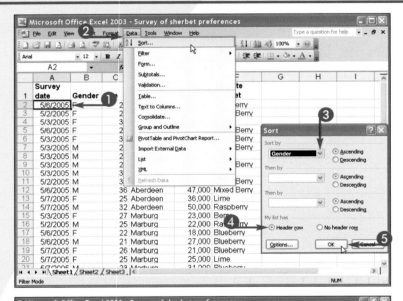

SORT A LIST

1. Click a cell in the list.

2. Click Data and then Sort.

   The Sort dialog box appears.

3. Click here and select the column by which you want to sort.

4. Click Header row
   (☐ changes to ☑).

5. Click OK.

● The entire list sorts according to the values in the selected column.

Note: For information about more complex sorting, see Task #39.

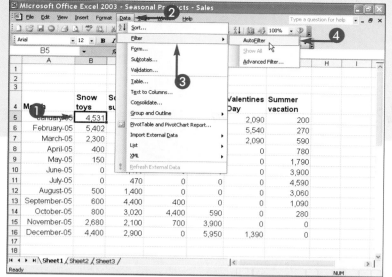

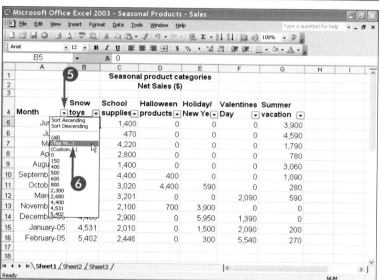

1. Position the cursor anywhere in the list.

2. Click Data.

3. Click Filter.

4. Click Autofilter.

DIFFICULTY LEVEL

Down arrows appear by each column head. You can click any arrow to view sorting options.

5. To filter by a column, click ⬇.

6. Click a menu choice.

Only the records that meet the specified criterion are displayed.

Note: *For more about complex filtering, see Task #41.*

Caution!

Make sure to check the radio button by Header Row in the Sort dialog box. That way, Excel will not try to sort the column headings along with the data values. In addition, make sure that there is only one row of column heads above the data cells. If you have several rows of headers, Excel may try to sort some of them.

Did You Know?

Your data is usually either continuous or discrete. *Continuous* data assumes a wide variety of values, such as incomes and names. *Discrete* data assumes only a few values — for example, male or female. Sorting continuous data imposes order by alphabetizing it or ranking it numerically. Sorting discrete data has the effect of grouping like values, enabling you to compare one category with another.

Sort by
MULTIPLE CRITERIA

Sorting a list by one criterion, like age, arranges your records for easy scanning. You can also sort by multiple criteria — a sort within a sort. When possible, first sort by a category such as gender, community, region, or department. That way, subsequent sorts apply to the multiple values contained within each category.

For example, after sorting your customer records by gender, you could sort them by income to display the *range* of men's incomes and women's incomes. Sorting by a third column, community, would then *show* where men and women with different income ranges live.

With your data sorted in this way, you can do subtotals, averages, and counts at every *break* in a category — that is, for all men, all women, all men in a specific community, and so on.

You define all sorts in the Sort dialog box. Ascending and descending are not your only choices. In the Sort dialog box, you can click Options to specify a custom order. For example, you could order months chronologically from January to December instead of alphabetically from April to November, which would not be very useful.

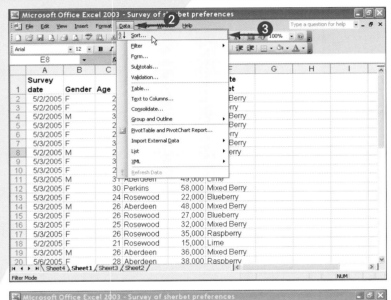

① Click a cell in the list.

② Click Data.

③ Click Sort.

The Sort dialog box appears.

④ Click here and select the column by which you want to sort.

⑤ Click Ascending or Descending to specify the sort order (○ changes to ◉).

⑥ Repeat steps **4** to **5** to sort by additional criteria.

⑦ Click Options.

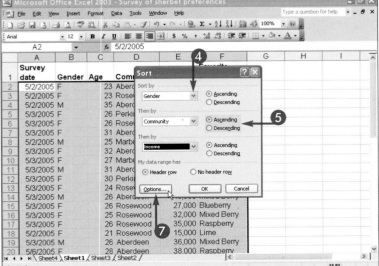

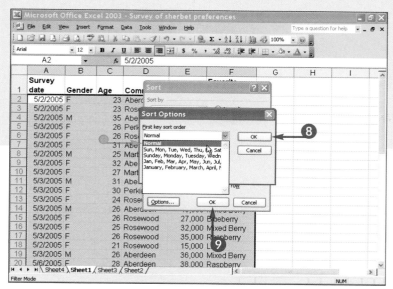

The Sort Options dialog box appears.

● If a column has days of the week, select a sort order to have them appear in chronological rather than alphabetical order.

39

DIFFICULTY LEVEL

⑧ Click OK.

⑨ Click OK in the Sort dialog box.

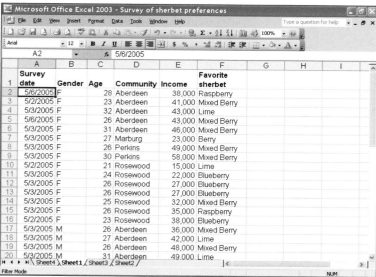

The list sorts according to the sort order specified, along with any options chosen.

Note: Sorting by columns with few categories shows information in groups.

Note: Sorting by columns with variable data arranges data for useful scanning.

TIPS

Did You Know?

Excel defines different sorts as follows. For numbers, ascending order goes from the smallest number to the largest. For text including numerals, as in U2 and K12, ascending order places numerals before symbols, and symbols before letters. Case does not matter unless you click Options in the Sort dialog box and click the Case Sensitive box.

Did You Know?

A custom sort tells Excel to sort *Wednesday* before *Thursday*, even though *T* comes before *W*. In the Sort dialog box, click Options and select an order from the drop-down menu in the upper-left corner.

Did You Know?

A *criterion* is a condition that you apply in filtering. If the criterion is State="Iowa", all Iowa records are included in your results.

FIND AVERAGES
in a sorted group

When you sort, you often aim to group your information into categories with a small number of possible values, such as gender. Excel provides the tools for you to perform simple calculations *within* such categories so that you can then compare one category with another. With a sort defined for one column, you can find the average, sum, or number of items for that column or another column. The Excel feature that enables you to perform calculations within categories is called *subtotaling*, even though it enables you to do more than subtotal.

Subtotaling uses outlining to hide data to allow you to compare rows or columns. When you calculate the average, or sum, or other calculation for a sorted list, outlining enables you to view only the results of the calculation.

Note that with subtotals, you can do a count on a column with text entries. In other circumstances, the Count function works only with numbers.

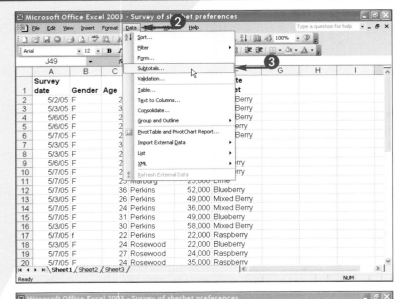

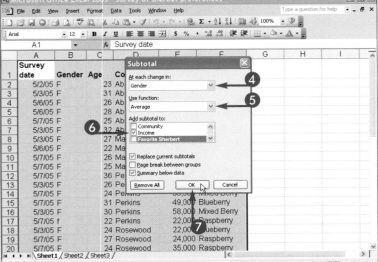

Note: To average a sort, start with a sorted list. For additional information, see Task #39.

① Click a cell in the list.

② Click Data.

③ Click Subtotals.

The Subtotal dialog box appears.

④ Click here and select the category by which you want to calculate.

⑤ Click here and select another type of calculation.

⑥ Click one or more columns in which you want the results to appear (☐ changes to ☑).

⑦ Click OK.

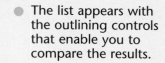

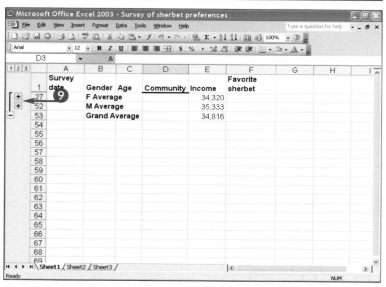

- The list appears with the outlining controls that enable you to compare the results.

⑧ To compare results in different rows, click the minus sign (-).

1 2 3		A	B	C	D	E	F	G	H	I
·	19	5/7/05	F	27	Rosewood	24,000	Raspberry			
·	20	5/7/05	F	24	Rosewood	35,000	Raspberry			
·	21	5/2/05	F	21	Rosewood	15,000	Lime			
·	22	5/3/05	F	26	Rosewood	27,000	Blueberry			
·	23	5/7/05	F	26	Rosewood	30,000	Raspberry			
·	24	5/3/05	F	25	Rosewood	32,000	Mixed Berry			
·	25	5/3/05	F	26	Rosewood	35,000	Raspberry			
·	26	⑧ 2/05	F	23	Rosewood	38,000	Blueberry			
−	27		F Average			34,320				
·	28	5 05	M	35	Aberdeen	50,000	Mixed Berry			
·	29	5/3/05	M	31	Aberdeen	49,000	Lime			
·	30	5/3/05	M	26	Aberdeen	48,000	Mixed Berry			
·	31	5/7/05	M	32	Aberdeen	50,000	Raspberry			
·	32	5/3/05	M	26	Aberdeen	36,000	Mixed Berry			
·	33	5/6/05	M	36	Aberdeen	47,000	Mixed Berry			
·	34	5/3/05	M	27	Aberdeen	42,000	Lime			
·	35	5/2/05	M	25	Marburg	22,000	Raspberry			
·	36	5/6/05	M	21	Marburg	27,000	Blueberry			
·	37	5/7/05	M	23	Marburg	31,000	Blueberry			
·	38	5/3/05	M	37	Perkins	50,000	Lemon			
·	39	5/7/05	M	36	Perkins	65,000	Lime			

Only the result rows appear.

⑨ To redisplay all results, click the plus sign.

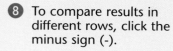

1 2 3		A	B	C	D	E	F	G	H	I
	1	Survey date	Gender	Age	Community	Income	Favorite sherbet			
+	27	⑨	F Average			34,320				
+	52		M Average			35,333				
−	53		Grand Average			34,816				
	54									
	55									
	56									
	57									
	58									
	59									
	60									
	61									
	62									
	63									
	64									
	65									
	66									
	67									
	68									
	69									

TIPS

Did You Know?
You can create several subtotals for a single sorted list. To display all your subtotals, make sure that the Replace Current Subtotals check box is *not* checked when you use the Subtotal dialog box.

Did You Know?
You can remove outlining by clicking Data, Group and Outline, and then Clear Outline.

Did You Know?
Remember that you can do a calculation on a different column from the one defining the sort. For example, if you sort by gender in one column, you can find the average salary or age for men or women, and place the results in the respective columns, such as income column or age column.

Filter by
MULTIPLE CRITERIA

Whereas sorting rearranges all records in ascending or descending order, filtering enables you to see only the records that match your criteria, hiding the rest. Criteria look like this: Age > 65 and State = "Missouri," where Age and State are the names of column heads. When you filter a list, down arrows appear to the right of every column head.

Click a column's arrow to select values, such as Missouri, by which to filter that column. By applying a filter, you display only those records that contain

certain values in the column, for example, all customers in Missouri, or all men who live in a specific community. You can also create a filter that displays the records for a column's top 10 values. With Excel, you can combine filters, applying different criteria to different columns.

By applying several filters, you can quickly narrow down a long list to the few records of interest to you. Criteria that apply to too narrow a range of values, however, might well return no records.

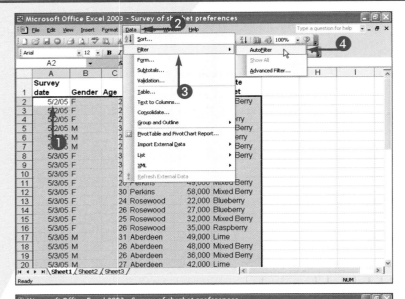

Note: To filter a list by multiple criteria, start with a worksheet formatted as a list, including column heads.

① Click a cell in the list that you want to filter.

② Click Data.

③ Click Filter.

④ Click AutoFilter.

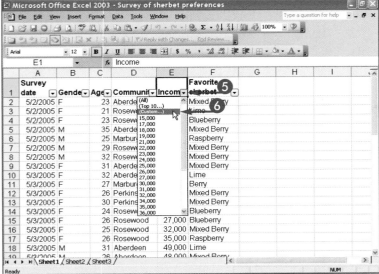

Down arrows (⏷) appear by each column head.

⑤ To create a filter, click ⏷

⑥ Click (Custom) to filter by one or two criteria for one column.

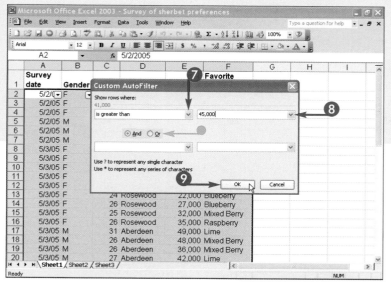

The Custom AutoFilter dialog box appears.

7 Click here and select an operator to indicate the values that you want to filter.

8 Type a value.

● Optionally, you can repeat steps **7** to **8** to create a second criterion.

9 Click OK.

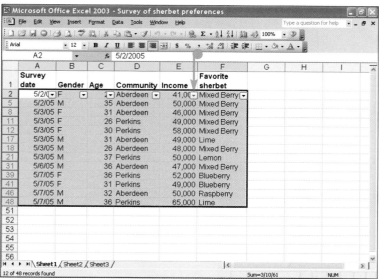

The list displays only records matching the criteria.

● A blue arrow ( ) indicates which columns have been used to filter.

Note: To sort the filtered records, click Data, Sort and then sort the filtered column in ascending order.

Note: To remove the filtering drop-down menu, click Data, Filter, and then AutoFilter.

Did You Know?

In the drop-down filtering menu, you can click Sort Ascending or Sort Descending to sort the filtered records. Click Top 10 to view the top 10 values or Bottom 10 for the bottom 10. You can also choose another number instead of 10. To perform a calculation on the top 10 values, see Chapter 2. To apply more than one filter to a column, for example, Age < 20 or Age > 30, click Custom. Also, see Task #44.

Did You Know?

AutoSum and Descriptive Statistics are not available for filtered lists because hidden details, or records not meeting the criteria, are included in the ranges. For more about addition, see Task #13. For more about statistics, see Task #54.

REMOVE DUPLICATE RECORDS
from a list

Excel provides many tools for managing long lists. With such lists, you may find that you need to identify and display unique records. A baseball-card collector, for example, may want to find out the number of unique players represented in his collection in order to create a catalog. Alternatively, a store manager may want to know the number of unique individuals represented in her survey in order to make informed decisions about customer behavior.

Excel provides tools for identifying unique records in a list. You start with a worksheet formatted as a list in which some of the records are duplicates, meaning that the values in every column of two or more records are the same. You use Excel's advanced filtering tools to identify and remove the duplicated records. Ordinarily, you use these tools to create filters in several columns and even several filters on a single column. When removing duplicate records, however, you do not specify any filter.

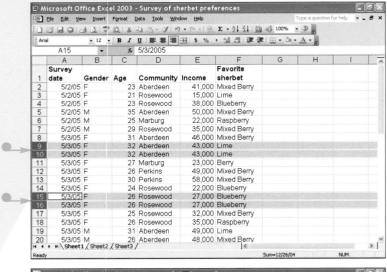

- Locate the duplicate records, which can create incorrect subtotals and other calculations.

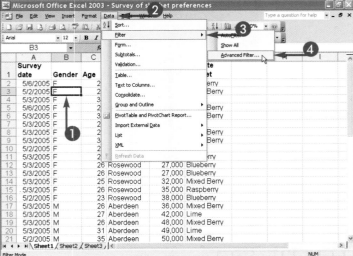

1 Click a cell in the list.
2 Click Data.
3 Click Filter.
4 Click Advanced Filter.

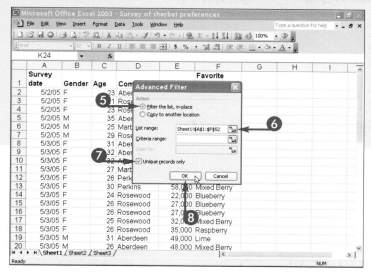

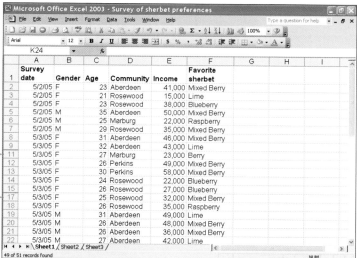

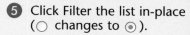
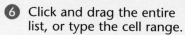

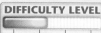

The Advanced Filter dialog box appears.

5 Click Filter the list in-place (○ changes to ◉).

6 Click and drag the entire list, or type the cell range.

Note: *Leave the Criteria Range empty.*

DIFFICULTY LEVEL

7 Click Unique records only (☐ changes to ☑).

8 Click OK.

The duplicate records are hidden from view.

Note: *You can tell the records are hidden because the row numbers are not continuous.*

● You can display the duplicate rows by clicking below the black line and clicking Unfreeze Panes.

Note: *To learn about analyzing, charting, and reporting on list, see Chapters 5, 6, and 7.*

TIPS

Did You Know?

A criteria range is used to provide the information that Excel needs to perform advanced filtering. It consists of one or more column heads displayed horizontally. For each column head, you type at least one criterion into the cell below the head. For examples, see Tasks #43 and #44.

Customize It!

As with any filtering, when you perform a calculation on a list from which duplicates have been filtered out, the hidden rows are included in the range of values included in the calculation. To correct this, in the Advanced Filter dialog box, click Copy to Another Location. Note that the location must be on the same worksheet. Click a cell where you want the copied, duplicate-free list to begin.

Count
FILTERED RECORDS

Like the standard worksheet functions, database functions enable you to perform calculations and summarize data patterns. Database functions are especially good at summarizing the subsets of your list created through filtering. Most database functions combine two tasks: They filter a group of records based on values in a single column; then, they count them or perform another simple operation on the filtered data.

Dcount() is a database function that counts the number of cells containing a number. Dcount() has

three arguments. The first argument, Database, identifies the cell range for the entire list. The second argument, field, identifies the cell range for the column from which you want to extract data.

In the third argument, criteria, you provide Excel a criterion for extracting information. For example, your criterion in a sales table could be Net Sales>5,000, where Net Sales is the column name. You build the criterion manually, copying a column head and in the cell beneath it, defining a condition.

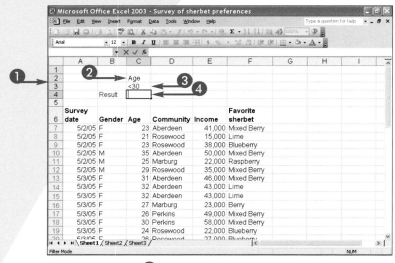

① Insert several rows above your list to hold the criteria range.

② Type the column head from which you want to count records.

③ Type the criterion for counting records.

④ Click a cell to hold your formula.

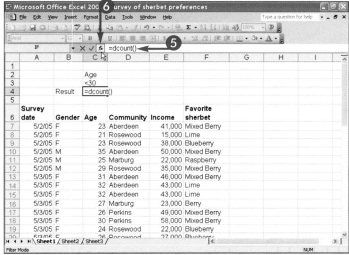

⑤ Type **=dcount()**.

⑥ Click the Insert Function button.

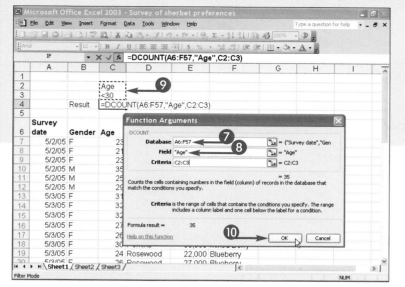

The Function Arguments dialog box appears.

7 Click and drag all the cells in the list, or type in the cell range.

8 Type the column name within quotation marks.

Or, type the column's number or the column's range.

9 Click and drag the cell range from steps **2** to **3**.

10 Click OK.

DIFFICULTY LEVEL

● The result appears.

Note: Remember, the Dcount () function counts only cells containing numbers. For non-numeric data, use the Dcount () function.

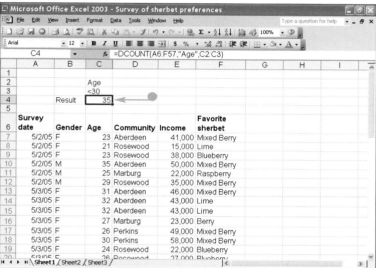

TIPS

Did You Know?

To add data to a list, you can insert a row or column at any time. To do so, select the existing row where you want the new row to appear and click Insert and then Row. The existing row is pushed down to make room for the new one. Similarly, you can insert a column by selecting the existing column where you want the column to appear, and clicking Insert, Column. Functions based on values whose positions change as a result of the insertions continue to work because cell references automatically change to accommodate the insertions.

Did You Know?

The names of database functions begin with a *D* to distinguish them from worksheet functions. Like worksheet functions, you can build database functions using the Function Wizard. Type the function into a cell, for example **=dcount()**, and click the Insert Function button. Other database functions use the same arguments as dcount () : database, field, and criteria range.

FILTER BY MULTIPLE CRITERIA
in the same column

Advanced filtering enables you to go beyond the limitations of using the AutoFilter command. With advanced filtering, you can create more than two filters for a single column and more easily coordinate a set of filters between columns. For example, you can filter a survey to find people age 30 or less who earn more than $35,000 *and* people age 30 or more who earn more than $45,000. Advanced filtering requires a bit of work, even when using the Advanced Filter menu command. You must find a block of cells

on the worksheet to create a *criteria range*. You create a criteria range to which you copy one or more column heads from a list. In the cells below each head, you type criteria by which each column is to be filtered, such as <30 and >30.

Using the Advanced Filter dialog box, you also specify the cell addresses of the entire list and the location of the filtered list. The filtered list must be on the same worksheet as the original list.

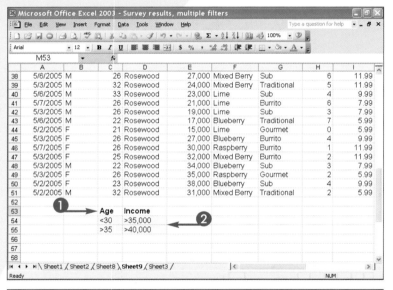

① On the worksheet with your list, copy the column head names of the columns you want to filter.

② Type criteria by which to filter values.

Note: *Use operators to define criteria and place text in quotes.*

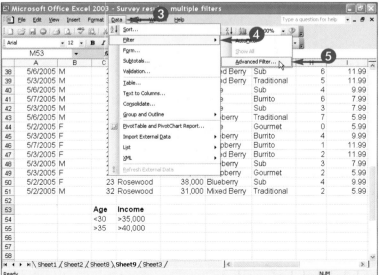

③ Click Data.

④ Click Filter.

⑤ Click Advanced Filter.

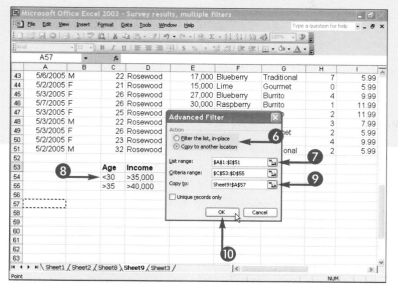

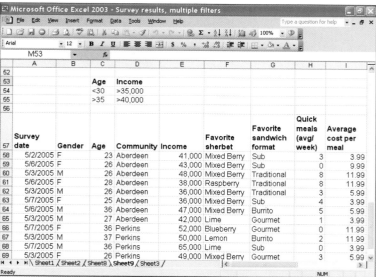

The Advanced Filter dialog box appears.

6 Click to indicate where to place the filtered list (○ changes to ⊙).

You can click Copy to another location to copy the information and retain the original.

7 Click and drag to select the entire list.

8 Click and drag to select the criteria defined in step **2**.

9 If you chose to copy the filtered list in step **6**, click the first cell for the filter.

10 Click OK.

The filtered list appears. You may need to format the results to accommodate wide columns.

Did You Know?

A criteria range can have several rows of criteria. When a row consists of two or more criteria, Excel looks through your list and returns only the rows that meet all criteria.

Caution!

Make sure that your criteria range has enough room below it to include all the values that may return in the filtered list. If you place the criteria range above your original list, the results may overwrite the list and prevent filtering from proceeding. Placing the criteria range to the right of the list or below it protects your original list.

Chart a
FILTERED LIST

With Excel, you can quickly create a chart showing the information in a worksheet or list. Charts show trends and anomalies that may be otherwise difficult to detect in columns of numbers. By choosing the appropriate type of chart and formatting chart features, you can share your results with others and quickly convey patterns in your data. For more about charting, see Chapter 6.

To chart a filtered list, first begin with a chart of an unfiltered list. Select the data you want to chart, click the Chart Wizard button, and follow the steps as prompted. Excel enables you to position the chart next to the data on which it is based, so you can make changes in the data and instantly observe changes in the corresponding chart.

The Plot visible cells only option in the Options dialog box shows you the filtered chart without the cells hidden as a result of filtering. If you turn the option off, you can view the unfiltered chart. Now, any filter you apply is immediately charted.

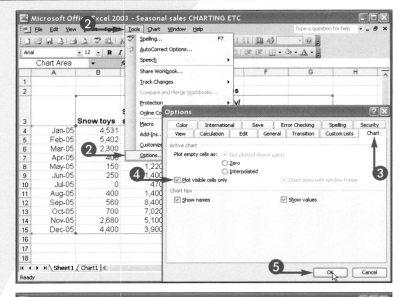

Note: To chart a filtered list, begin with a chart of an unfiltered list.

① Click the chart to select it.

② Click Tools and then Options.

The Options dialog box appears.

③ Click the Chart tab.

④ Click Plot visible cells only (☐ changes to ☑).

⑤ Click OK.

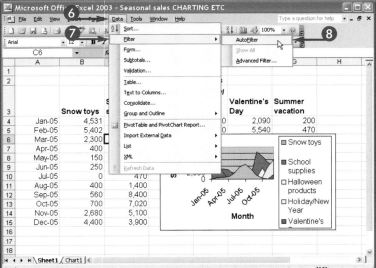

⑥ Click Data.

⑦ Click Filter.

⑧ Click AutoFilter.

98

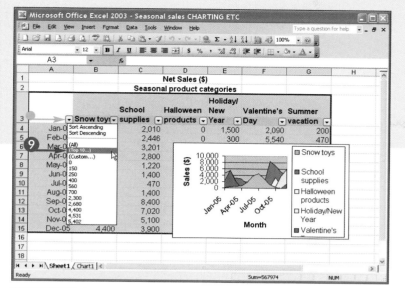

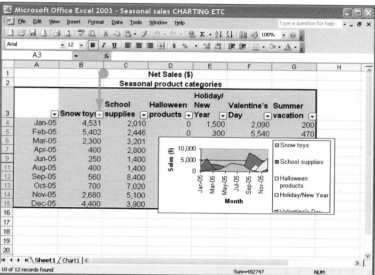

- Down arrows appear by each column head.

9 Click here and select the filter that you want to apply.

10 Repeat step **9** for additional filters that you want to apply.

DIFFICULTY LEVEL

Note: The Top 10 filter shown in this example selects and displays the records with the ten highest values.

The chart changes to reflect the Top 10 filter.

- The down arrow for the column with the filter is now blue.

Note: You can restore the pre-filtered view by clicking the blue down arrow and clicking All.

Caution!

Changing the information in a list automatically changes a chart based on the list as well. The reverse is also true, however. You can change and potentially invalidate list data by simply dragging a chart's data series. When formatting a chart, avoid clicking and dragging the lines or points that represent data!

Did You Know?

A chart represents only data you have selected. To view the effect of a filter on a single column and suppress the values in other columns, right-click the entire chart and click Source Data. On the Series tab, click and remove the list information that you do not want to appear. To restore the information, you need to regenerate the chart.

LOOK UP INFORMATION
in a list

With Excel's vertical lookup function, `Vlookup()`, you can identify a value in one row based on a value in a column in the same row. For example, in a product list, you could enter a product's ID to retrieve its price; product ID and price form are part of the same row. You use lookup functions when you know one value, such as a state name, and need to look up a value in that state's record, such as the sales tax.

To use `Vlookup()`, you type a value in one column; the function retrieves a value from the column that

you specify. You set up the function so that the first column in the list contains the values that you use to retrieve the other value.

To use `Vlookup()`, you enter three required arguments into the Function Wizard: the cell address where you enter the value that you want to look up, the list's cell range, and the column in which the retrieved value can be found. For simplicity, you can call the first column in the list *1*, the second column *2*, and so on.

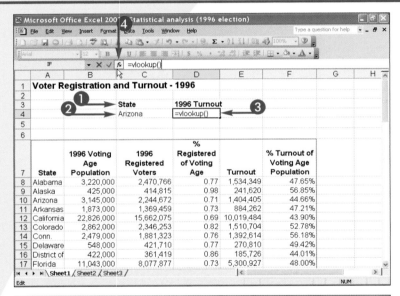

① In a blank cell, create a label to describe the lookup value that you will type to retrieve another value.

② In an adjacent cell, type a sample value that you may use to look up a related value.

③ In an adjacent cell to the right, type **=vlookup()**.

④ Click the Insert Function button.

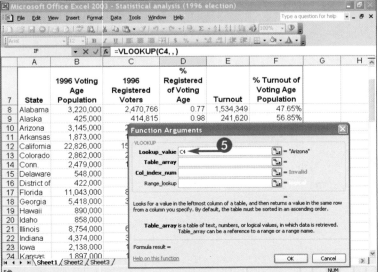

The Function Arguments dialog box appears.

⑤ Click in the first field and then click the cell with the value entered in step **2**.

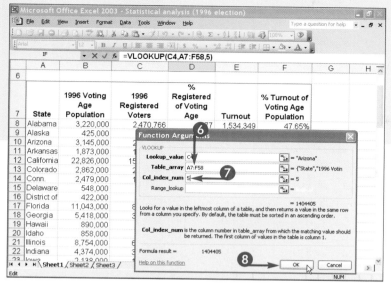

6 Shift+click to select all the values in the list.

7 Type the number of the column containing the value that you want to retrieve.

● Alternatively, you can type the column name (**"Turnout"**) or range (**E:E**).

8 Click OK.

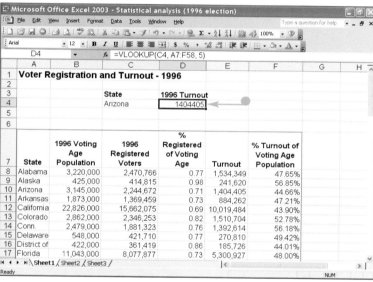

● The box containing the formula displays the value corresponding to the lookup value.

Note: You can click the cell with the current lookup value, for example, Arizona, and type another lookup value.

TIPS

Did You Know?

The less common horizontal lookup function finds a value in a column based on another value in the same column.

Did You Know?

The lookup functions have an optional fourth argument called range lookup. If you use TRUE or leave the argument blank, the function looks for the closest match to the value that you seek. If you use FALSE, the function returns only an exact value.

Did You Know?

To further simplify your function, give your list a name such as Sales or Customers. Likewise, use column names instead of column numbers to designate a column in which you can find the result. For more information, see Task #3.

Exploring Patterns in Data

Excel offers you much more than a way of keeping track of your data and doing calculations. It adds even more value by providing you with the tools to analyze your data and thus to understand it better and make better decisions. In this chapter, you find a range of tools that can give you rich insights into your data.

One of the most useful tools in Excel, the PivotTable, is also one of the least understood. A PivotTable performs similar work to cross-tabulation in statistics. It shows how data is distributed across two categories. With a PivotTable, for example, you can analyze survey data and display how different products sell among men and women in three different communities. Alternatively, you can analyze income distribution and consumer preferences by gender and age bracket. Excel makes it

easy for you to create PivotTables and answer useful questions about your data.

This chapter introduces Excel's statistical functions, too, which you can use to analyze your data. These statistics were once available only through large, expensive statistical software packages. You learn to use descriptive statistics to characterize your data and to explore associations between data series, using the Correlation function. Excel includes more advanced functions for the statistically adept.

Finally, you learn to do two related analytical tasks in Excel: what-if analysis and goal seeking. With what-if analysis, you vary an input to find how it affects a result. With goal seeking, you do the opposite. You start with a goal and try to achieve it efficiently by varying a single factor.

Top 100

Create a
PIVOTTABLE

PivotTables enable you to answer incisive questions about your worksheet data. A PivotTable consists of rows and columns, just like a worksheet.

The rows and columns of a PivotTable usually have *discrete* information, meaning that the values fall into categories. Gender is a discrete variable because all values are either M or F. Community is another discrete variable because many people live in one community. Salary, sales, and frequent-flier miles are not discrete, however, but *continuous,* meaning that a wide range of values is possible for each.

The body of a PivotTable — the data area — usually has continuous data to show how the data are distributed across rows and columns. For example, you could show how income is distributed among men and women living in different communities.

You can optionally organize PivotTables by pages with a separate table on each page. You can define each page by a region, showing regional sales data broken down by gender and income bracket.

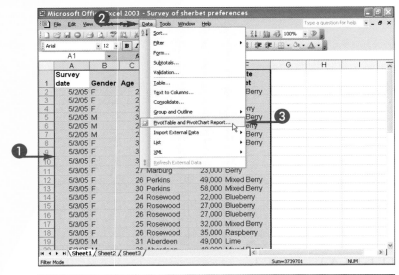

Note: *To create a PivotTable, begin with an Excel list; see Task #36.*

① Click and drag to select the list.

Note: *Make sure to include the column head.*

② Click Data.

③ Click PivotTable and PivotChart Report.

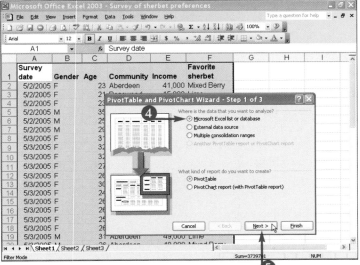

The PivotTable and PivotChart Wizard appears open to step **1** of the Wizard.

④ Click the source of data for the table (○ changes to ◉).

⑤ Click Next.

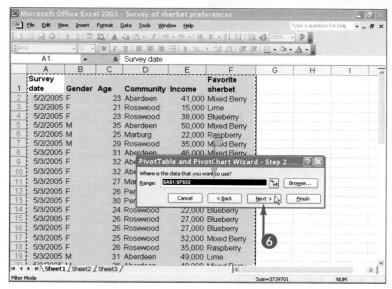

● Step 2 screen of the Wizard appears displaying the cells selected in step **1**.

Note: You can type in a range name or click and drag to select a different cell range.

⑥ Click Next.

Step **3** screen of the Wizard appears.

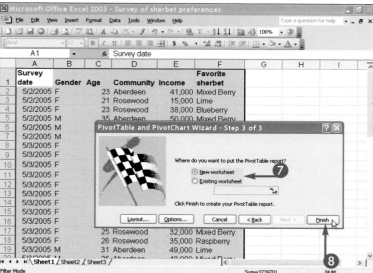

⑦ Click to create the PivotTable on a new worksheet or to include it on the same page as the list (○ changes to ◉).

⑧ Click Finish.

TIPS

Did you know?
In step 3 of the PivotTable and PivotChart Wizard, click Layout if you know which data you want to use for the columns, rows, and data area, as well as for the page views. Actual data does not appear in the Layout window, but will appear when you click OK to leave the Layout view and Finish to leave the Wizard.

Did you know?
Pivot simply refers to the ability to rearrange row and column fields so that you can get different views of your data. The PivotTable concept may be familiar to you from statistics, where the more familiar terms are *cross-tab* and *contingency* tables.

Did you know?
The term *field* refers to a column or row head, such as Income or Age.

Create a
PIVOTTABLE

The PivotTable layout consists of several elements. The PivotTable Field List shows all the fields, columns and rows in your list. When working with a PivotTable, you can always restore the Field List to view by clicking the button on the far right of the PivotTable toolbar. The toolbar appears whenever you display a PivotTable.

The table itself first appears as a set of blank elements designed to hold rows, columns, and data. To construct a PivotTable, you drag fields from the

PivotTable Field List onto the row, column, and data areas of the blank PivotTable. You can click and drag more than one field into an area. Row fields showing Community and Age information would show, for example, the percentage of senior citizens in each of several communities. To change a PivotTable, simply click and drag the table-shaped fields off the table or from one area — column, row, data, or page — to another. For more information, see Task #48.

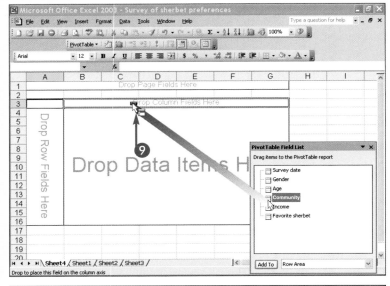

The PivotTable layout appears on a new worksheet.

The PivotTable Field List also appears.

⑨ Click and drag a field to the PivotTable column.

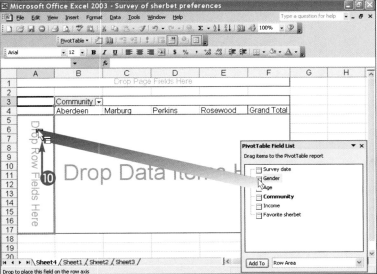

⑩ Click and drag a field to the PivotTable rows.

Optionally, you can add a page field.

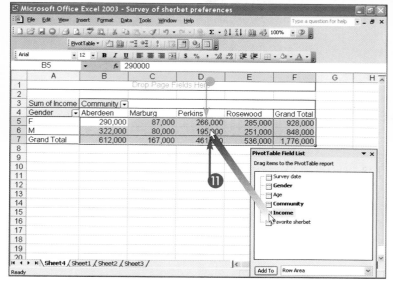

⓫ Click and drag the data that you want to distribute across the rows and columns of the PivotTable.

● As you build the PivotTable, your changes are reflected instantly.

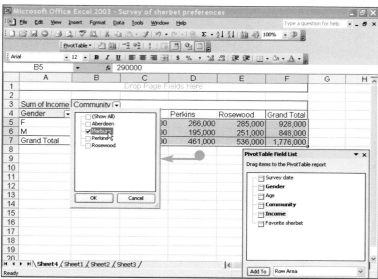

The PivotTable shows how the data chosen in step **11** is distributed across the cells created in steps **9** and **10**.

● The drop-down lists of field names enable you to display one or more specific rows and columns.

TIPS

Did you know?

You can click any cell in a PivotTable to display the PivotTable Field List. The list displays the fields used in the table in bold.

Did you know?

It often makes sense to use the same field from the Field List for both the row and the data area. You would do this to create a simple count, for example. That is, you can use the Age variable in the column area and then show Age in the data area. Select the data cells, right-click, click Field Settings, and select Count to find out how many individuals of each age you have. To create discrete categories out of continuous data, you could create a histogram, as shown in Task #67.

PIVOTTABLE DATA AND LAYOUT

PivotTables enable you to ask essential questions of your data. To extend the value of PivotTables, Excel allows you to update the data upon which they are based and the manner in which they are laid out.

PivotTables can easily get quite complex as you refine them. Fortunately, you need not regenerate and re-edit a table every time the underlying data changes. Instead, you can refresh a table and any charts by clicking the Refresh Data button on the PivotTable toolbar. The refresh button applies even to

data imported from Access in step 1 of the Wizard. Any charts generated from a PivotTable change to reflect updated data.

You can change the layout of a PivotTable in different ways. You can simply click and drag the tablet-like field names to rearrange row and category fields, try out different page views, and redistribute data in the table proper. You can drag the field tablets off the table altogether, enabling you to start again at any time.

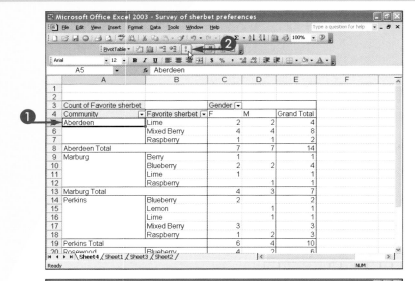

REFRESH DATA

① Click any cell in the table to open the PivotTable toolbar.

② Click the Refresh Data button.

Note: The Refresh Data button appears only if changes have been made to the underlying data.

● Numbers and any calculations based on the changes are revised to reflect changes in the data.

Note: This example shows changes in sherbet preferences.

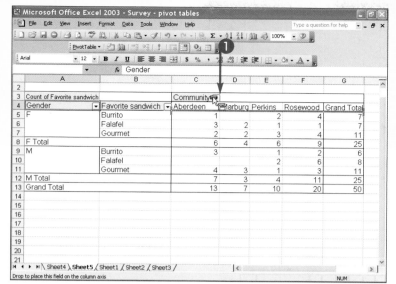

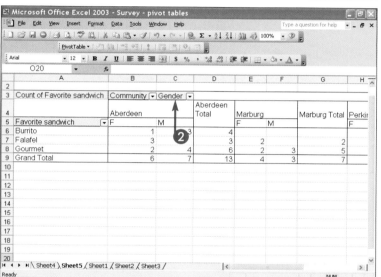

DIFFICULTY LEVEL

① To convert a row into a column field, click the row tablet to change the cursor arrow into a four-point arrow and then drag it to the column area.

Note: To make a column a row, click and drag the column tablet to the row area.

The PivotTable instantly shows the change.

Note: You can move any tablet to any location: data, row, column, or page.

② To remove a field from a PivotTable, click and drag it away from the page, row, column, or data area.

The field is removed.

TIPS

Did you know?

You can have two levels of rows and columns to break down your data by different variables, such as salaries among men and women in different communities.
If you have two row fields, their order can be reversed to give you different views of the information — for example, age broken down by community or community by age.
A drop-down tablet called Data enables you to control which field is shown in the table.

Did you know?

To add fields not present in a PivotTable, click and drag fields from the Field List onto the column, row, data, or page area.

Did you know?

Another way of breaking out a row by two categories is to drag two or more fields into the data area.

Find the AVERAGE OF A FIELD

PivotTables enable you to compare and contrast the distribution of data across categories. You may need a variety of statistics to measure differences between categories. PivotTables automatically calculate Grand Totals for the columns in your list.

You have a choice of calculations other than Grand Total to use in summarizing data, including sum, average, count, standard deviation, minimum, and maximum. To change the summary statistic, select any value in the row or column with values that you want to calculate differently. Use the PivotTable toolbar, or right-click and then click Field Settings.

Use the PivotTable Field dialog box to select a different summary statistic.

Changing the type of calculation used to generate values in a row or column can result in oddly formatted data. To remedy this, the PivotTable Field dialog box has a Number button that gives you access to the number-formatting capabilities of the Format Cells dialog box. You may, for example, want to eliminate decimal points or to add a thousands separator so that you see 7,236,273 instead of 7236273.

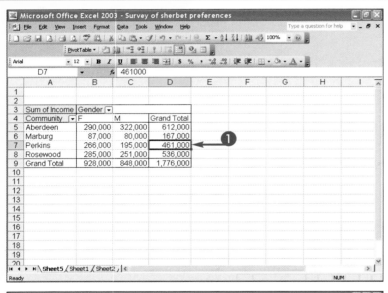

FIND THE AVERAGE OF A FIELD

① Click any cell in the Grand Total row or column.

② On the PivotTable toolbar, click the PivotTable drop-down button.

③ Click Field Settings.

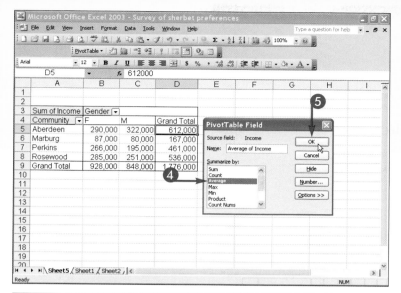

The PivotTable Field dialog box appears.

④ Scroll down and click Average.

⑤ Click OK.

New values appear in the table. Any chart based on the PivotTable automatically changes to reflect the new summary statistic.

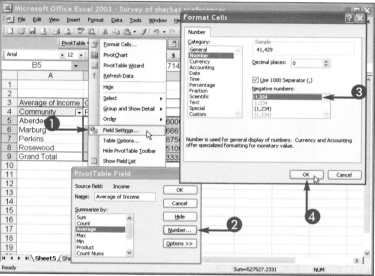

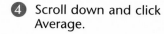

REFORMAT NUMBERS

① Right-click the cell or cells you want to reformat and select Field Settings from the menu.

② Click Number.

The Format Cells dialog box appears, displaying only the Number tab.

③ Click to select formatting options for your values.

④ Click OK.

The reformatted numbers appear.

TIPS

Did you know?

To add new columns or rows to a PivotTable, you can return to the step in the PivotTable Wizard at which you specify information. Click any cell in the PivotTable. From the PivotTable drop-down menu, click PivotTable Wizard. You return to step 3 of the Wizard, where you can click and select another row or column from the same worksheet. Alternatively, you can click Browse to incorporate information from a different worksheet.

Did you know?

If you do not want Excel to calculate grand totals for rows or columns, or both, click anywhere in the table. Using the PivotTable menu on the PivotTable toolbar, click Table Options, and click to uncheck the Grand Total for columns and Grand Total for row options. Click OK.

Create a
CALCULATED FIELD

With a PivotTable, you can create new fields, called *calculated fields,* based on the values in existing fields. You create a calculated field by multiplying or performing another simple operation on every value in the existing field.

You usually use calculated fields with continuous variables such as incomes, prices, miles, and sales. For example, you can multiply each value in a field called *Price* by a constant sales tax to create a calculated field called *Tax.* However, within the PivotTable you cannot multiply two sets of different values by each other. To do that, return to the

worksheet and create a new column. Multiple the cell values in that column, then include the column in a PivotTable.

To create a calculated field, you use the Insert Calculated Field dialog box, which consists of two fields: one to name the new field and the other to build a formula defining the new field. When you create a calculated field, it becomes available in the PivotTable Field List box for use in a PivotTable. You can use the values in the calculated field only in data cells, not in rows, columns, or pages.

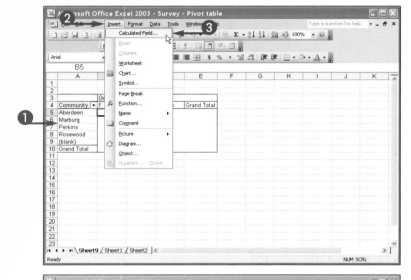

CREATE A CALCULATED FIELD

1 Click any value in the data area of the table.

2 Click Insert.

3 Click Calculated Field.

The Insert Calculated Field dialog box appears.

4 Type a name for the new field.

5 Double-click an existing field to use in defining the field.

6 Type a value by which to multiply or perform other operations upon the field and an operator, such as *.

7 Click OK.

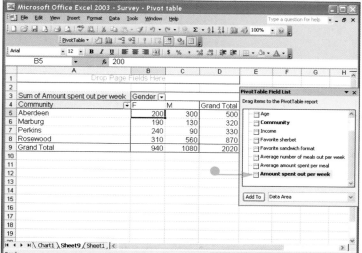

Values for the calculated field fill the data area.

To continue adding fields to the table, right-click any cell in the table and click Field List.

● The calculated field appears at the end of the Field List.

You can access the Field List from the PivotTable toolbar.

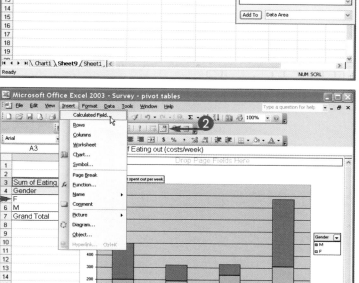

CHART RESULTS

❶ Click any cell in the data area.

❷ Click the Chart Wizard button.

The chart appears, showing who spends more money eating out — men or women — and in which community.

Did you know?

Each cell in a PivotTable summarizes several rows of information. To view this underlying information for any cell, double-click it. The rows appear in a new worksheet, which cannot, however, be edited.

Did you know?

Instead of the Insert menu, you can use the PivotTable toolbar to create a calculated field. If you do not see the PivotTable drop-down button on the toolbar, click the small triangle on the right side of the toolbar. Click the Add or Remove Buttons down arrow and then click PivotTable. From the long drop-down list, click the PivotTable option.

HIDE ROWS OR COLUMNS
in a PivotTable

DIFFICULTY LEVEL

Formatting data changes its appearance, but formatting is not just a matter of cosmetics. Rather, formatting is useful because the complexity of the table elements can make it difficult to see data patterns. Formatting can improve data legibility.

Two formatting tasks available in Excel when working with PivotTables are outlining and autoformatting. Outlining enables you to suppress detail and more easily compare results. For more information, see Task #52.

TIP

Did you know?
To format a PivotTable cell or range, click and drag the cells, and then click Format and Cells. On the Number tab, click a category such as Number or Custom on the left and make appropriate changes on the right.

① Click and drag to select the rows or columns.

② Click the PivotTable drop-down button.

③ Click Group and Show Detail.

④ Click Group.

A new margin appears, with a Minus button.

⑤ Click the Minus button.

The rows or columns are hidden, and the minus sign on the button turns into a plus sign.

Note: You can click the Plus button to see the hidden cells again.

114

AUTOFORMAT
a PivotTable

Autoformatting applies ready-made layouts to your data so that they are easier to read and more attractive. These formats create effects such as enlarging column heads and removing grids. Autoformats also replace field-name tablets that you cannot format with ordinary-looking text, but you can still drag them to a new location.

Applying autoformatting does not prevent you from working on your data. The PivotTable controls remain in place, so you can continue rearranging row and column fields, adjusting summary calculations, and revising the underlying data.

Did you know?
You can autoformat any worksheet. Click any cell in the sheet. Then click Format and Autoformat. The AutoFormat dialog box shows small pictures of sample, ready-made formats. Click any format and OK to apply that format to your worksheet. Use the Options button to restrict formatting to worksheet elements such as numbers, borders, and fonts.

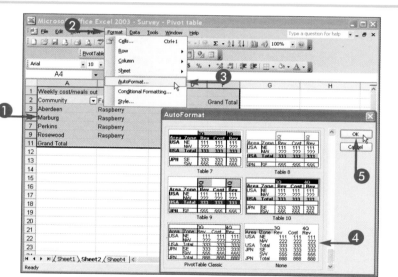

① Click any cell.

② Click Format.

③ Click AutoFormat.

The entire worksheet is highlighted.

The AutoFormat dialog box appears, showing sample formats.

④ Click a format.

⑤ Click OK.

Your table appears in the new format.

Note: Chances are that you will want to try out different formats. You can repeat steps 1 to 5 until you find one that you like.

Note: To make field (tablet) text more readable, click the cell, then click Format and Cells. In the Format Cells dialog box, click the Alignment tab, and then click Shrink to Fit.

Create a
PIVOTCHART

PivotTables can clarify patterns in your worksheets. Charts based on PivotTables, called *PivotCharts,* make such patterns even more evident. Like all charts in Excel, PivotCharts consist of several elements, including chart type, axis, legend, and data series, all of which you can modify at any time to meet your needs.

You can create a chart based on a PivotTable. This method gives you flexibility in using summary statistics and adjusting row and column layout before generating the chart.

You can also create a PivotChart using the PivotTable and PivotChart Wizard, as explained in Task #47. In Step 1 of the Wizard, under What Kind of Report Do You Want to Create, click PivotChart Report to make a chart and proceed with the other Wizard steps. (When you create a chart from an existing PivotTable, Excel generates the PivotChart on a new worksheet.)

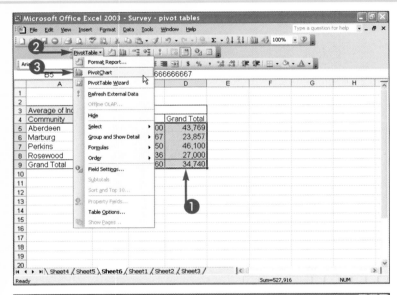

① Click any cells.

② Click the PivotTable down arrow on the PivotTable toolbar.

③ Click PivotChart.

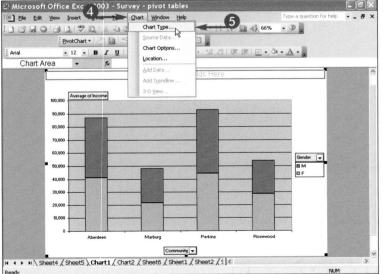

The PivotChart appears in its own worksheet, labeled *Chartx,* where x is greater than 1 if there are already charts on their own sheets.

④ To edit the chart type, click Chart.

⑤ Click Chart Type.

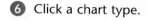

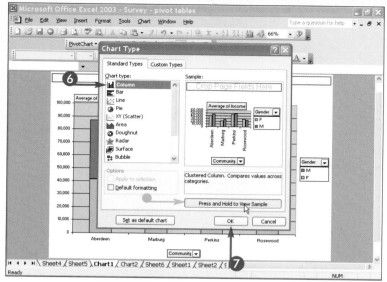

The Chart Type dialog box appears.

6 Click a chart type.

● To review a chart type's effect, you can click this button.

7 To apply a chart type, click OK.

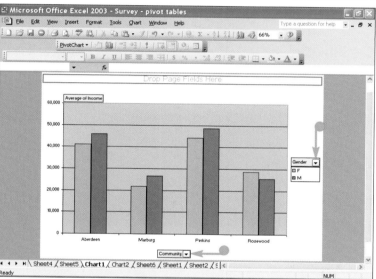

The new chart type takes effect.

● As in a PivotTable, down arrows appear by field names whenever row or column fields have categories that you can view one at a time.

TIPS

Did you know?

You can also modify the colors used for the chart background, the degree of grid detail, the styling of the axis, and more. See Task #59 for information about modifying chart elements.

Caution!

Excel uses its default chart type, the column chart, to generate a PivotChart. In the example shown here, the stacked column chart produces misleading results by adding incomes of men and women instead of comparing them. To chart the default chart type, click Chart and then Chart Type. Select a type and subtype, and then click the Set As Default Chart button. See Task #60 for information about the characteristics of different chart types.

DESCRIBE DATA
with statistics

Excel includes more than 80 statistical functions. You can find these functions using the Function Wizard in the Statistics category. Some of them are also available in the Descriptive Statistics dialog box. If some statistical functions are not available to you, install the Excel Analysis ToolPak as described in Task #93.

Among the statistical functions, you will find more than a dozen types of *descriptive statistics*. With these statistics, you characterize both the "central tendency" of your data, such as mean, mode, and median, and its "variability," such as sample variance

and standard deviation. The Function Wizard has the benefit of providing a guide to using the individual functions. With the Descriptive Statistics dialog box, you can apply all descriptive statistics at the same time, but without the guide to individual functions.

To use descriptive statistics, first display a worksheet with the data you want to analyze. The worksheet can be generated within Excel or imported from Access or other data source. Many functions work only with numeric data. For imported data that remains in non-numeric text form, see Task #28.

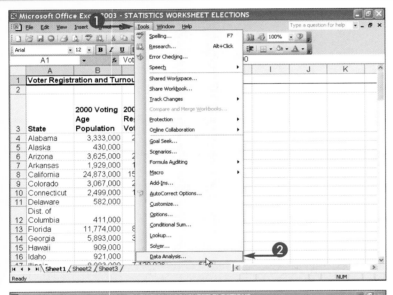

① Click Tools.

② Click Data Analysis.

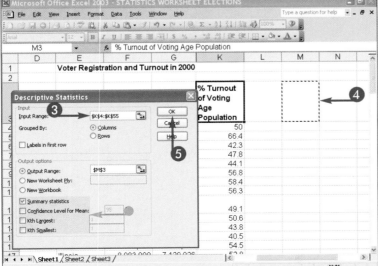

The Descriptive Statistics dialog box appears.

③ Click and drag the cells that you want to describe, or type the cell range.

④ Click the cell in which you want the statistics to appear.

● Optionally, you can include other statistics.

⑤ Click OK.

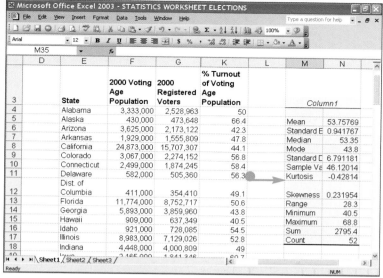

- The statistics appear in a boxed area.

54

DIFFICULTY LEVEL

⑥ To see all your statistics, widen the column heads by clicking the border between column letters and dragging.

TIP

Did You Know?

There are descriptive statistics available as Excel functions.

Excel Functions			
Descriptive Statistic	**Excel Function**	**Descriptive Statistic**	**Excel Function**
Mean	`Average()`	Skewness	`Skew()`
Standard Error	`Steyx()`	Range	`Max()-min()`
Median	`Median()`	Minimum	`Min()`
Mode	`Mode()`	Maximum	`Max()`
Standard Deviation	`Stdev()`	Sum	`Sum()`
Sample Variance	`Var()`	Count	`Count()`
Kurtosis	`Kurt()`		

Discover
ASSOCIATIONS
within your data

With a statistical correlation, you can measure the relationship between two variables. With Excel's Correlation function, you can explore questions such as whether long-term customers purchase more each year or baseball players hit fewer home runs as they age.

A correlation does not prove that one thing causes another. The most you can say is that one number varies with the other. Their variation may be an accident, the result of how your numbers were measured, or the result of some factor underlying both variables. To use correlation, you need to start

with a hunch about the likely influence. If there is a correlation, you must gather evidence and develop plausible reasons accounting for the correlation.

`Correl()` has two arguments: the two lists of numbers. The result of the function is a number, r, that varies between -1 and 1. The closer r gets to -1 or 1, the stronger the likely relationship. If r is negative, the relationship is negative — for example, as age increases, batting averages decrease. A positive result suggests that as one variable increases, so does the other. Squaring r (r^2) provides an absolute measure of the strength of the relationship.

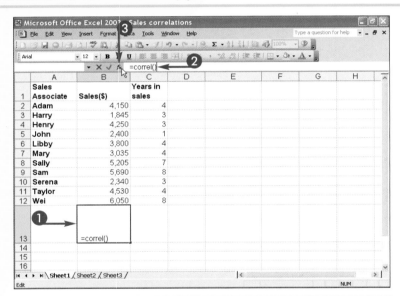

① Click the cell where you want to place your answer.

② Type =**correl()**.

③ Click the Insert Function button.

The **Correl()** Function Arguments dialog box appears.

④ Click and drag one of the series of numbers, or type in the cell range.

⑤ Click and drag the other series, or type in the cell range.

Note: You can select a subset of a list, but make sure that the same subset is selected for the other list.

⑥ Click OK.

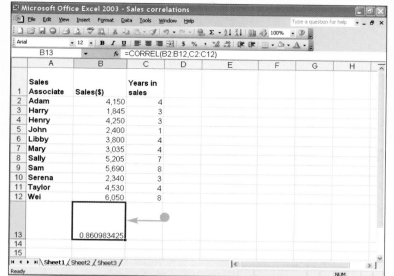

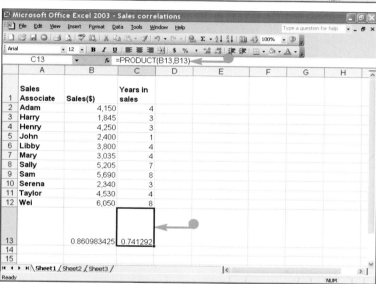

- The correlation coefficient appears.

  Note: The sign suggests whether the relationship is positive (+) or negative (-).

- You can use the `product()` function to find the square of the number (r^2), a measure of its strength.

  Note: To find product and square root, see Task #25.

TIPS

Did you know?

Most statistical measures have tests of significance. Such tests tell you how likely it is for a result to have happened by accident. In correlations, one relevant test is the f test — the Excel `ftest` function. Also, you can use the RSQ function to generate r^2. RSQ() uses the two ranges selected in steps **4** and **5**.

Apply It!

Choose your analytical tool based on the kind of information you have. PivotTables work best with *categorical* data, for which only a few values are possible — M and F for the Gender variable, for example. Correlation requires continuous data, which means that a limitless number of values are possible, such as miles and income.

Explore outcomes with
WHAT-IF ANALYSIS

When you use a function, your purpose is often to find out how one thing influences another. When you use the Payment function, for example, you can find out how a change in the loan amount, loan length, or interest rate — or some combination of these factors, or all three together — affect the monthly payment. By typing in different amounts, rates, and periods, you can see how different scenarios affect the monthly payment.

What-if analysis is a systematic way of finding out how a change in one or more variables affects a result. Scenario Manager lets you vary one or more "inputs" to find out how the result changes. The advantage of using the Scenario Manager is that it stores a series of values and enables you to create a single report or table showing how each value or combination of values influences the result — your monthly payment, in this example. You can even present this information as a PivotTable, with all the flexibility it offers.

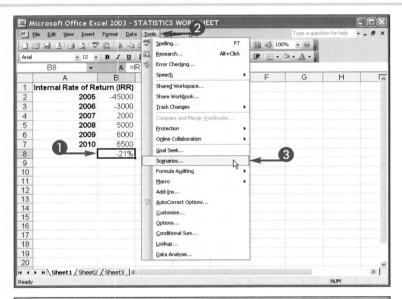

Note: To create scenarios, you must first enter the values required for a function into a worksheet and type a function that calculates an answer for one set of values. This example uses the IRR function, discussed in Task #20.

① Click the cells that contain the values you want to vary.

② Click Tools.

③ Click Scenarios.

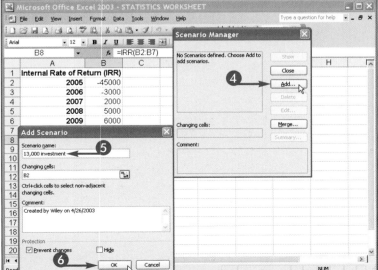

The Scenario Manager appears.

④ Click Add.

The Add Scenario dialog box appears, indicating the cells selected in step **1**.

⑤ Type a name for the scenario.

⑥ Click OK.

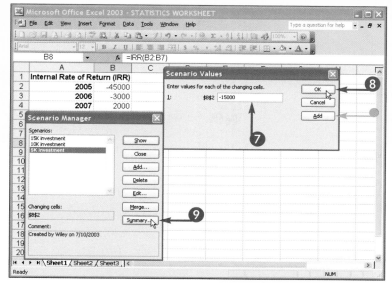

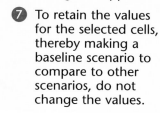

The Scenario Values dialog box appears.

7 To retain the values for the selected cells, thereby making a baseline scenario to compare to other scenarios, do not change the values.

● You can click Add to create more scenarios.

8 Click OK instead of Add when you are done.

The Scenario Manager comes up again.

9 Click Summary.

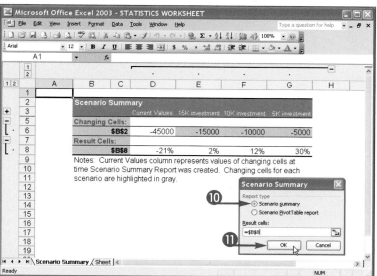

The Scenario Summary dialog box appears.

10 Click the type and location of your report (○ changes to ⊙).

11 Click OK.

The type of report that you requested appears on a new worksheet, displaying how each value affects the result.

TIPS

Did you know?
If you share copies of a workbook and people add their own scenarios, you can merge these scenarios into a single list. To do so, open the workbooks, and click Tools, Scenarios. In the Scenario Manager, click Merge. In the Merge Scenarios window, select the workbooks and individual worksheets to consolidate. Click OK when you are done.

Did you know?
When you vary several inputs, PivotTables can be a powerful tool. PivotTables, the subject of chapter 4, enable you to show how values are distributed among cells, each of which is defined as the intersection of a row and a column. By naming cells, for example *Interest Rate* instead of A2 and *Number of payments* instead of A3, your PivotTable becomes easier to read. To name cells, see Task #3.

Optimize a result with
GOAL SEEK

Excel gives you a powerful tool for reaching your goals. Suppose you need a loan for a new home. Your goal might be to pay a specific monthly payment. You would use the Goal Seek feature to reach your goal by adjusting *one* of the loan terms—interest rate or loan amount, for example.

In the case of a loan, you could have Goal Seek find the interest rate required to reach your payment goal, given a loan amount. Alternatively, you could have Goal Seek find the loan amount required to reach your goal, given a specific interest rate. Some

goals cannot be met, as when you try to reduce your monthly payment to nothing; the interest rates and loan amounts would be unrealistic.

Goal Seek is an excellent tool when you have more control over some variables than others. In this case, the variable might be the amount of down payment you can afford.

To find multiple specific inputs that result in a specific goal, you need to use Solver, an add-in. See Task #93 for more about add-ins.

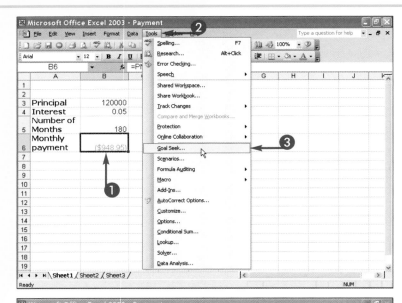

1 Click the cell that will contain the value you want to reach.

2 Click Tools.

3 Click Goal Seek.

The Goal Seek dialog box appears.

4 Type a value that you want to reach.

5 Click and drag the cells whose value you want to change in order to reach the goal.

6 Click OK.

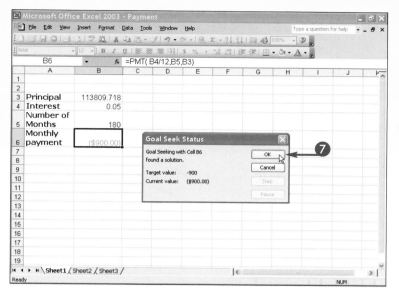

The result appears both in the worksheet and in the dialog box.

⑦ Click OK to accept the change.

Alternatively, you can click Cancel to restore the original values.

DIFFICULTY LEVEL

#57

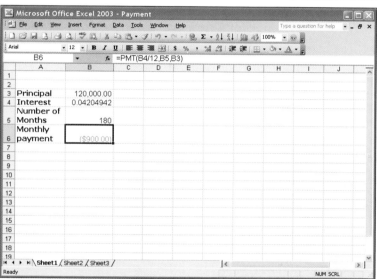

⑧ Repeat steps **1** to **7** for another value.

In this example, principal is kept the same, and the $900 monthly payment can be reached by finding an interest rate of 4.2 percent.

Did you know?

You can save each set of cells on its own worksheet by clicking Edit and then Move or Copy Sheet. In the Move or Copy dialog box, indicate where to place the cell.

Did you know?

The example shown in this task shows the loan amount required to bring the monthly payment down to $900 ($113,809). You would have to contribute a down payment of just over $6,000 to bring the loan down to that amount. You could construct a worksheet that allows you to enter various down payment amounts.

Did you know?

If you are not getting a result, try clicking Tools and then Options. In the Options dialog box, click the Calculation tab to increase the maximum of iterations.

Creating Charts

Excel gives you tools for quickly generating a chart, or visual representation, of the numbers in your worksheet. Charts clarify patterns that can get lost in columns of numbers and formulas, and they make your data more accessible to people who are not familiar with the details.

Charts make a greater impression than rows and columns of numbers because the mind perceives, processes, and recalls visual information more quickly than textual or numerical information; shapes and colors can have a real impact. This effectiveness can be a liability. Charts can be inadvertently misused in a way that emphasizes unimportant or misleading patterns. This chapter helps you become comfortable with the Excel tools, so you can communicate your content as effectively as possible.

In this chapter, you find out how to generate a chart quickly. You then learn to modify chart details, change chart type, and add as well as remove data series. One tip reviews options for representing missing data in charts. Another tip shows how to create a trendline that visually summarizes the direction and magnitude of change over time.

Anyone who uses Excel to manage and analyze experimental data can benefit from the tip relating to error bars. Several tasks provide insight into specific chart types, such as pie charts for showing the relationship of a part to the whole and histograms for plotting frequencies.

Two tips show how to insert both a static chart and an editable chart into a Word document. Chapter 9 elaborates on the theme of exchanging Excel data with other applications.

Top 100

Create a
CHART

A wizard is a software feature that can help you get started with complex tasks in Excel. When you use a wizard, the software collects information from you by presenting a series of screens. In each screen, you click buttons, make choices, and otherwise provide data, clicking Next to get to the next screen. When you are done, the wizard takes your information and quickly generates sophisticated worksheet objects such as pivot tables and charts. The Chart Wizard in particular quickly steps you through the required choices, generating a chart as attractive and accurate as you choose to make it.

As with any wizard in Excel, the Chart Wizard simplifies the creation of a complex object. The Chart Wizard consists of four steps. At each step, you make one or more decisions regarding the data, type, elements, and location of your chart. You can undo your choices by editing the chart. When the chart is done, Excel enables you to modify every element the wizard generates.

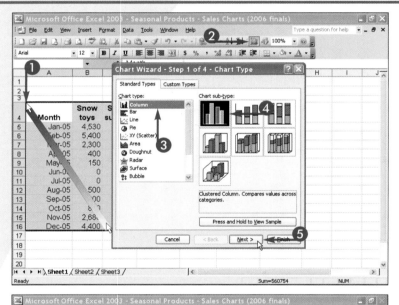

① Click and drag to select the worksheet data you want to chart.

② Click the Chart Wizard button.

The Chart Wizard appears.

③ Click a chart type.

④ Click a chart sub-type.

⑤ Click Next.

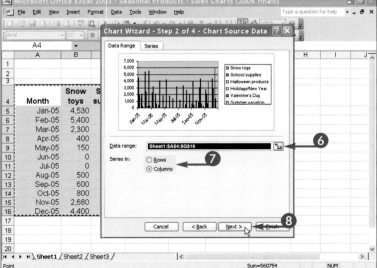

The Chart Wizard Step 2 screen appears.

⑥ Confirm the selected data range.

⑦ Click to arrange data in rows or columns (○ changes to ⊙).

⑧ Click Next.

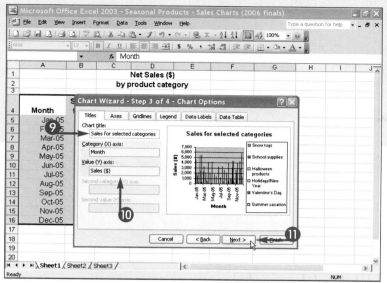

The Chart Wizard
Step 3 screen appears.

⑨ Type a chart title.

⑩ Type a name for the x and y axes.

⑪ Click Next.

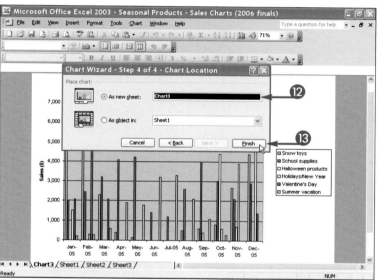

The Chart Wizard Step 4 screen appears.

⑫ Click to indicate whether to locate your chart on a separate sheet.

⑬ Click Finish.

The chart appears with the type and details you specified and in the location you requested.

Note: To improve the look and accuracy of a chart, see Task #60.

TIPS

Did You Know?

You do not need to complete every step of the wizard. At any point, you can click Finish to generate a chart based on the choices you have made. Excel uses its default settings in place of choices you have not made. The default chart type is the bar chart.

Did You Know?

The fastest way to create a chart using all of Excel's charting defaults is to select your worksheet and press F11.

Caution!

Changing the chart by clicking and dragging its data points and columns also changes the underlying worksheet data. By working with a copy of your data, you can avoid changing and thus invalidating it.

Modify
CHART DETAILS

After your chart is generated, Excel gives you a wide variety of options for editing the various chart elements. In the *chart area,* you combine the border, background color, and other features that define overall appearance. In the *plot area,* you define the background of the data itself. Your *legend* explains the meaning of the colors and patterns used to represent data, and your *title* summarizes chart content.

On the *axis,* you define the unit of measurement and its styling. The *grid* consists of the vertical and horizontal lines that relate your data points to the axis. Finally, you can modify *data series* and individual *data points* using labels, special fonts, and the positioning of series relative to another.

You can make charts more effective by modifying these elements. To identify an element used in a chart, pass your mouse arrow slowly over it until descriptive text in a small box appears by the mouse arrow, or click any element and its name appears in the Name box in the upper-left corner of the Excel window.

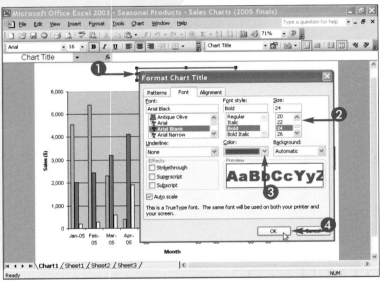

① Double-click the chart title to modify it.

② Click here to increase the font size.

③ Click here to select a text color palette.

④ Click OK.

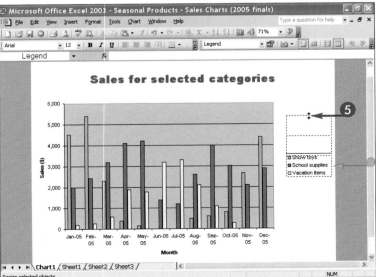

⑤ To increase the legend size, click and drag it.

You may remove an item in the legend by right-clicking it and selecting Clear.

● You can edit legend text by double-clicking the legend, selecting the Font tab, and clicking your preference in the Size menu.

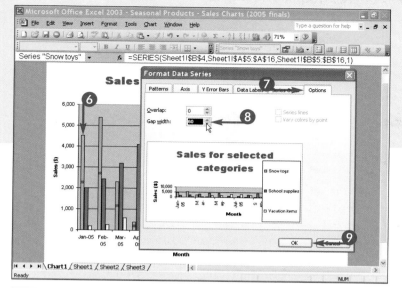

6 To widen columns, double-click a column to select all.

The Format Data Series dialog box appears.

7 Click the Options tab.

8 Click here to decrease the width between the columns.

9 Click OK.

59

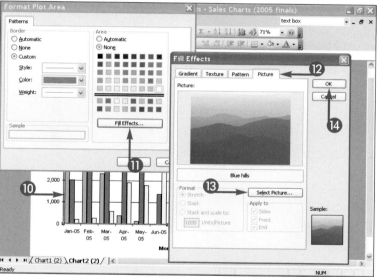

10 To add a background picture, double-click the plotted data.

The Format Plot Area dialog box appears.

11 Click Fill Effects.

The Fill Effects dialog box appears.

12 Click the Picture tab.

13 Click Select Picture and select a digital picture from your computer by double-clicking it.

14 Click OK.

The picture forms the background of the chart.

TIPS

Did You Know?

The Chart toolbar has a drop-down menu of editable chart elements. Using the toolbar, you can select any element to edit.

Did You Know?

To edit an element, you can double-click it, or right-click it and select Format. You can modify many elements at once using the Options command on the Chart menu. To make charts that are larger and easier to edit, you can select As new sheet in step 4 of the Chart Wizard. See Task #58.

Caution!

To resize a chart, click the chart near its edge. A bold border with square handles surrounds it. Click and drag the side or corner handles to resize. Resizing a chart skews the chart and distorts the content by emphasizing data peaks or flattening them.

Change the
CHART TYPE

Different chart types enable you to choose the visual form for your data that best matches the kind of information you are working with. For example, sometimes your data is grouped in categories such as gender or age bracket. To compare such categories, you can use a bar chart, where each horizontal bar represents a category, or a column chart, where vertical bars represent categories.

Stacked bar and column charts show the relative contribution of a single category to the whole at a specific moment. The 100 percent stacked column or bar chart shows each category as a percentage of the whole. Pie charts also show how a category contributes to the whole, but for one data series at a time. Some charts, such as the stacked area chart, show the relative contribution of different categories over time.

Sometimes, your data are continuous instead of categorical; they can take many values. With such data, you can use a line or area chart. Special kinds of data have their own chart types: *stock charts* for stock prices, for example, and *scatter charts* for scientific data.

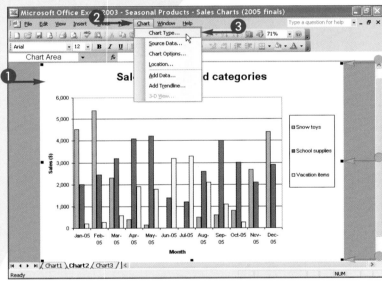

① Click near the chart outside border to select it.

● Square selection handles appear around the chart.

② Click Chart.

③ Click Chart Type.

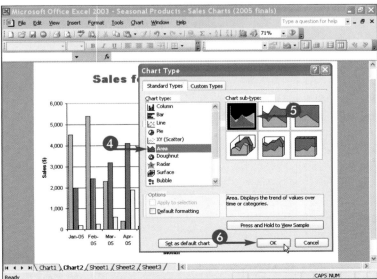

The Chart Type dialog box appears.

④ Click a different chart type.

⑤ Click a different sub-type.

⑥ Click OK.

The chart appears, formatted with the new chart type and sub-type.

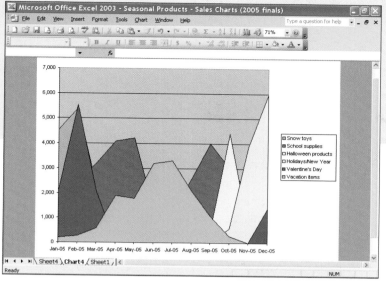

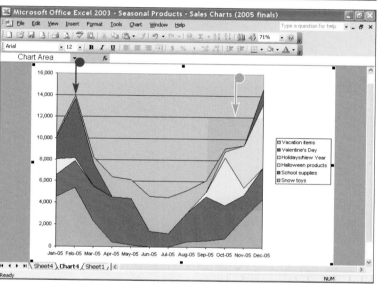

- The stacked area chart, showing the same data, adds the combined values of the series. The lines show the amount contributed by each series.

- Notice that the highest value is about 14,000, the total for all categories, compared to just over 5,000 on the previous figure, the amount of a single category.

TIPS

Did You Know?
If you show more than two data series in a single graph, you can change the type of either series and create a *combination graph*. Using different chart types can make it easier to distinguish continuous data, such as income from categorical data, such as community or gender.

Did You Know?
You can think of an area chart as a line chart with the area below it filled in. Each data series has its own area. A stacked area chart adds the areas of more than one data series in order to show their relative contribution to the actual total. A 100 percent stacked area chart precisely shows the contribution of each series to the total.

Add a
TRENDLINE
to a chart

With Excel, you can add trendlines to your charts, which helps you see both the size and the direction of changes in your data from category to category or over time. Creating a trendline enables you to ask questions such as: Is there a pattern in the recent surge of new orders?

When you add a trend to your chart, you begin with data charted as any chart type except 3-D, stacked, or pie. Excel superimposes trendlines on charts.

A *trend* is defined as the one line through your data series that is as close as possible to every point in

the data series. You can have Excel generate a straight or curvy line. A straight line identifies the direction of change but obviously lacks the flexibility to accommodate data that is not distributed in a linear shape.

Excel offers you a variety of trendlines based on common mathematical formulas for fitting lines to data points. If you want, Excel can generate a statistic called R^2 that indicates how well a given trendline fits your data. The higher R^2, the better the line fits your data.

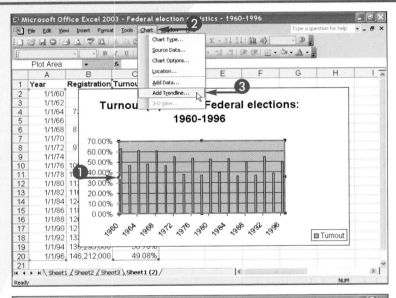

① Click any part of the chart to select it.

② Click Chart.

③ Click Add Trendline.

The Add Trendline dialog box appears.

④ Click a chart that appears to match the visual patterns in your data.

● For Polynomials and Moving Averages, click ⬍ to select an appropriate number.

⑤ Click the Options tab.

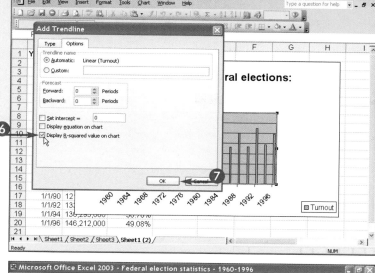

6 Click the square root option (☐ changes to ☑).

R^2 gives you an idea of the accuracy of the line generated in step **4**. The closer R^2 is to 1, the better the fit.

7 Click OK.

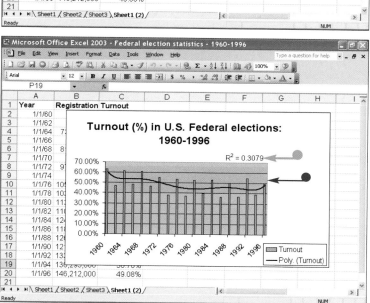

● This polynomial trendline appears on the chart.

● This trendline had a R^2 value higher than the R^2 generated by other lines.

The chart indicates a decline in turnout over the years, but also indicates the difference in turnouts for presidential and non-presidential elections.

To remove a trendline, right-click the line and click Clear.

TIPS

Did You Know?
A *moving average* creates a trendline based on the sum of a value and an equal number of values before and after it in the series. You use moving averages to smooth out bumps and reveal trends. For example, a moving average that adds three values on either side of a data point cannot begin until the fourth value in your data series. Thus, the longer the moving average, the more values you need in your series.

Did You Know?
In the Options tab of the Add Trendline dialog box, you can forecast future values and infer historical values based on the trendline generated for existing values. Use the spinners to set the number of past or future periods to project.

Add and remove
CHART DATA

You can add and remove entire columns or rows of information without changing a chart's type or other properties. In fact, when you update any data on which your chart is based, you do not have to regenerate the chart. Instead, an Excel chart automatically updates itself to reflect data changes.

Adding and removing data involves a similar series of steps. Start by displaying the chart. From the Chart menu, located under View, Toolbars, and Chart, click Source Data. You use the Series tab of the Source

Data dialog box to add and remove a data series. The tab lets you add and remove several series at a time.

You can also redefine an existing data series using the Source Data dialog box. Select the series, and in the Values field, reselect the cell addresses that define it. If you only want to add data to a chart, click Add Data on the Chart menu, and then select the row or column head if any and the new series.

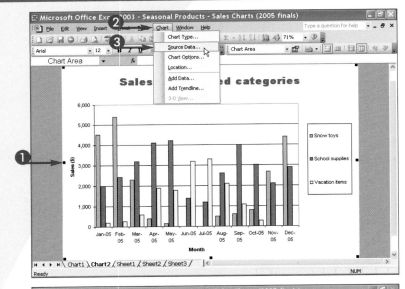

ADD DATA SERIES

If the chart is on the worksheet, position it so that it does not overlap the data you want to add.

1 Click to select the chart in which you want to add new data.

2 Click Chart.

3 Click Source Data.

The Source Data dialog box appears.

4 Click the Series tab.

5 Click Add.

6 Click and drag to indicate the cell addresses for the new series.

7 Repeat steps **4** to **6** for additional series you want to add.

8 Click OK.

The chart updates to reflect the new series.

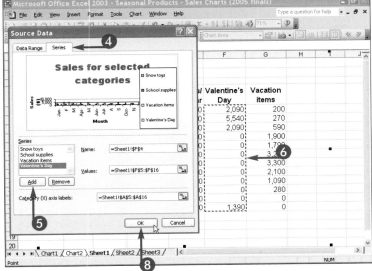

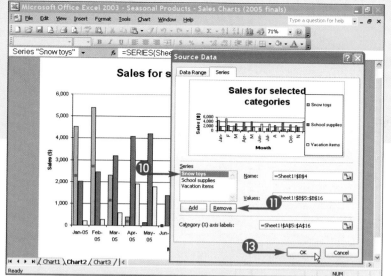

REMOVE DATA SERIES

⑨ To remove a data series, repeat steps **1** to **3** if the Source Data dialog box is not already open.

⑩ Click a data series to remove.

⑪ Click Remove.

⑫ Repeat steps **10** and **11** to remove additional series.

⑬ Click OK.

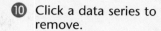

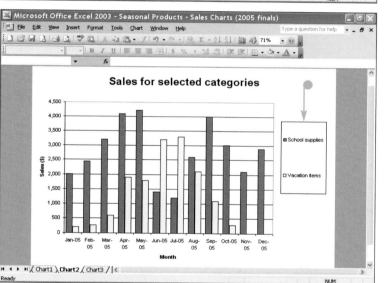

● The chart no longer shows the data series; only two columns are shown, instead of three.

Note: After adding and deleting data, you may need to modify old and new chart details. You can use the Patterns tab of the Format Chart dialog box to select coordinated column colors.

TIPS

Did You Know?

In the Source Data dialog box, the Category Labels field may automatically display the cell addresses of any labeled column heads on your worksheet. These heads appear on the chart to describe the corresponding data series. For some chart types, Excel also picks up axis labels. If Excel fills in this field automatically, you need not provide a name for the data series in the Name field of the Source Data box.

Did You Know?

Here is a quick way to add data to a chart. Click and drag to select the data you want to include in the chart. Click the toolbar Copy button. Click the chart to select it and click Paste. The chart reflects the added data series.

Visually represent
MISSING CHART DATA

Sometimes, you find yourself without a value for a period, transaction, or whatever you happen to be tracking. Perhaps the data was not recorded, not validly recorded, or is just missing. The term *missing data* means a data series has *no* value for one or more cells. Excel makes it easy for you to show that data is missing.

Using the Charting tab of the Options dialog box, you have three options for representing missing data. To take advantage of any of these choices, you must use a line chart.

First, you can choose not to plot the missing data, leaving a gap in your line. This option makes it clear that data is missing, which is important where precision is important or not much data is missing. Second, you can have Excel treat missing data as a zero, which creates ugly and misleading charts but may be desirable if you rely on functions that cannot handle a missing value. Third, you can have Excel interpolate the data, constructing data series based on the values of neighboring points.

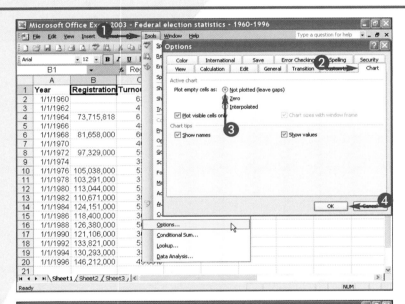

① Click Tools and then Options.

● The Options dialog box appears.

② Click the Chart tab.

③ Click Not plotted (○ changes to ⊙).

④ Click OK.

● A chart appears showing missing data as a blank area in the worksheet.

● The missing data is shown as gaps in the line.

⑤ Repeat steps **1** to **4**, selecting Zero in step **3** to represent missing data with a zero value.

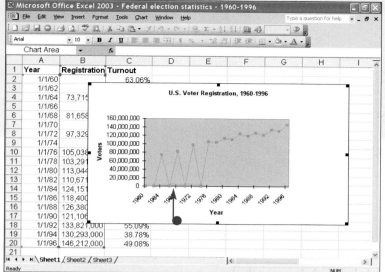

- The missing data is represented as zero.

6 Repeat steps **1** to **4**, selecting Interpolated in step **3** to represent missing data as interpolated, or estimated.

- The missing data appears interpolated. This graph shows no noticeable break in the data series.

  Interpolated means that Excel estimates missing values based on adjacent values.

TIPS

Did You Know?

Charts can handle missing data, but some statistical functions, such as Correl(), require that you pair every value in one data series with a value in the other series. The function does not work if data is missing. You may have to throw out missing values, or records containing them, decreasing your sample size but possibly increasing the validity of the results.

Did You Know?

When plotting missing values, any chart type other than a 2-D line chart may result in unsatisfactory results. With a 3-D line chart, for example, you can only show missing data as zeroes.

Did You Know?

When you decide how to handle missing values for a chart — whether as a gap, as interpolated, or as zero — your choice applies to every data series in the chart.

Use
ERROR BARS
in a chart

With Excel, you can easily generate error bars to provide an estimate of the potential error in experimental or sampled data. In science, marketing, polling, and other fields, people make conclusions about populations by sampling the population or devising controlled experiments. When data is sampled or generated in laboratory conditions, the resulting numbers approximate the larger reality you are exploring. An *error bar* shows the range of possible values for these experimentally derived numbers.

With Excel, you can show the range of possible values in several ways: as a fixed number, measured in the same units used to measure data, above or below each data point in your data series; as a percentage of the data point; or in terms of standard deviation units.

Standard deviation units indicate whether an experimental number is reasonably close to the population characteristic being studied. Usually, you can have a *confidence level* of 95 percent that the *population* mean, which you want to find out, falls within two standard deviation units of the *sampled* mean, which you know.

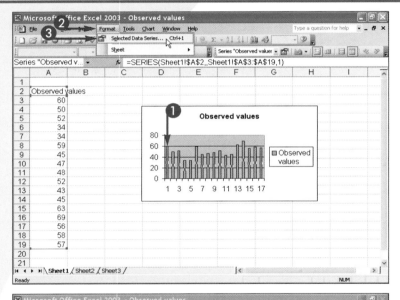

① Click any column to select the entire data series.

② Click Format.

③ Click Selected Data Series.

As an alternative to performing steps **1** to **3**, you can simply double-click any column.

The Format Data Series dialog box appears.

④ Click the Y Error Bars tab.

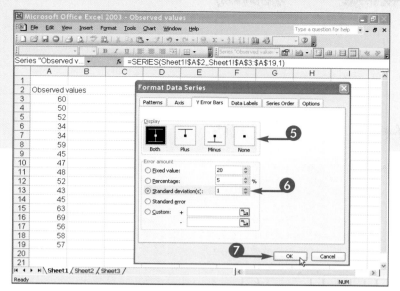

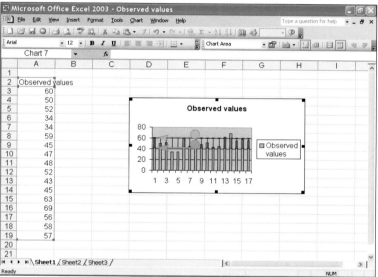

The Y Error Bars options appear.

⑤ Click a positive, negative, or both view.

⑥ Click here to adjust the error range (○ changes to a ◉).

⑦ Click OK.

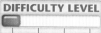
DIFFICULTY LEVEL

The chart appears with error bars.

● Upper limit of error range.

● Lower limit of error range.

Note: *The confidence that the population characteristic falls between these limits is about 68 percent. In step 6, this example uses only one standard deviation unit.*

TIPS

Did You Know?
Your confidence level in estimating population characteristics assumes that the sampled values are *normally* (evenly) distributed around the mean, as in a bell curve.

Did You Know?
You can find a clear review of statistical concepts at the Research Methods Knowledge Base, a Web site developed by Cornell professor William Trochim at http://trochim.human. cornell.edu/kb/. The Knowledge Base includes a glossary of statistical terms.

Did You Know?
Only certain chart types support error bars, including 2-D area, bar, column, line, and XY scatter charts. These types let you create error bars for the values measured by the *y* axis. For the scatter chart, you can create both X and Y error bars.

PULL A SLICE
from a pie chart

Pulling out a slice of the pie chart lets you emphasize its contribution to the whole pie. In presentations, it is also a good way to emphasize a piece that is too small to easily see. The space between the slice and the pie creates visual contrast: the more space, the greater the emphasis. Pulling out slices close to a pie's horizontal diameter is easier to see than pulling out a slice near its vertical axis.

Remember that a pie chart provides a snapshot, usually at a moment or within a period, showing the

contribution of each of several units to the whole; you would use the *donut* chart type for several data series. Pie charts are most effective when few categories are involved and when the differences between categories are clear enough for the viewer to quickly grasp the relative importance of each piece. Excel enables you to assign percentages to each pie slice in order to display more precisely their relative importance.

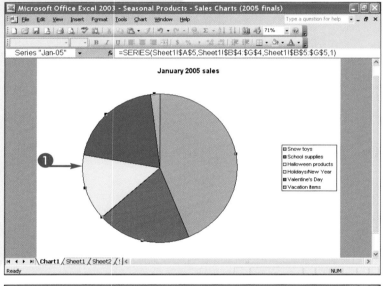

1 Click the pie to select it.

You can drag the selected pie chart to pull out, or emphasize, every slice; however, it is hard to control the display.

2 Click the one slice you want to pull out.

3 Click Format.

4 Click Selected Data Point.

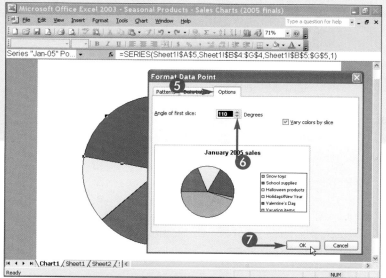

The Format Data Point dialog box appears.

⑤ Click the Options tab.

⑥ Click here to select the degrees by which to move the slice to a place where it can be pulled out.

⑦ Click OK.

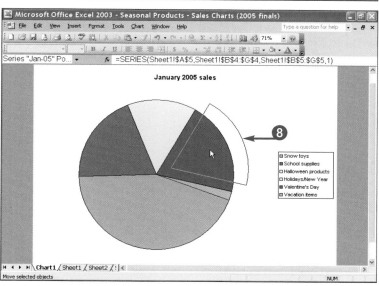

⑧ With the slice facing right, click and drag the slice to the right as desired.

TIPS

Did You Know?
You can pull a slice from either a 2-D or 3-D pie chart. To convert a 2-D pie with a pulled slice into a 3-D one, right-click the pie and click Chart Type. Change its sub-type as described in Task #60. One interesting pie sub-type enables you to represent the smaller slices as a miniature pie chart — a pie within a pie — showing the relative importance of the smallest slices.

Did You Know?
In the Chart Wizard, step 1, the Custom list includes pie-chart variants — Black-and-White, Pie Explosion, and Blue. The Black-and-White pie automatically includes the percentage contribution of each slice. The Exploded pie shows a 3-D pie, with each piece pulled out. The somewhat garish Blue pie shows a 2-D pie with each piece pulled out.

LABEL THE SLICES
of a pie chart

Pie charts enable you to quickly compare how different slices contribute to a whole. For example, you could use a pie chart to show the percentage of a nation's budget, represented by the whole pie, that is devoted to education, health, and defense, each represented by slices of the pie. Or, you could show how a store's costs are divided among labor expenses, overhead, inventory, and so on. Excel simplifies the task of labeling individual slices and automatically computing a percentage for each label, making it easier to compare the slices. When slices include percentages and labels, they can do the work

of the chart legend. By varying the colors of the slices and pulling out slices, you can emphasize the contribution of different slices, making a strong visual impact and clarifying, although sometimes simplifying, relationships.

Creating labels requires a bit of editing to ensure that the slices are large enough and the labels readable and well-positioned enough to convey information at a glance. You can add labels while using the Chart Wizard. However, additional options are available if you create the chart first and then add labels.

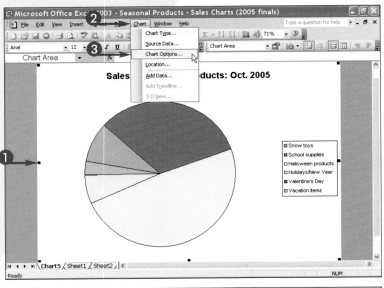

① Click the chart to select it.

② Click Chart.

③ Click Chart Options.

The Chart Options dialog box appears.

④ Click the Data Labels tab.

⑤ Click Category name (☐ changes to ☑).

● Optionally, you can select Percentage to include a percentage.

⑥ Click OK.

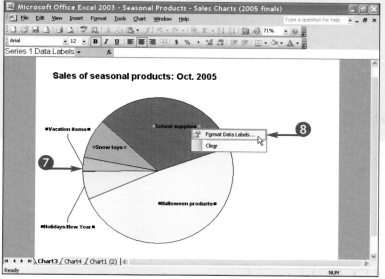

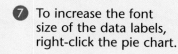

In this example, the pie appears with labels and without a legend.

⑦ To increase the font size of the data labels, right-click the pie chart.

⑧ Click Format Data Labels.

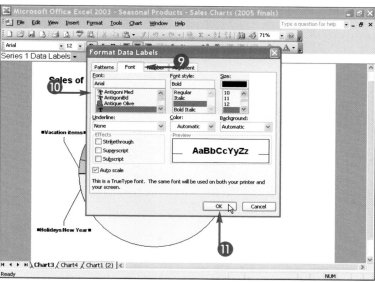

The Format Data Labels dialog box appears.

⑨ Click the Font tab.

⑩ Click to make your selections.

⑪ Click OK.

You may have to reposition labels by clicking and dragging.

Did You Know?

When creating a pie chart with the Chart Wizard, you may wish to spend some time at step **3**. In the Legend tab, clear the Show legend check box to prevent the legend from displaying. In the Data Labels tab, make the changes shown in steps **5** and **6**. You can also create labels on a completed pie by clicking it and then clicking Format, Format Data Series.

Did You Know?

When you create data labels, use the check box on the Data Labels tab to add *leaders*, which are lines connecting labels to slices. Excel uses leaders when labels are located outside a pie. When you drag a label into the slice it refers to, the leader disappears.

Create a
HISTOGRAM

With Excel you can create histograms, which you use to group many values into a smaller number of categories. When charted, a histogram looks like a bar or column chart. A bar or column chart can measure just about anything, such as the height of a child at regular intervals over ten years. You use histograms to group individual values into categories in order to compare the categories. In the world of histograms, these categories are called *bins*.

To display the prices of different cereals, for example, your first bin would be *<3*, representing prices under

$3.00 per box, your second bin *2.00-2.99*, and so on up to a bin for all boxes priced at over $5. You then sort prices into bins, and finally count the number of values in each bin to see which price ranges are most and least common.

The histogram tool is part of the Analysis ToolPak, which you may need to install, as explained in Task #93. You must provide three pieces of information. First, you define the raw data you want to sort. Then you define the bins. Finally, you specify in which cell you want the result to appear.

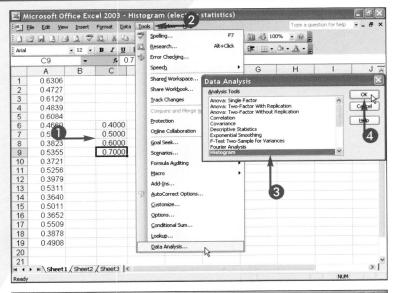

① Type the highest value in an adjacent vertical cell to define bins.

Note: *The bins must be in ascending order, but need not be the same size.*

② Click Tools and then Data Analysis.

The Data Analysis dialog box comes up.

③ Click Histogram.

④ Click OK.

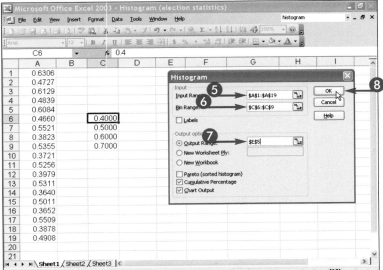

The Histogram dialog box appears.

⑤ Click and drag the range of numbers to categorize, or type the cell range.

⑥ Click and drag the range of bins created in step **1**, or type the cell range.

⑦ Click the cell where you want the results to start, or type the cell range.

⑧ Click OK.

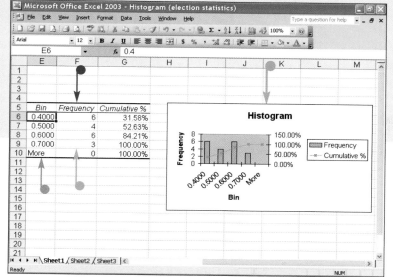

● The results appear on the same worksheet as the original data.

● A histogram chart appears.

● *Frequency* means number of values per bin.

● *More* refers to the uncategorized values in the highest bin.

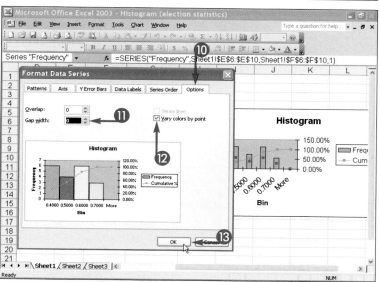

You can edit the histogram.

9 To widen the columns, double-click any column to open the Format Data Series dialog box.

10 Click the Options tab.

11 Click here to decrease the Gap width.

12 To vary column colors, click Vary colors by point (□ changes to ☑).

13 Click OK.

The Histogram chart assumes the appearance shown in the Format Data Series box.

TIPS

Did You Know?
You can distinguish a column or bar chart from a histogram by increasing the width of the histogram bars to the point where the sides of each column overlap. To distinguish one histogram column from another, you can vary their colors. Both options are available by double-clicking any column in the histogram. In the Format Data Series dialog box, click the Options tab. Use the Gap width spinner (🔼) and Vary colors check box as appropriate.

Did You Know?
You can create a histogram consisting of descending bins such as 90-100, 80-89.9, 70-79.9, and so on. To do so, click the Pareto option in the Histogram dialog box.

Did You Know?
The Frequency function gives you the same capabilities as the Histogram tool. To find out more, type **frequency function** into the search box in the upper-right corner of the Excel window and press Enter.

Paste a
CHART INTO WORD

By using Excel charts, you can add attractive visual elements to documents created in other Office applications. In a Word document, for example, you might use charts to illustrate quarterly reports and technical documentation.

You have a choice in importing a chart into Word. You can *paste* it as a simple image. When you paste, you can edit the data within Word. The original worksheet data in Excel is untouched. As an alternative, you can paste-link the chart. This means that any changes you make affect the original Excel document as well

as the one in Word. For more on paste-linking, see Task #70.

When importing, you have a choice of formats. When you paste a chart as an Excel Chart Object, you can edit the chart, but your edits do not affect the original worksheet. However, when you paste-link an Excel Chart Object, you can then make changes to the actual Excel worksheet from within Word. The bitmap and Windows metafile file formats are discussed on the opposite page.

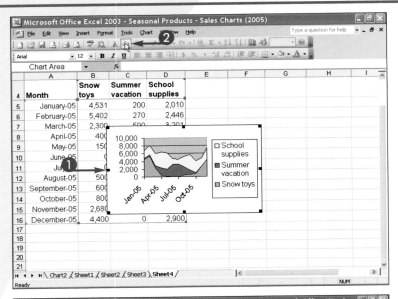

① Click to select the chart you want to copy.

② Click the Copy button.

The selected chart is surrounded by a marquee, or box consisting of blinking dashes.

③ Switch to the Word document.

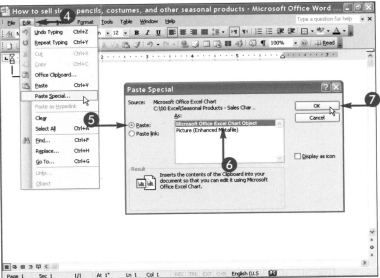

④ In Word, click Edit and Paste Special.

The Paste Special dialog box comes up.

⑤ Click Paste (○ changes to ◉).

⑥ Click Excel Chart Object.

⑦ Click OK.

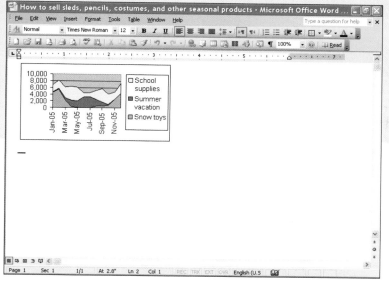

 # 68

DIFFICULTY LEVEL

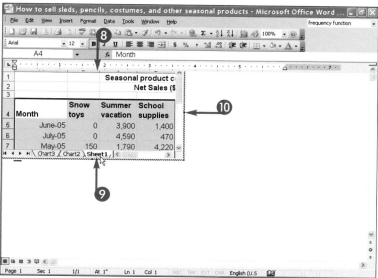

8 To edit a worksheet on which the chart is based, click the chart.

9 Click the worksheet.

You remain in Word, and your changes do not affect the original worksheet.

10 Click and drag the image borders to resize it and simplify editing.

![TIPS]

Did You Know?

Excel gives you two other ways to use an Excel worksheet in other programs. First, you can generate an Excel object within the other program. Second, you can create a hyperlink from Excel to the other program. For more about these techniques see Tasks #84 and #85.

Did You Know?

A metafile is what graphics experts call a *vector file*. It is an efficient way of representing an image by using formulas, unlike *bitmaps*, which use individually colored pixels. Metafile images tend to display better at larger sizes while also requiring less disk space. For most purposes and with smaller images, you may not notice a difference in the way they look. You can paste or paste-link both bitmaps and metafiles.

Paste-link a
CHART INTO WORD

When you paste-link a document from one Windows program into another Windows program, you keep control of the original document. This means that when you double-click the paste-linked document and change it, the changes are reflected in the original document, not just in Word's copy of it. Double-clicking the chart in Word brings up the chart ready for editing in Excel. When you are done in Excel, save your work and switch back to Word, where your changes are reflected.

Whether you are pasting or paste-linking, you can have the Excel chart appear in the Word document either as a chart or as an icon. You double-click the chart or the icon to edit the chart.

The advantage of paste-linking for you is content control. Pasted documents, when you edit them, diverge from the original document, making it confusing for other people using the document. When you paste-link, however, the embedded and original documents remain the same. When many people use the same document, everyone can work with the same document.

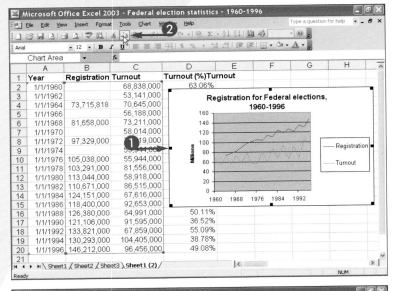

① Click to select the chart you want to copy.

② Click the Copy button.

The selected chart is surrounded by a marquee, or box consisting of blinking dashes.

③ Switch to the Word document.

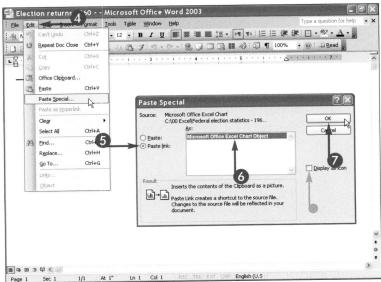

④ In Word, click Edit and then Paste Special.

The Paste Special box comes up.

⑤ Click Paste Link (○ changes to ◉)

⑥ Click Excel Chart Object.

● Optionally, you can display the chart as an icon.

⑦ Click OK.

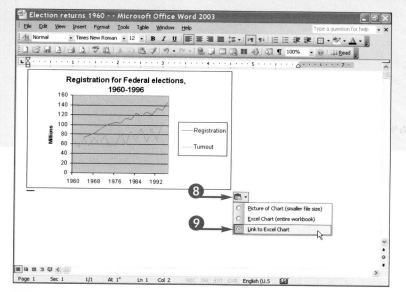

The chart appears in Word.

⑧ Click the Paste Options menu button.

⑨ Click to paste-link in either the entire workbook or the chart without its worksheet.

69

Ordinarily, you want to select the default Link to Excel Chart. Pressing Esc removes the menu and accepts the default.

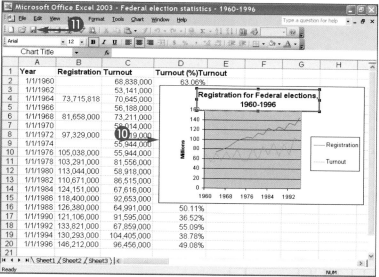

Note: You are in Excel, not Word.

⑩ Double-click the chart to edit it within Excel.

If the chart is on its own sheet, click the appropriate worksheet to change the underlying data for that sheet.

⑪ When you are finished, click Save and return to Word.

You can click the paste-linked chart to see your changes.

TIP

Did You Know?

You can use the Paste Options menu to change your mind — to paste instead of paste-link or vice versa. It appears by the lower-right corner of charts imported into Word. The menu gives three somewhat confusing choices. *Picture of chart* is equivalent to merely pasting a chart. You cannot edit the chart except as a Word object that you can resize, flow text around, surround with a border, and so on. Double-click a pasted picture to use Word's Format Picture dialog box. *Excel chart* gives the broadest choice, letting you bring into Word the entire workbook, with all charts and worksheets. *Link to Excel chart* is equivalent to paste-linking. For these last two choices, double-click the chart in Word to edit the Excel chart in Word or Excel, respectively.

Chapter 7

Presenting Worksheets

With Excel, you can adjust almost every aspect of how your worksheets and charts appear. Such control involves more than making text bold or coloring cells blue. Formatting enables you to make your worksheets easier to read and understand and thus more useful to others.

This chapter includes tips on formatting many cells at the same time, applying formats quickly with Format Painter, and combining formats into reusable styles. It concludes with tips on integrating images into your worksheets.

Excel gives you several tools for simplifying the work of formatting. The *Format Cells dialog box* provides all the controls for changing the look and properties of both text and numbers in one place. You can also use it for adjusting the color, border, pattern,

texture, and numerous other cell properties. When you create effective formats, Excel's *Format Painter* lets you quickly apply them to other cells. With styles, Excel goes even further, giving you the flexibility to reuse integrated groupings of formats in any workbook. While AutoFormats provide pre-packaged formats, with styles and Format Painter you can create custom designs that meet your specific needs.

Images can enhance worksheet presentation in many ways. Chapter 6 includes tips for making charts that communicate worksheet content. This chapter has a pair of tips for using images and worksheets together. Transparencies are images that are overlaid on data in such a way that the data shows through the image. You can place background images behind your data, getting people's attention and perhaps enhancing the content itself.

Top 100

FORMAT NUMBERS
as percentages

Excel enables you to convert raw numbers into percentages. If your data are already in the form of percentages, formatting them as such causes a percentage sign (%) to appear and enables you to perform complex calculations. Numbers formatted as percentages can be readily compared with one another and tracked over time.

To generate a percentage based on numbers, first format a cell using the Excel Percentage format: Click Format and Cells, in the Number tab click the Percentage category, and click OK.

In the cell, for example, type an equal sign (=) and 13/17, or the data of your choice. Press Tab or Enter, and 76.47% appears in the cell. If the values are in other cells, you could click those cells instead of typing the values directly, separating the cell addresses with a forward slash (/).

To enter percentages directly, enter the data and format the cells as percentages. Excel considers 1 as 100% — and 100 as 10000%! — so make sure to adapt your data accordingly.

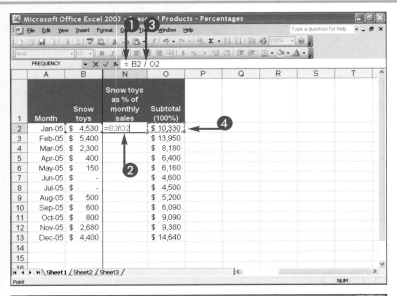

1 Type an equal sign.

2 Click the cell with the numerator.

3 Type a forward slash (/).

4 Click the cell with the denominator.

5 Press Enter.

The percentage appears in the cell.

6 Click the cell with the percentage.

7 To convert the other cells into percentages, click the Fill handle and drag to the bottom of the column.

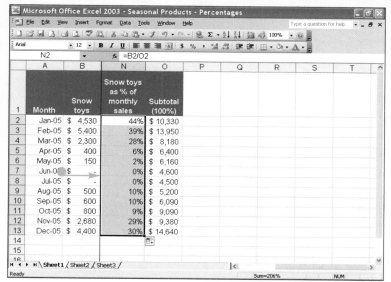

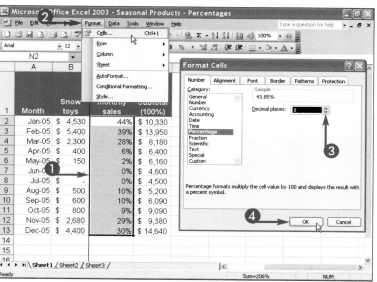

- Percentages are automatically generated for the other cells.

Note: *For more about AutoFill, see Task #5.*

#70

DIFFICULTY LEVEL

CHANGE NUMBER OF DECIMAL POINTS

① Click and drag to select cells.

② Click Format and then Cells.

The Format Cells dialog box appears.

③ Click here and select the number of decimal points you want.

④ Click OK.

The percentages now appear with the changed format.

TIPS

Did You Know?

You can quickly change a decimal number into a percentage by clicking it and then clicking the Percentage button (%) on the Formatting toolbar. Just as when using the percentage format, Excel displays .06 as 6%, including the percentage symbol (%) in the display.

Caution!

The percentage format allows you to indicate how many decimal points you want to appear. The more decimal points you use, the more accurate — but possibly harder to read and interpret — your results. Using too few decimal points can lead to columns of percentages that do not seem to add up precisely.

Format a
COLUMN OF CURRENCIES

Formatting numbers as currencies clearly identifies cell content, aiding analysis and limiting confusion. For some business reports, you may even want to provide a currency symbol next to every monetary value. Excel does not usually allow you to use a symbol and number in the same cell and then perform a math operation on the number. However, it does provide two formats — Currency and Accounting — that display currency symbols without preventing math operations.

The two formats, Currency and Formatting, are similar. Both allow you to choose from dozens of currencies and currency symbols or descriptors. The Accounting format was designed to comply with accounting practice and to make it easier to read columns of numbers. The format aligns the currency symbol, such as the $, along the left cell border. Decimal points, too, are aligned. The Accounting format places the symbol right before the number, converts a zero (0) into a dash (-), and shows a negative value as $(20,000). The Currency value gives you a choice in displaying negative values.

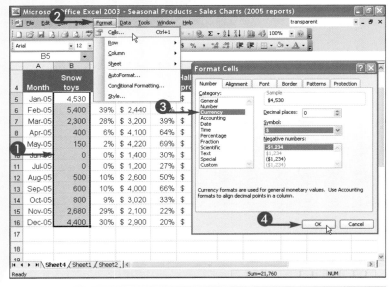

APPLY CURRENCY FORMAT

① Click and drag to select the cells you want to format.

② Click Format and then Cells.

The Format Cells dialog box appears.

③ Click the Number tab and select Currency from the Category list.

You may change the decimal points, currency symbol, and styling of negative numbers as desired.

④ Click OK.

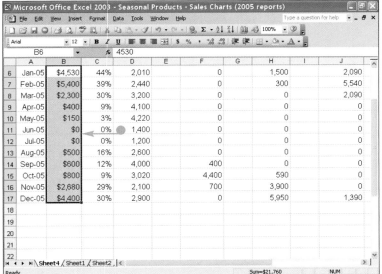

● The cells appear in the Currency format.

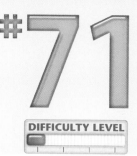

Apply Accounting Format

#71

DIFFICULTY LEVEL

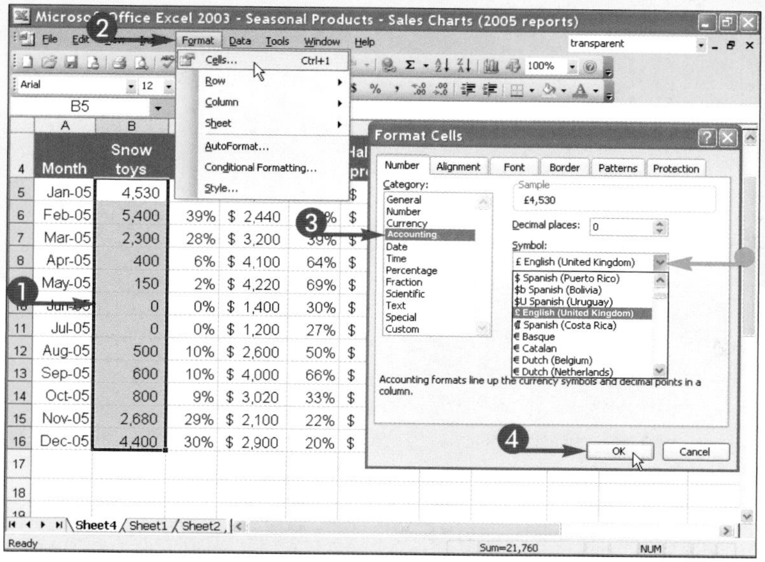

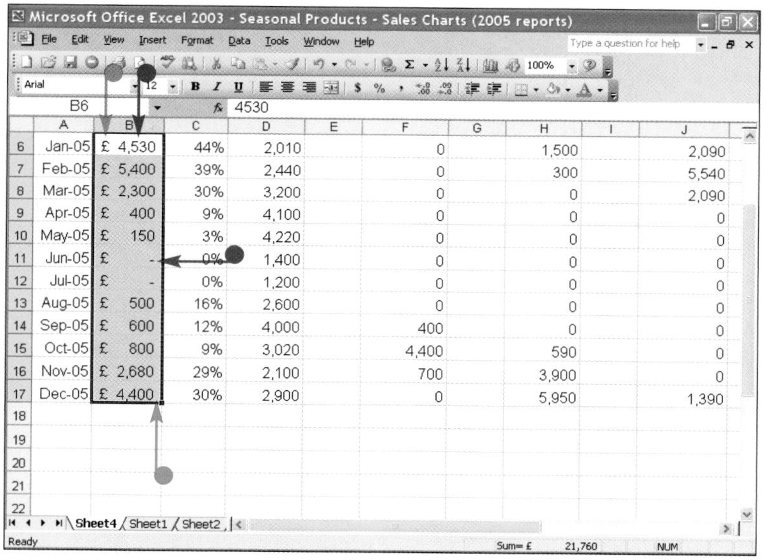

1. Click and drag to select the cells to format.
2. Click Format and then Cells.

   The Format Cells dialog box appears.
3. Click the Number tab and select Accounting from the Category list.
   - You may change the decimal points and currency symbol as desired.
4. Click OK.

- The cells appear in the Accounting format.
- The currency symbol is aligned.
- Space is reserved for right parenthesis if there are negative values.
- A dash appears instead of a zero.

TIPS

Did You Know?

Changing number formats often increases the number of digits that a cell contains, as when you increase the number of decimal points or convert a number into its Excel serial number. Excel does not automatically widen columns to accommodate larger numbers. If a number does not fit in a column, Excel fills the cell with pound signs (######). To view the number, simply double-click the border at the very top of the worksheet between the current column and the column to its right. Dragging the border gives you more control of its placement.

Did You Know?

To adjust a column width to a specific size, click Format and Column, and on the sub-menu click Autofit Selection. You can use this technique with several columns of numbers at the same time.

Format
COLUMN HEADINGS

Formatting one cell at a time takes little effort, but the real benefits of formatting come when you apply many formats at the same time. Formatting row and column heads can be especially helpful in a printed or online report, where the row provides visual orientation and important information about the structure and content of your data. Formatted column heads also make it easier to use lists.

Using the Format Cells dialog box, you can set off a row of column heads by bolding, wrapping, and aligning the text; applying a colored or patterned

background; changing the font size and type; using borders; and applying still other effects. You can continue making changes using the different tabs of the Format Cells dialog box and click OK when you are done.

With formats defined, you can apply them to other column headings using Format Painter and styles. See Tasks #73 and #74 for more information.

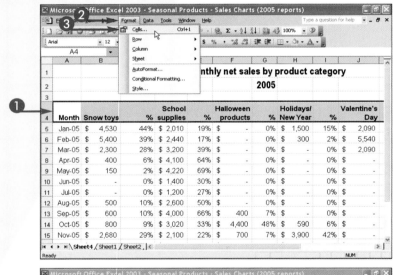

① Click and drag to select the cells you want to format.

② Click Format.

③ Click Cells.

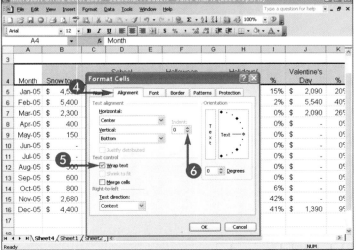

The Format Cells dialog box appears.

④ Click the Alignment tab.

⑤ Click Wrap text (☐ changes to ☑).

When you reduce the column width, the text wraps.

⑥ Click here and select Center.

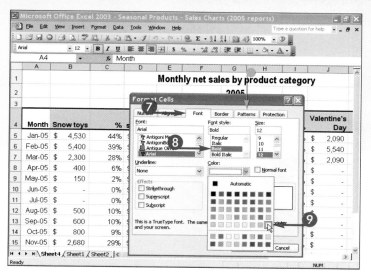

7 Click the Font tab.

8 Select the Bold font style.

9 Click here and select White as the font color.

The white text appears against a color.

10 Click OK.

● You can click the Patterns tab and add a pattern with color.

DIFFICULTY LEVEL

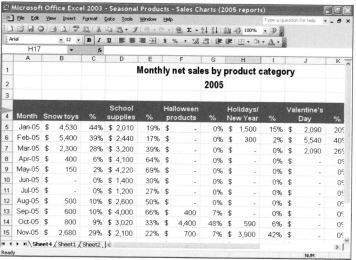

● The column heading appears with the selected formatting.

To make additional edits or additions, reselect the cells and repeat steps **2** and **3**.

Did You Know?

Creating consistent column widths can be difficult when the width of column heads differs; the amount of text differs in each heading. If you have a repeating column, such as percentage, you can format one column width and apply its setting to other columns. Select the column by clicking the column letter. Click Format, Column, and then Autofit Selection or manually adjust the width. With the cell selected, click Copy. Then select one or more other columns and click Paste Special. Click Column width in the Paste Special box and then click OK.

Format quickly with
FORMAT PAINTER

Excel can save you time when you apply formats that you have used before. The easiest technique for applying a format used in one cell to another cell, or range of cells, is Format Painter, a feature now found in other Office 2003 programs, including Word and PowerPoint. Format Painter makes sense for the one-time copying of formats, especially within a workbook. Styles, discussed in the next task, make sense when you plan to apply common formats throughout a workbook and across workbooks. See Task #74.

You can find the Format Painter tool on the Standard toolbar, not the Formatting toolbar, where you might expect it. To use it, first click a cell with the format you want to copy. Then, click the Format Painter icon, which is shaped like a brush. Finally, click a cell or cells that will receive the formatting. You can click and drag to apply the formatting to many cells at the same time. The formats are applied instantly. If you make a mistake, you can undo the formats by pressing Ctrl+Z.

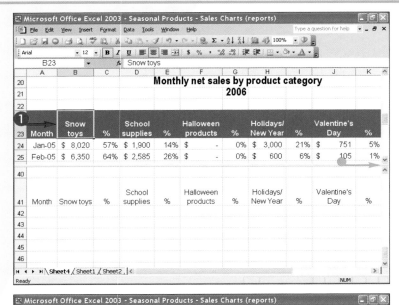

1 Click the cell of the format you want to copy.

● You can split the screen to see different parts of the worksheet at the same time by clicking and dragging the Split box.

Note: For other ways of viewing large worksheets, see Tasks #7 and #8.

2 Click the Format Painter button.

To apply the format you selected in step **1** several times, double-click the button.

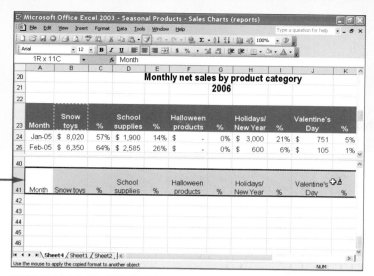

③ Click the cell in which you want to duplicate the format.

You can also click and drag to select the range of cells you want to format.

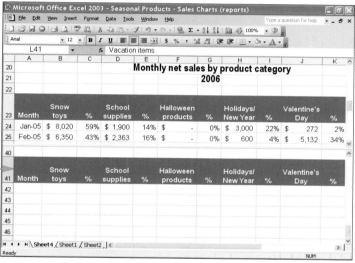

● The cell or range instantly takes on the formatting of the cell.

If you double-clicked in step **2** to apply the format several times, continue clicking other cells. Then press Esc when you are done.

TIPS

Did You Know?

You can apply a format using the Format Painter tool only once. However, if you want to copy a format more than once, applying one format to several non-adjacent cells, double-click the tool instead of single-clicking it in step **2**.

Did You Know?

You can use Format Painter to transfer the properties from one image, such as clip art, to another image. The properties you transfer include background color, text flow around the image, and so on. Click the formatted picture, click the Format Painter button ( ), and then click the picture you want to format.

GROUP FORMATS
in a style

Using the Format Cells dialog box, you can easily format numbers, text, and cells. A *style* is a named collection of formats that you can share among users and apply across workbooks. Styles streamline the work of formatting and enable others to apply a consistent set of formats to worksheet elements such as row heads, column heads, and data values. A worksheet can contain several styles, and you can view the collection of formats for them by using the drop-down menu in the Style box.

With Excel, you are always using either the default (Normal) style or a style you created. To view the settings of the style currently in effect, click Format, Style to bring up the Style dialog box.

To create a new style based on the current one, click the Modify button. A version of the Format Cells dialog box appears. Use the dialog box to select one or more formats. Click OK when you are finished. Back in the Style box, give your new style a new name and click OK.

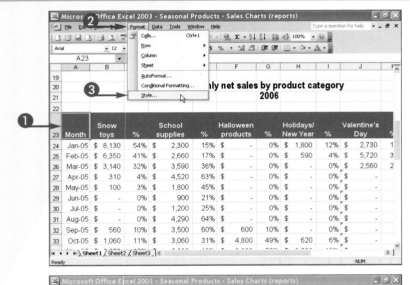

GROUP FORMATS AS A STYLE

1. Click a cell with formats you want to use as the basis of a style.

2. Click Format.

3. Click Style.

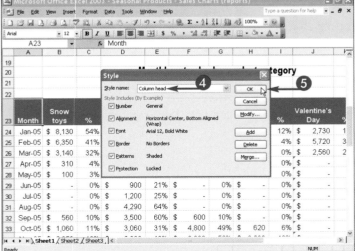

The Style dialog box appears.

4. Rename your style by typing over the existing style name.

5. Click OK.

You can now apply the style throughout the current workbook.

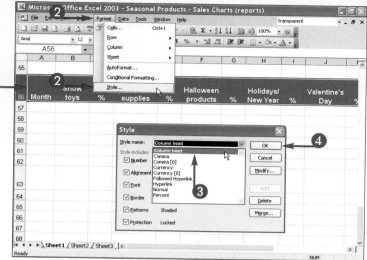

① Click and drag to select the cells to which you want to apply the style.

② Click Format and then Style.

The Style dialog box comes up.

③ Click here and select the style you created in step **4**.

④ Click OK.

DIFFICULTY LEVEL

The style is applied.

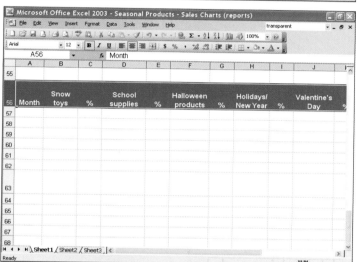

TIPS

Did You Know?

To copy a style from one workbook to another, open both workbooks. In the workbook into which you want to import a style, click Format and Style, and click the Merge button. In the Merge Styles box, click the workbook with the styles to be imported. For more information, see Task #31.

Apply It!

You can also build a style from the ground up rather than basing it on a formatted style. Click a cell to receive the style, and click Format and then Style. Click Modify and use the formatting dialog boxes to apply the number, alignment, font, border, and patterns formats. When you are done, just type a new name in the Style name box and click OK.

INSERT A BACKGROUND IMAGE
into your worksheet

Placing a background image behind a worksheet can draw attention and enhance the appearance of otherwise drab columns of numbers. Backgrounds can set the tone. Using a company logo, for example, can convey official status. Backgrounds can also create a dramatic or decorative effect related to worksheet content. A storekeeper, for example, could place pale red hearts behind a worksheet showing trends in the sale of Valentine Day's cards.

A background shows a color or image underneath the text and covers the entire surface of the worksheet. To apply a background image, you start with the

Format menu, and click Sheet, Background. You then navigate to the folder on your PC or network with the image you want to use as background, and double-click it. You can use images in any standard format, such as JPG, BMP, PNG, or GIF.

Note that any images you bring in by using the Insert menu, such as clip art and digital pictures, appear as resizable objects floating *over* your worksheet. You can drag them around, resize them, or set them inside a border, but they are different from backgrounds.

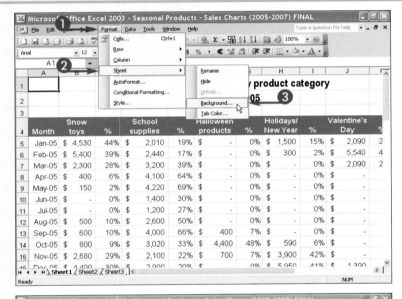

① Click Format.

② Click Sheet.

③ Click Background.

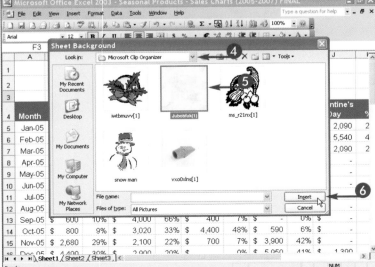

The Sheet Background window appears.

④ Click here and locate the image you want to use.

⑤ Click the image.

⑥ Click Insert.

In this example, the selected texture gives the worksheet the look of rough paper.

75

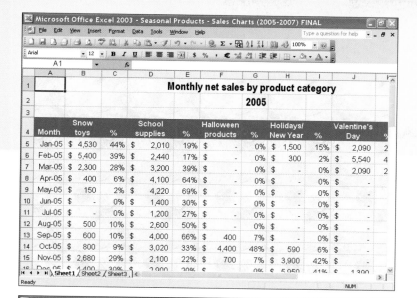

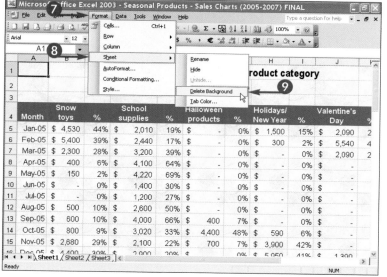

7 To remove the image, click Format.

8 Click Sheet.

9 Click Delete Background.

The background disappears.

TIPS

Did You Know?

To apply a color background to individual spreadsheet cells, select the cells and click Format, Cells. In the Format Cells dialog box, click the Patterns tab. Use the Cells shading section to click a color. Cell gridlines do not appear when you apply a color to adjacent cells, even though any text or numbers you type into colored cells are situated within the individual cells.

Did You Know?

You can apply backgrounds to other objects in Excel. For example, Task #59 shows how to place a background image behind charted data. You can also place a background behind the entire chart, including title, by clicking near the chart border instead of selecting just the plot area, and then using the Format Chart Average dialog box to make your choices.

Create a
TRANSPARENT IMAGE

Excel enables you to use objects along with worksheets. *Objects* include charts, clip art, WordArt, text boxes, digital pictures, and various shapes available by using the Drawing toolbar.

Making an object transparent allows anything underneath it, and thus covered by it, to show through. You can adjust the degree of transparency depending on how much of the underlying information you want to show. Transparent images blend smoothly with other objects in the same vicinity and obstruct less of your content.

In Excel, you can create transparent chart titles, legends, and data series. Text boxes enable you to create additional descriptive content. To create a text box, display the Drawing toolbar and click the Text Box tool.

You make an object transparent by double-clicking it. In the Pattern tab of the Format box, click the Fill Effects button. Use the Transparency slider to control the amount of transparency, from opaque to transparent, with 0 being opaque and 100 transparent.

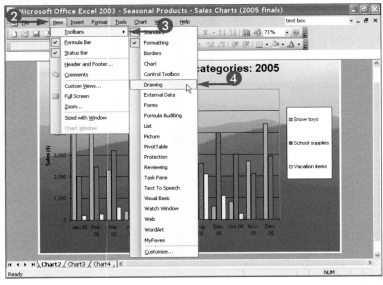

① Open a chart.

② Click View.

③ Click Toolbars.

④ Click Drawing.

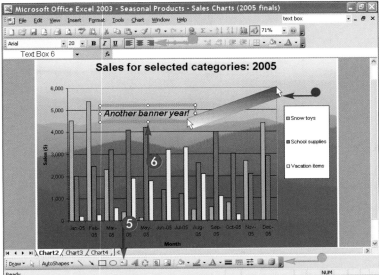

● The drawing toolbar appears.

⑤ Click the Text Box tool.

⑥ Type anywhere on the chart to generate a text box.

● You can select the text and change the text type, size, and style as desired.

● You can select the text and drag it anywhere.

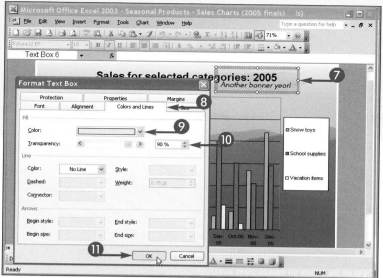

7 To set the text against a transparent color, double-click the text box.

The Format Text dialog box appears.

8 Click the Colors and Lines tab.

9 Click here and select a color.

10 Click here to adjust the color transparency.

11 Click OK.

● The text box appears with a pale colored background.

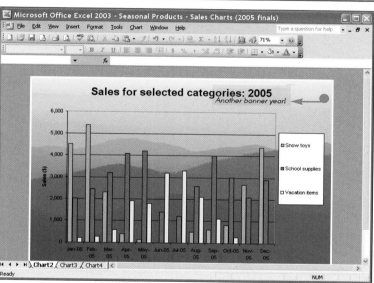

TIPS

Did You Know?
When you use clip art, the Picture toolbar includes a Set Transparent Color button (🖉). Use this button to remove a single color from the picture. This effect differs from the effect described in this task, which evenly renders an entire image transparent.

Did You Know?
With charts, you can add a text box anywhere to add descriptive or other text. Position your cursor and start typing. When you are finished, make the text box transparent by double-clicking it. In the Format Text Box dialog box, under the Colors and Lines tab, use the transparency slider. You can also add decorative WordArt titles anywhere. Click Insert, Pictures, WordArt. On the WordArt toolbar, click the Format button (🖫) to view the Format dialog box, which includes a transparency slider.

Chapter 8

Saving and Printing Worksheets

After you complete the work of entering, analyzing, charting, and formatting your data, you can share it with others. Most often, sharing data means either saving it and sharing the file or saving it and sharing the printout.

The tips in this chapter make it easier to share your work with others. By saving a workbook as a template, you eliminate the chore of re-creating special-purpose worksheets in the future. By saving your workbooks in XML, especially in corporate environments, you give non-Excel users the ability to use and edit your Excel worksheets. The printing tips in this chapter focus on managing the printing of multiple-page worksheets and multiple-sheet workbooks.

In this chapter, you find out how to display dispersed cell ranges in one place, so that you can print them together. You also find out how to select multiple cell ranges and print them across several pages. Repeating row and column labels across several pages helps your readers find information. Finally, by printing functions along with the Excel-based row numbers and column letters, you can troubleshoot your functions.

The two key printing tools are the Page Setup dialog box and the Print Preview window. Spend time familiarizing yourself with the many choices they offer.

Chapter 9 carries forward the themes introduced in this chapter. There you find out how to publish interactive spreadsheets on the Web and learn more about exchanging data between Excel and other applications.

Top 100

Save a workbook as a
TEMPLATE

Templates are special-purpose workbooks that you use to create new worksheets. They can contain formats, styles, and specific content such as images, column heads, and date ranges that you want to reuse in other worksheets. Templates save you the work of re-creating workbooks that you use for recurring purposes, such as filling out invoices and preparing monthly reports.

When you work with a template, you edit a copy, not the original, so that you retain the original template for use in structuring other worksheets. Excel

worksheets ordinarily have the XLS file extension. Saving an Excel worksheet as a template creates a file with the XLT extension. You can create any number of templates and store them wherever you want.

To use a template you have created, click File, New. In the worksheet pane, click On my computer in the Templates section. After opening and using a template, Excel prompts you to give it a new name when you save in order to avoid overwriting the original template.

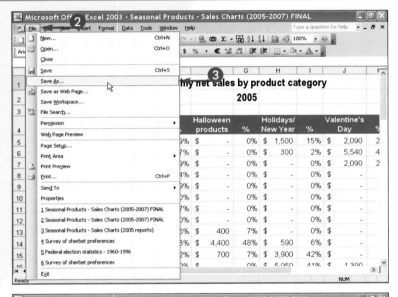

① Open the workbook you want to use as a template.

Templates can consist of actual data, column labels, and empty cells with specific number formats such as percentage.

② Click File.

③ Click Save As.

If the file has not been previously saved, clicking the Save button will open the Save As dialog box.

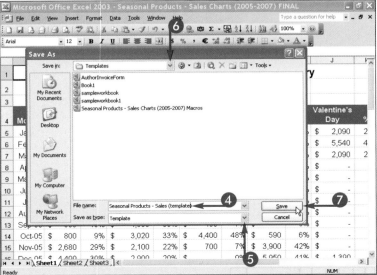

The Save As dialog box appears.

④ Type a name for the template.

⑤ Click here and select Template.

⑥ Click here and select the folder where you want to store the template.

Excel automatically keeps track of Excel templates regardless of where they are stored.

⑦ Click Save.

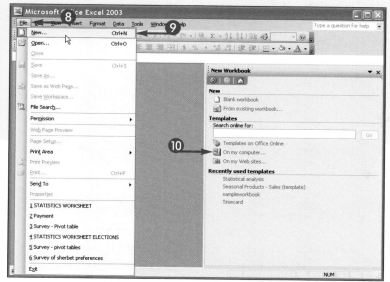

8 When you want to use the saved template, click File.

9 Click New.

10 In the New Workbook task pane, click On my computer in the Templates section.

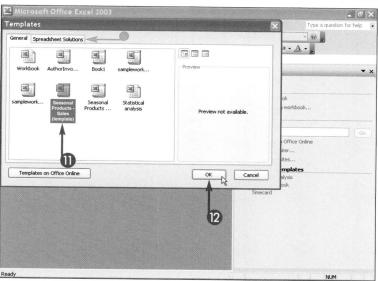

The Templates window appears, displaying templates you have made.

11 Click the template you want to use.

12 Click OK.

● Use the Spreadsheet Solutions tab for ready-made templates.

TIPS

Did You Know?

The Office InfoPath application provides template-like forms that you can use to structure Excel worksheets. You can read about this new application in Task #12.

Did You Know?

Excel comes with ready-made templates that serve basic business purposes such as invoicing. To open and use one of these templates, click File, New. In the New Workbook task pane, click On my computer in the Templates section. You can find the templates under the Spreadsheet Solutions tab of the Templates window. You can also find templates to download and use at the Microsoft Web site. Click File, New, and in the task pane click Templates on Office Online. For Excel templates, look in categories such as Finance and Accounting.

Save a workbook as an
XML SPREADSHEET

When you work in a spreadsheet and click Save, the document is saved as an Excel file and can be reused only by Excel, or a program that can read Excel files, or a database program. When you save a worksheet as a Web page, you can open the spreadsheet in any Web browser, all Office applications, and the countless programs that can read Web pages.

XML is an emerging standard that goes beyond HTML in many respects. Saving a spreadsheet as an XML Spreadsheet (XML-SS) enables you to make a spreadsheet available to any application that can read XML. Office 2003 is based on XML, and numerous business applications support the standard as well.

When you save as an XML, you have a choice of formats. *XML Spreadsheet* automatically applies a set of XML tags to your document that structure it as a spreadsheet, so that other applications can use it. *XML Data* gives you the option of applying custom tags to your document.

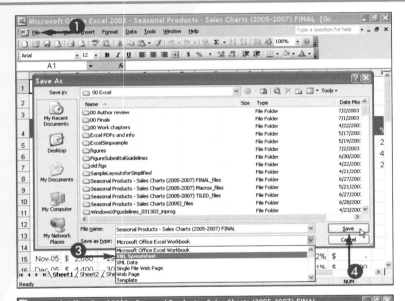

SAVE A WORKSHEET AS XML

1. Click File.
2. Click Save As.

   The Save As dialog box appears.
3. Click here and select XML Spreadsheet.
4. Click Save.

Your spreadsheet appears unchanged, but is now an XML Spreadsheet document, which you can share or continue editing.

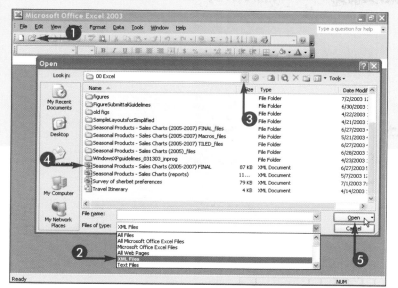

#78

① To open an XML document, click the Open button.

The Open dialog box appears.

② Click here and select the XML Files.

③ Click here and select the directory where the file is located.

④ Select an XML file.

⑤ Click Open.

DIFFICULTY LEVEL

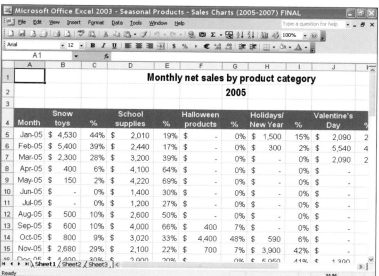

The document opens ready for editing.

Note: *If the XML List dialog box appears, click XML List to open and edit the document.*

TIPS

Did You Know?

When you open a workbook saved as XML-SS, it is indistinguishable from the standard Excel (XLS) format. Thus, in a business environment, you can use XML-SS as your standard Excel format. You can also use HTML as your standard format, but HTML generates a number of ancillary files that can be a nuisance to maintain.

Did You Know?

XML is an emerging data-exchange standard that has been of special interest to large organizations. Like HTML, XML allows you to apply tags to your content to determine how it looks. However, XML goes beyond HTML by allowing you to create custom tags that define every aspect of different types of content and to render it usable by many applications and devices.

PRINT MULTIPLE CELL RANGES
on one page

Using the Excel Camera feature, you can take snapshots of different cell ranges from different worksheets, combine them for viewing, and print them together. Using the feature requires that you add the Camera button to any one of your existing toolbars.

Using the camera is simple: Select cells to copy and click the Camera button. Unlike copying cells, the Camera does something very similar to taking a picture of them. It creates a single image of the

selected cells and their values, but it captures no information about the contents of individual cells — formats, formulas, and values. This means that when you paste an image, you have a single graphical image to work with. You can resize the image as a whole and drag it to a new position on a worksheet, but you cannot edit the values represented in the image. Note that you will likely have to resize the image to get it to line up with the grid lines of the worksheet cells.

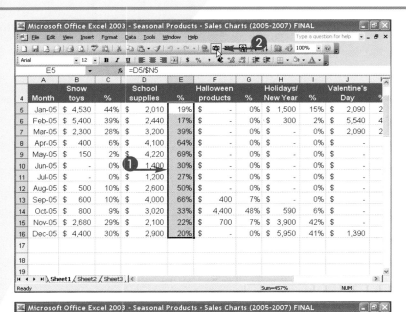

1 Click and drag the cells you want to copy to a new location.

2 Click the Camera button.

3 Click the worksheet tab where you want to place the cells.

4 Click the cell where you want to paste the image.

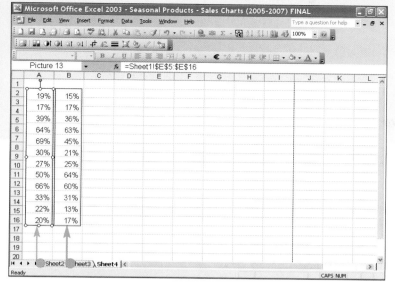

- The cells appear surrounded by selection handles. You can drag and resize the image.

- Repeat steps **1** to **4** to copy and arrange other ranges that you want to appear together.

#79

DIFFICULTY LEVEL

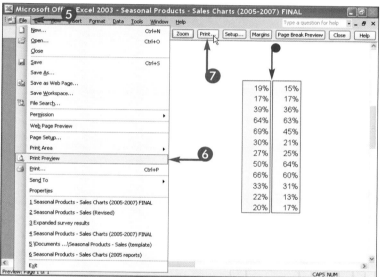

⑤ To preview what your cell images will look like when you print them, click File.

⑥ Click Print Preview.

- Excel displays the worksheet as it will look when you print it.

⑦ Click the Print button to print the image.

Your selected ranges print out on one page.

TIPS

Did You Know?

To add the Camera button (📷) to the toolbar, click Tools, Customize. In the Commands tab of the Customize dialog box, click Tools in the Categories column. In the Commands column, scroll down to the Camera button. Now click and drag it to any position on any displayed toolbar. To remove the Camera, return to the Customize box. In the Toolbars tab, click the name of the toolbar containing the camera, and click the Reset button.

Did You Know?

An alternative to using the camera is to select the cells you want to copy. Then navigate to the new location, press and hold the Shift key, and click Edit and then Paste Picture from the menu.

Did You Know?

You can copy cell images as pictures into other Office applications, where you can use them in presentations and reports. However, they lose their live connection to the Excel data. See Task #69.

PRINT MULTIPLE AREAS
of a workbook

Excel gives you flexibility in deciding which portions of a worksheet to print. For your long worksheets and multipage workbooks, this means you can print just what you need, so you do not waste paper but instead print only the information of relevance to you and others. This feature involves little more than selecting the *print area*, defined as the cell or cells you want to print.

Sometimes you may want to print out several print areas. For example, if you have several years of sales data, you can select the columns showing sales

for the same item over several years. To do so, you use the Page Setup box. In the Print Area field, click and drag to specify several ranges, separating each range with a comma.

When you print a worksheet with multiple selected areas, each area prints on its own page. This technique thus gives you an alternative to setting page breaks.

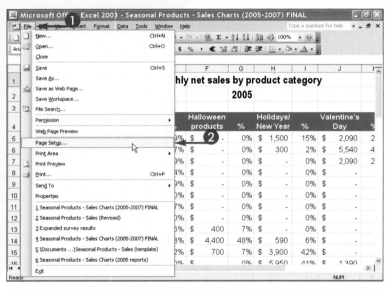

① Click File.

② Click Page Setup.

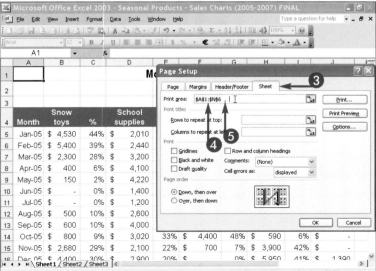

The Page Setup dialog box appears.

③ Click the Sheet tab.

④ Click and drag the first group of cells you want to print, or type the cell range.

⑤ Type a comma (,).

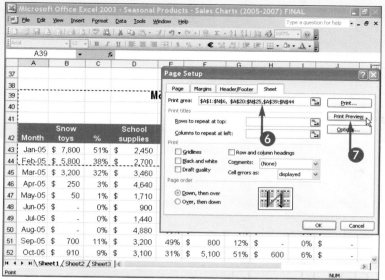

6 Repeat steps **3** to **5** for each area you want to copy.

7 Click Print Preview.

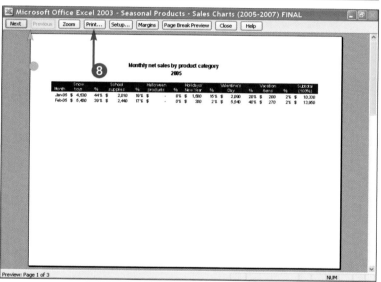

The Print Preview window shows the first page of the printout containing the area you selected in step **4**.

● You can press the Next and Previous buttons to view subsequent and previous pages.

8 Click Print when you are satisfied with the layout.

Did You Know?

If you need to print one worksheet per page, use the Page Setup dialog box to fit the worksheet to the size of the page. In the Page tab, Orientation section, first click Portrait if you have few columns or Landscape if you have many. Then, in the Scaling section, click the Fit to radio button and Pages spinner boxes to specify the dimensions of the printout, that is, the number of pages wide and tall.

Did You Know?

To add page numbers as well as a header or footer, or both, use the Header/Footer tab in the Page Setup dialog box. Click Custom Header or Custom Footer to automatically generate dates and page numbers on each page, and even add an image to the header or footer.

PRINT MULTIPLE WORKSHEETS
of a workbook

Excel prints, by default, either the entire active worksheet or a selected print area within the worksheet. You can also select several worksheets and print them all at the same time. You may want to select this option if you have created charts on separate sheets.

To select several worksheets, Press and hold the Ctrl key and click the relevant worksheet tabs in the lower-left corner. The sheets do not have to be

sequential; for example, you can Ctrl-click to select Sheet1 and Sheet3. Clicking the Print button prints all of the selected worksheets.

When you select several worksheets, any data you enter into a selected worksheet is also entered into cells of the other worksheets. On occasion, you may want to enter data into multiple worksheets at the same time, but you also run the risk of overwriting data in the other worksheets. When you need to use the same data in multiple worksheets, copying and pasting is safer.

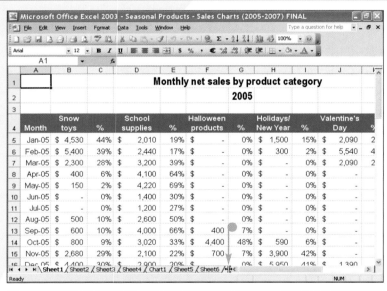

PRINT MULTIPLE WORKSHEETS

- To view all the sheets, click and drag the border to the right of the tab.

1 Press and hold the Ctrl key.

2 Click the individual tabs you want to print.

You can click Chart tabs, Sheet tabs, and tabs you have renamed.

3 Release the Ctrl key.

The selected tabs are white.

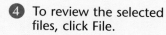

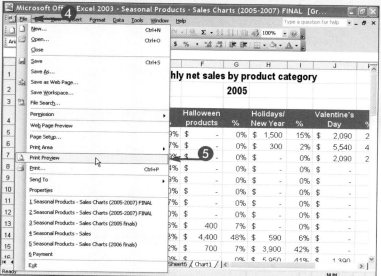

④ To review the selected files, click File.

⑤ Click Print Preview.

Monthly net sales by product category
2005

Month	Snow toys	%	School supplies	%	Halloween products	%	Holidays/ New Year	%	Valentine's Day	%
Jan-05	$ 4,530	44%	$ 2,010	19%	$ -	0%	$ 1,500	15%	$ 2,090	20%
Feb-05	$ 5,400	39%	$ 2,440	17%	$ -	0%	$ 300	2%	$ 5,540	40%
Mar-05	$ 2,300	28%	$ 3,200	39%	$ -	0%	$ -	0%	$ 2,090	26%
Apr-05	$ 400	6%	$ 4,100	64%	$ -	0%	$ -	0%	$ -	0%
May-05	$ 150	2%	$ 4,220	69%	$ -	0%	$ -	0%	$ -	0%
Jun-05	$ -	0%	$ 1,400	30%	$ -	0%	$ -	0%	$ -	0%
Jul-05	$ -	0%	$ 1,200	27%	$ -	0%	$ -	0%	$ -	0%
Aug-05	$ 500	10%	$ 2,600	50%	$ -	0%	$ -	0%	$ -	0%
Sep-05	$ 600	10%	$ 4,000	66%	$ 400	7%	$ -	0%	$ -	0%
Oct-05	$ 800	9%	$ 3,020	33%	$ 4,400	48%	$ 590	6%	$ -	0%
Nov-05	$ 2,680	29%	$ 2,100	22%	$ 700	7%	$ 3,900	42%	$ -	0%
Dec-05	$ 4,400	30%	$ 2,900	20%	$ -	0%	$ 5,950	41%	$ 1,390	9%

Preview: Page 1 of 4

● Each worksheet appears on its own page. Use the Previous and Next buttons to review the selected sheets.

⑥ When you are ready to print, click Print.

The selected worksheets print.

Did You Know?

When printing multiple *worksheets*, you may find worksheets that include both worksheet data and charts based on the data. To prevent a chart from printing and potentially blocking the underlying worksheet data, open the worksheet with the chart. Click the chart near its border to select it. From the Format menu, click Selected Chart area. In the Format Chart Area dialog box, click the Properties tab and uncheck the Print Object box. Click OK.

Did You Know?

To print several *workbooks* at the same time, click File, Open. In the Open dialog box, Press and hold the Ctrl key and click the workbooks you want to print. From the Tools drop-down menu in the upper-right corner, click Print.

REPEAT HEADINGS
of a row and column

By repeating your formatted row or column headings on multipage reports, you make it easier for readers to scan long reports for information. One worksheet must contain the row or column you want to repeat. The other worksheets must appear as the first row or column of every page.

To repeat a row, use the Page Setup dialog box to identify the row you want to repeat. To review where new pages begin — page breaks — click View and then Page Break Review.

TIP

Did You Know?

You can print row numbers and column letters on every page. In the print section of the Page Setup dialog box, click Row and column headings (☐ changes to ☑) before printing your worksheet.

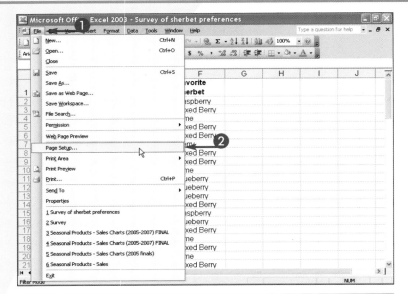

① Click File.

② Click Page Setup.

The Page Setup dialog box appears.

③ Click the Sheet tab.

④ Click and drag to select a repeating row, or type the cell range.

Optionally, you can click and drag to select a repeating column, or type the cell range.

The row and column headings repeat.

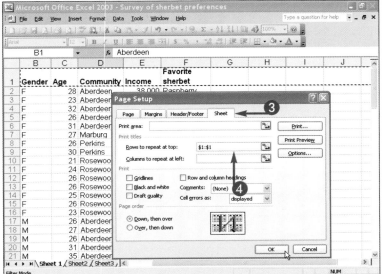

PRINT FUNCTIONS
to show calculations

By displaying and printing functions, you can troubleshoot your worksheets and share your calculations with others. Any cell whose value is based on a function displays the function instead of the value; all other data cells display the value. Because functions usually consist of operations applied to cells, you may want to display and print row numbers and column letters. When you print, a row of letters appears along the top and a column of numbers along the left; each column-row intersection (D3, A2) defines a cell address, which can help you in troubleshooting functions.

Did You Know?

To print all comments for a workbook, click File and Page Setup. In the Sheet tab of the Print section, select an option next to Comments. You can print comments adjacent to their cells or gather them at the end of the report.

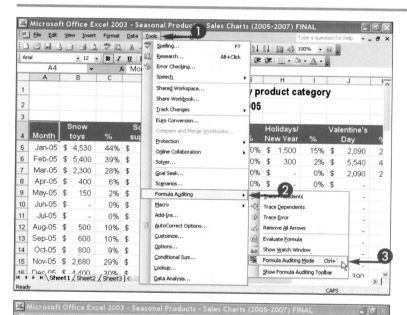

❶ Click Tools.

❷ Click Formula Auditing.

❸ Click Formula Auditing Mode.

Columns widen to display functions.

❹ Click the Sheet tab.

❺ Click Row and column headings (☐ changes to a ☑).

❻ Click OK.

❼ Click Print.

Extending Excel

Excel does not limit you to creating and maintaining workbooks and worksheets. Through data exchange, you can extend Excel in two ways. First, you can use data from other programs within Excel and apply worksheet capabilities to the data not available in the other programs. Second, you can use Excel data within other programs, thus extending the capabilities for using, analyzing, and presenting your data.

This chapter focuses on the techniques for querying Web sites and Access databases within Excel. A *query* enables you to bring non-Excel data, such as a Microsoft Access table, into Excel. After you create a query, you can sort, filter, analyze, and chart it, as you would any worksheet data. Queries are a powerful database tool for analyzing data sets. With minor changes, you can extend the tasks

in this chapter to data exchange with corporate databases based on Oracle, SQL Server, and other such products.

Less well known are the query features that enable you to query a Web site within Excel. You might query a Web site to import Web content into Excel, such as statistics that are presented as HTML tables and thus available in tabular format.

This chapter opens with hyperlinks, which enable you to create links from your worksheets to other worksheets and information in programs outside of Excel. Along the way, you learn to incorporate Excel data in Word documents, Access tables, and PowerPoint presentations.

HYPERLINK A WORKSHEET
to another Office document

You may be familiar with the many benefits of *hyperlinks* on Web pages. When you click one of these hyperlinks, or just *links*, you jump to a new Web page, with more links, creating an enormous and seamless web of information. Like most Office applications, Excel lets you create links, too. These links can take users to a place in the same worksheet or workbook, a document created by another Office application, or even a Web page.

Hyperlinking documents differs from linking objects, which you can read about in Task #69. Instead of

pulling data created by one application into Excel, a hyperlink enables you to jump from one worksheet to a related document. When you click a hyperlink on an Excel worksheet, you jump to a different document containing related information.

You can use hyperlinks to jump directly to a chart or PivotTable based on the worksheet. Or, you can link a worksheet to a Word document providing detailed information or identifying the assumptions used in the worksheet.

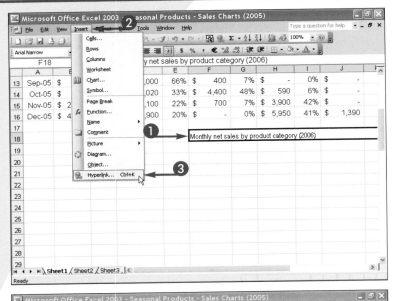

INSERT A HYPERLINK

① Click the cell where you want the hyperlink to appear.

② Click Insert.

③ Click Hyperlink.

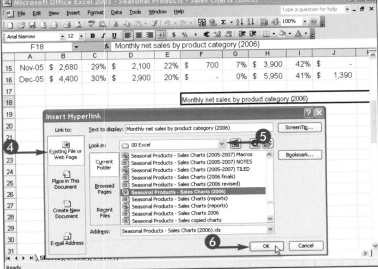

The Insert Hyperlink dialog box appears.

④ Click Existing File or Web Page.

⑤ Click here and select the folder with the Word document.

⑥ Click OK.

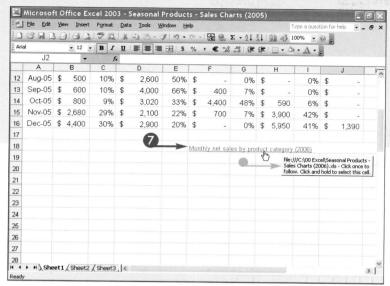

- The cell content appears as a hyperlink. You can pass your mouse over the link without clicking to see the name of the linked-to file.

7 Click the link to jump to the document.

DIFFICULTY LEVEL

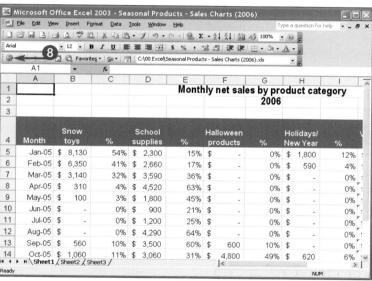

The linked-to document appears, and includes Excel's Web toolbar.

8 To return to the worksheet, click the Back arrow.

To remove the hyperlink, right-click the linked worksheet cell and click Remove Hyperlink.

TIPS

Did You Know?

Creating a hyperlink to a Word document provides an alternative to annotating worksheets using comments and text boxes. Unlike comments, Word hyperlinks can be of any length and complexity. Unlike text boxes, hyperlinks do not obstruct worksheets or distract readers.

Did You Know?

You can create hyperlinks from workbook images such as clip art and WordArt. Right-click the object, click Hyperlink, and use the Insert Hyperlink dialog box to select a destination in the same document, in other document, or on the Web.

Did You Know?

For interactive worksheets published online, as discussed in Task #89, include an e-mail link so users can send you e-mail. Click E-mail Address in the Insert Hyperlink box shown in step **4**.

EMBED A CHART
within PowerPoint

When you create PowerPoint presentations that include Excel charts and worksheets, you can edit your worksheets and modify your charts entirely within PowerPoint. Such control enables you to change your work as needed to demonstrate, for example, different business scenarios as you are giving a presentation. To do this, you *embed* your Excel chart or worksheet into your PowerPoint file. You can start with an existing Excel file or generate a new file entirely within PowerPoint.

When you embed Excel documents, the Excel worksheet or chart becomes part of the PowerPoint document and accessible only through it. However, the resulting PowerPoint file can become quite large in the process.

Embedding differs from linking. When you link a worksheet or chart to PowerPoint, you can edit the original Excel file from within PowerPoint, but the worksheet file remains distinct from the PowerPoint file. Changes made to embedded documents, however, affect only the PowerPoint file.

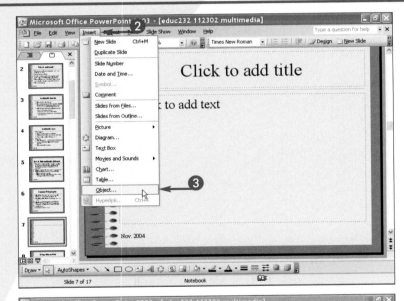

EMBED A CHART IN POWERPOINT

① Open the PowerPoint presentation to the slide where you want the chart.

② Click Insert.

③ Click Object.

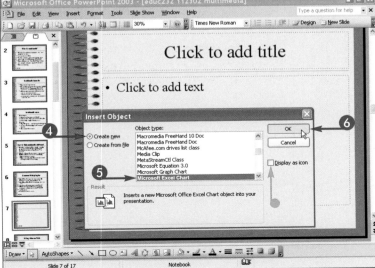

The Insert Object dialog box appears.

④ Click Create new to generate a new chart (○ changes to ⦿).

⑤ Scroll down and click Microsoft Excel Chart.

● You can click Display an icon to display a small icon enabling you to access the chart.

⑥ Click OK.

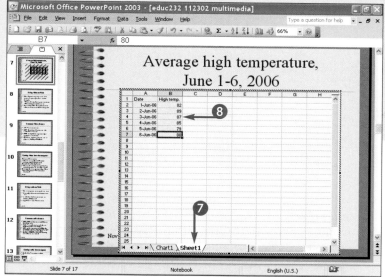

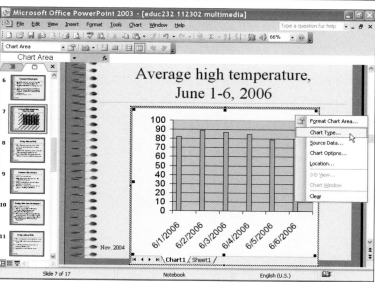

A chart based on placeholder data appears.

7 Click Sheet1.

8 In the worksheet, type new data.

Alternatively, you can copy data from another worksheet and paste it in the worksheet.

DIFFICULTY LEVEL

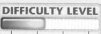

The chart changes to reflect the worksheet.

***Note:** To change the chart type and details, and add a trend line, see Chapter 6.*

TIPS

Did You Know?

When you create a new Excel chart in PowerPoint, you see a fake data set and associated chart. Change the data and replace it with your own, either by typing in new data or by copying and pasting data from part of an existing Excel worksheet. You can use the new or copied data as the basis of a chart, which you can modify as you would any chart. For more information on creating charts, see Chapter 6.

Did You Know?

If you click Create from file in step **4**, the dialog box changes and prompts you to type in a filename or to click Browse to select a workbook to embed.

Publish an
INTERACTIVE WORKBOOK

With Excel, you can publish your worksheets as Web pages that retain some of the features of the original worksheet. Saving an interactive worksheet on the Web lets you share your work with others. They can then carry out rudimentary spreadsheet operations such as summing numbers, inserting worksheets, sorting and filtering columns, formatting text, and editing data. Changes made to the Web-based pages have no impact on the original data, however.

Interactive workbooks have a toolbar that differs from the Excel toolbar. Sheets are available from a drop-down list instead of a series of horizontally arranged tabs. The toolbar includes only basic functions for summing, copying, pasting, sorting, and applying a small set of commands and options. The Export to Microsoft Excel button enables any user to save a copy of the page as an Excel workbook. To make the page available, you must upload it to a Web server.

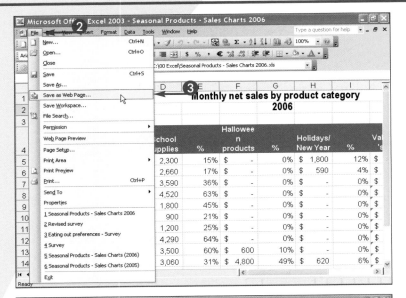

PUBLISH AN INTERACTIVE WORKSHEET

① Open the worksheet you want to publish on the Web.

② Click File.

③ Click Save as Web page.

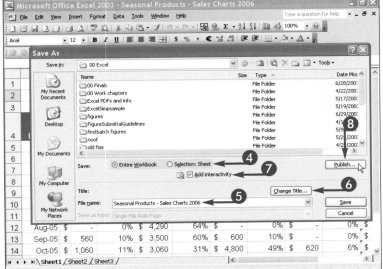

The Save As dialog box appears.

④ Click whether you want to publish the current worksheet or the entire workbook (○ changes to ⊙).

⑤ Type a name for the Web page.

⑥ Click here to type a title for the page.

⑦ Click Add interactivity (☐ changes to ☑).

⑧ Click Publish.

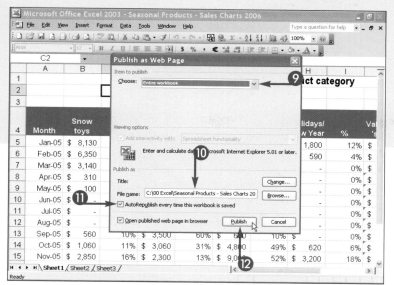

The Publish as Web Page dialog box appears.

⑨ Click here to select which elements to publish.

⑩ Confirm the filename and title.

⑪ Click to refresh the Web page every time you save the Excel workbook on which it is based (☐ changes to ☑).

⑫ Click Publish.

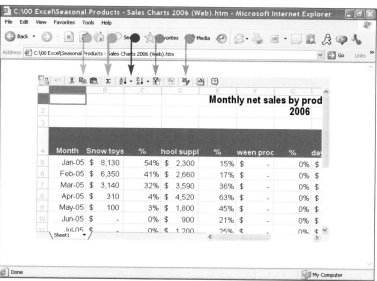

The worksheet appears in a browser.

● Cut, copy, and paste cell values.

● Sum selected cells.

● Sort selected cells.

● Filter a list.

● Save as a workbook.

Format data, use formulas, and add a worksheet.

TIPS

Did You Know?

When you choose Save As Web Page, you must choose a file type in the Save As dialog box: Web page or Single Web page. *Web Page* creates an HTML file that opens in any browser. *Single File Web Page* creates a proprietary Microsoft file that you can view only in Microsoft Internet Explorer version 5.01 or above.

Did You Know?

In Web parlance, a *title* is the text that appears in the browser title bar. It differs from the Web page filename, which is part of the Web address for your worksheet if you upload it to a server.

Did You Know?

To publish without interactivity, leave the check box in step **7** unchecked. The resulting worksheet appears without gridlines, clickable cells, or toolbar.

IMPORT A WORKSHEET
from the Web

Many government agencies, at all levels and around the world, make public statistics available on the Internet. Often, these business, census, employment, and related statistics are made directly available as Excel spreadsheets. You can open these Web-based worksheets from within Excel, edit them, and save them on your own computer.

Different Web browsers handle XLS files in different ways. Recent versions of the Microsoft Internet Explorer browser are capable of opening and displaying XLS worksheets. When you click a link to a

worksheet using MSIE or a browser based on it, such as AOL, you usually get the choice of opening the file in the browser or downloading and saving it on your hard drive. When you view a worksheet in your browser, you can save it on your hard drive by clicking File and Save, and then using the Save As dialog box to assign the file a name and folder.

The Netscape browser does not display XLS files, but it does give you the option of opening them within Excel or saving them as files on your hard drive.

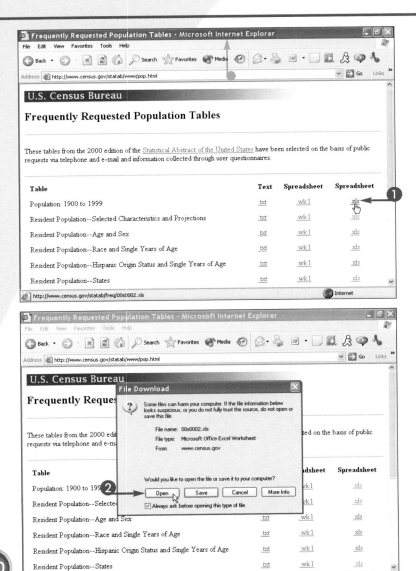

IMPORT A WORKSHEET FROM THE WEB

1 In a browser, click a link to an XLS file.

Usually, such links are labeled as such.

● This example uses MSIE version 6.0.

The File Download dialog box appears, giving you a choice of saving the file or opening it.

2 Click Open.

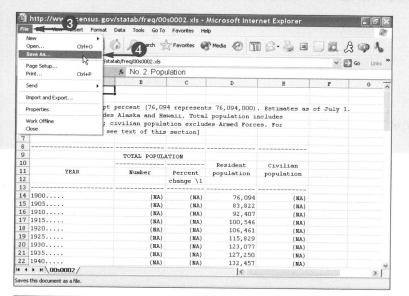

The worksheet appears in the browser.

No Excel controls appear.

③ To save the worksheet, click File.

④ Click Save As.

DIFFICULTY LEVEL

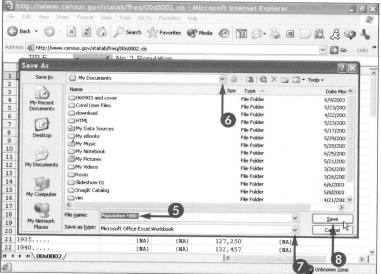

The Save As dialog box appears.

⑤ Type a name for the worksheet.

⑥ Click here and locate a folder to hold the worksheet.

⑦ Click here and select the Excel file type.

⑧ Click Save.

The worksheet is saved and can now be opened from within Excel using File, Open.

TIPS

Did You Know?

Worksheets formatted as Comma Separated Value, (CSV), files use commas to separate columns and double commas to indicate the end of a row. When you click Web links to such files, Excel should display the data without problem. You can also query the data by clicking Data, Import External Data, and Import Data, and then selecting the text as the file type. The Text Import Wizard prompts you to indicate whether the data is delimited, by what character it is delimited, and what data type to use for each column.

Did You Know?

When viewing a Web site through Internet Explorer, you can bring it into Excel to edit. Right-click a Web page and select Export to Microsoft Excel.

Query a
WEB SITE

You can find structured data in many forms on the Web, including online Excel worksheets and CSV files, as described in the previous task. Even ordinary Web pages can be considered structured if they contain tabular content — that is, rows and columns of numbers or other data.

Excel gives you two options for opening and using Web-based tabular data. You can use the File, Open command. Simply type or paste in a Web address to open a page containing the data. Or, into the Filename field you can import the data as a query

using Data, Import External Data, and New Web Query menu.

Both techniques allow you to view and edit numbers, but querying a Web site has advantages. Importing data as a query enables you to filter data, viewing only records of interest. A query also lets you refresh data if it is subject to updates. With the data in Excel, you have complete access to data analysis and presentation tools, including functions, pivot tables, and charts.

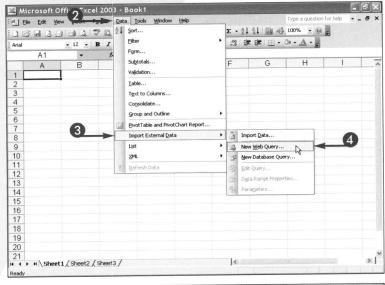

QUERY A WEB SITE

① Open a new Excel worksheet.

② Click Data.

③ Click Import External Data.

Note: The first time you click Import External Data, you may be prompted to install MS Query. If so, follow the instructions to do so.

④ Click New Web Query.

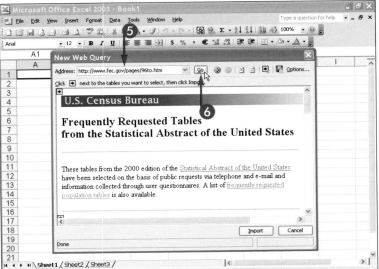

The New Web Query dialog box appears displaying a previously queried page.

⑤ Type or paste in a Web address.

This example uses www.fec.gov/pages/96to.htm.

⑥ Click Go.

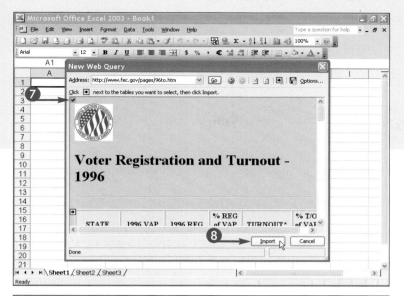

The Web page appears in the dialog box.

7 Click the elements you do not want to appear in your query.

A check mark indicates you do not want to query an element. An arrow indicates you want it.

DIFFICULTY LEVEL

8 Click Import.

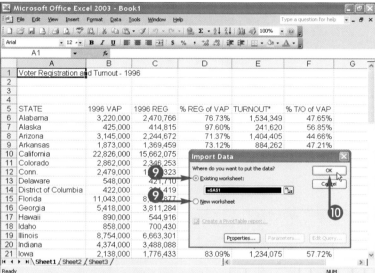

The Import Data dialog box appears.

9 Click to select a location for the page (○ changes to ◉).

10 Click OK.

The selected Web elements appear within Excel, ready for analysis, charting, and so on.

TIPS

Did You Know?

To find statistical data you need on the Web, you can do a Google search. You can download U.S. federal statistics in multiple formats from the official FedStats site at www.fedstats.gov/cgi-bin/A2Z.cgi. State and municipal data is also available in great abundance. You can find central access to this material at the federal compendium, FirstGov, available at www.firstgov.gov. Be aware, however, than many XLS files are also published as PDF files, readable only with the free Adobe Acrobat reader.

Did You Know?

A query is a file containing a definition of the data you import into Excel from an external source. The query definition indicates the data source, the rows to include, how rows added to the source are accommodated by the query, and the frequency with which the data is updated. You can view and modify query properties by clicking Data, Import External Data, and then Data Range Properties.

Query an
ACCESS DATABASE

Many organizations use more than one application to manage structured data. Excel shines in the area of managing, analyzing, and presenting numbers. Databases such as Access help you store, filter, and retrieve data in large quantities and of every type. With Excel, you can apply easy-to-use data analysis techniques with complex Access databases.

Database security and management features come at the cost of complexity. Instead of worksheets, in Access you must carefully organize your information into data tables, each of which stores information about one part of the entity of interest to you:

customers, products, employees, transactions, and so on. To help you keep track of these tables, Access enables you to create identifiers, called *keys*, and can automatically assign each customer, product, employee, transaction, and so on, a unique key. Tables are linked to each other through these keys.

Excel simplifies the use of highly structured Access data tables. When you import a database, you can select columns of interest from multiple tables and display the results in a single worksheet. The imported data set, or query, and can be easily refreshed.

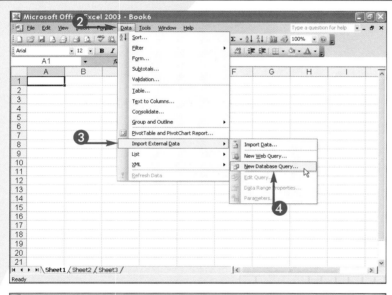

❶ Open the workbook where you want to view Access data.

❷ Click Data.

❸ Click Import External Data.

❹ Click New Database Query.

The Choose Data Source dialog box appears.

❺ In the Database tab, click a database type.

This example uses an Access database, which comes with Office.

❻ Click OK.

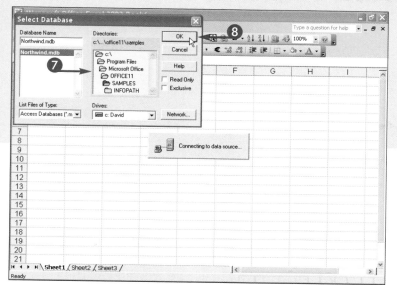

89

The Select Database dialog box appears.

The Connecting to data source message box appears on-screen until step 8.

DIFFICULTY LEVEL
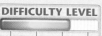

7 Click here and select the Access database you want to import from a folder.

8 Click OK.

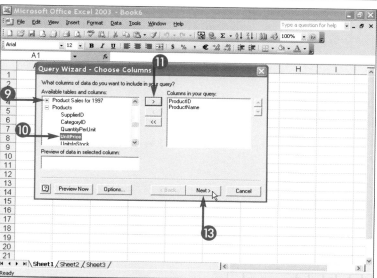

The Query Wizard - Choose Columns dialog box appears, listing database tables.

9 Click the Plus sign (+) to view columns in a table.

10 Click a column to use in query.

11 Click the arrow.

The column is moved to the pane on the right.

12 Repeat steps **9** to **11** to add more columns.

13 Click Next.

Did You Know?

This tip uses the Northwind database, a large database elaborated over many years and distributed with Access on the Office CD. The database includes information about the products, customers, employees, and other attributes of a fictional gourmet food store. To follow along with this tip, or to experiment importing and querying a database, you may need to install the database from the Office CD located in the Microsoft Access, Samples folder. After you install the database, it is available in the Program Files/Microsoft Office/Office 11/SAMPLES folder.

Did You Know?

You can apply the technique described in this task to any database that has an ODBC (Open Database Connectivity) driver, a standard interface. With Excel, you can query server databases including Oracle, Microsoft SQL Server, and desktop databases such as Visual FoxPro.

Query an
ACCESS DATABASE

The Query Wizard forms part of Microsoft Query, a separate application that comes with Microsoft Office. Microsoft Query is a *front end* that makes it easy for you to generate queries in SQL (Structured Query Language), a standard in the corporate world. The Wizard provides a point-and-click interface you can use to filter and sort imported data. After the data has been imported into Excel, you can use Excel's tools for further sorting and filtering.

You can go beyond the Wizard to directly manipulate the Access tables from which your query is to be drawn. Click View data or edit query in Microsoft

Query and then Finish for a graphical view of the underlying data tables. You can work directly with criteria fields, add tables, and connect tables by shared fields.

You can also run and view queries within Microsoft Query, instead of Excel. When you are done, you can save the query. That query becomes available in Excel for viewing, analysis, charting, and so on. For more information, see Task #90.

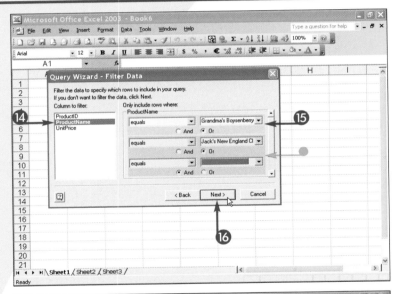

The Query Wizard - Filter Data dialog box appears enabling you to filter the database.

⑭ Click the column you want to filter.

⑮ Click a comparison operator and value from the drop-down menus.

● You can apply a second or third filter to a column.

⑯ Click Next.

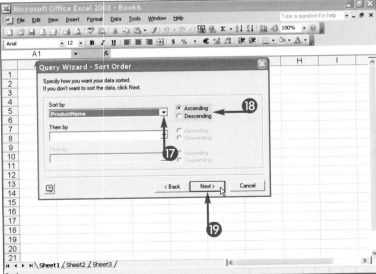

The Query Wizard - Sort Order dialog box appears.

⑰ Click here and select the column by which to sort the filtered results.

⑱ Click Ascending or Descending order (○ changes to ◉).

Optionally, you may make a selection in the second and third columns to sort *within* a sort. For each, click Ascending or Descending.

⑲ Click Next.

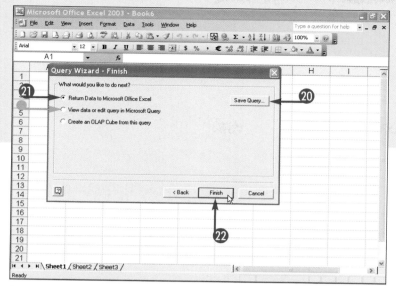

The Query Wizard - Finish dialog box appears.

⑳ Click here to save the query definitions to reuse them in the future.

89 CONTINUED

㉑ Click Return Data to Microsoft Office Excel to view the selected, filtered, and sorted data in Excel now (○ changes to ⊙).

● Click this option for the advanced SQL, filtering, and the table-linking options available in MS Query.

㉒ Click Finish.

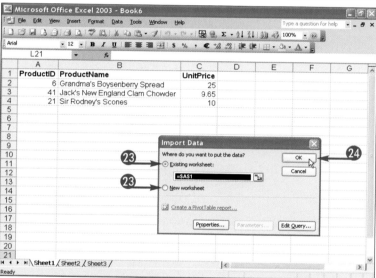

The Import Data dialog box appears.

㉓ Click to indicate whether to place the data in the selected cell of the current worksheet or in a new worksheet (○ changes to ⊙).

㉔ Click OK.

The imported data appears.

Did You Know?

Only one copy of Microsoft Query can be open at a time.

Did You Know?

Filtering data improves performance when working with large databases. Northwind, for example, exceeds Excel's maximum number of rows. Using Microsoft Query further speeds up performance. If you work with large databases and want to apply numerous filters and sort orders, MS Query is worth learning.

Did You Know?

You can quickly rerun the query by saving your query in step **18,** clicking Data, Import External Data, and then Import Data. If you will be processing the query in Microsoft Query — the option in step **20** — you can save the query from that program by clicking File and Save, or click the Disk toolbar button. For more information, see Task #90.

Reuse a
SAVED QUERY

Running a query has benefits relative to simply downloading a Web page or opening a database within Excel. For large pages or databases, you can restrict which parts of the page or which columns of the database to view and filter. By saving the query, you can quickly return to the queried data, refresh the data, and perform all worksheet operations, such as applying functions, using pivot tables, and creating charts.

Regardless of the data source, queries have a similar format. You can reload them quickly by clicking Data, Import External Data, and Import Data. You can

recognize saved queries by the icons used to represent them in the Select Data Source dialog box: Web queries ( ) and database queries ( ). While opening a saved query, you have the opportunity to review query properties and change them as needed.

You can import queries into existing or new worksheets. After you import them, they look like any worksheet. Saving changes in a workbook file leaves the original query definition untouched, so that you can reuse it later.

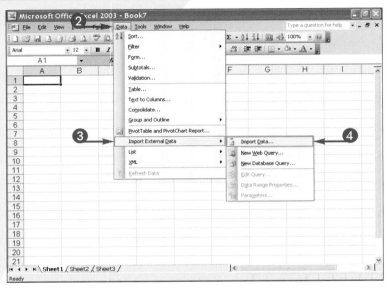

① Open a new Excel worksheet.

② Click Data.

③ Click Import External Data.

④ Click Import Data.

The Data Source dialog box appears.

⑤ Click a saved Web or database query.

⑥ Click Open.

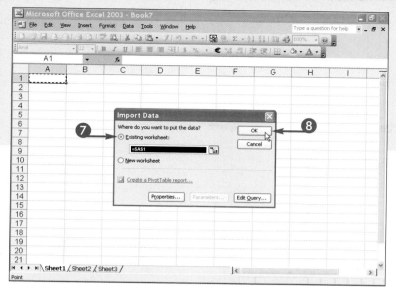

The Import Data dialog box appears.

7 Click to indicate whether to import the query into the current worksheet or a new worksheet (○ changes to ◉).

Note: When using a database query, click Edit Query to apply new filters and sort orders. Repeat steps **9** to **19** in Task #89.

8 Click OK.

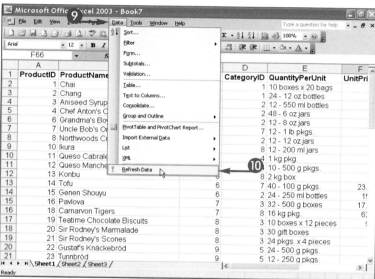

The query range appears in worksheet.

9 To refresh the data, click Data.

10 Click Refresh Data.

Customize It!

While using a query, the External Data toolbar gives you the tools required to refresh and edit the query, for example, the Edit Query button (🖼️), Edit Data Range Properties button (🖼️), and the Refresh Data button (🔲). To view the External Data toolbar, click View, Toolbars, and then External Data. Click the Edit Query button to return to the Query Wizard. You can add and remove the data you want to query. In the case of Web queries, click Edit Query to choose different items on the Web site to query. See Tasks #88 and #89.

External Data

IMPORT A WORKSHEET
into Access

Lists enable you to take advantage of basic database features like sorting and filtering within Excel. By bringing Excel lists into Microsoft Access, you can better manage growing lists by taking advantage of additional database features.

As a relational database, Access offers the benefits of integrated wizard and design tools that enable you to build customized forms, queries, and reports. Another benefit is size. Unlike a workbook, a database is, for practical purposes, limited only by the amount of available disk space.

Before importing a worksheet into Access, you need to format it as a list. Columns must have text headings, and cells may not be blank, as discussed in Task #34. Exported Excel lists should also avoid repeating information. For example, instead of including a customer's name and address in every record of a transaction list, you should split the worksheet into two lists: one with customer information, the other with transaction information. The two lists become, in Access, two tables linked by the customer field.

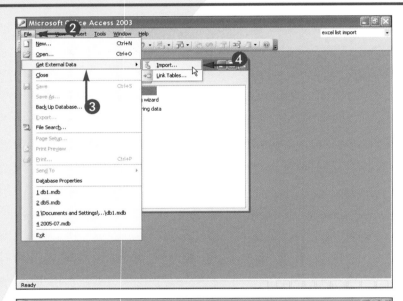

1. Open a new database in Access.
2. Click File.
3. Click Get External Data.
4. Click Import.

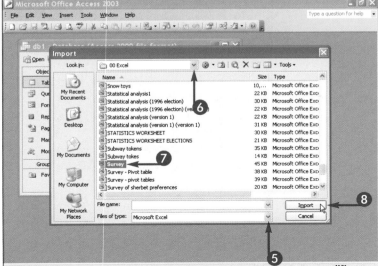

The Import dialog box appears.

5. Click here and select Microsoft Excel as file type.
6. Click here and select an Excel workbook.
7. Double-click to select a workbook.
8. Click Import.

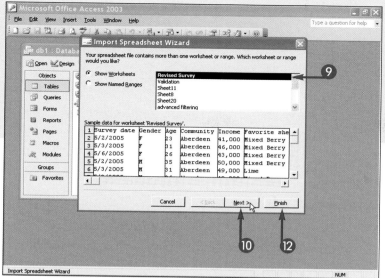

The Link Spreadsheet Wizard dialog box appears.

9 Click the worksheet to import.

10 Click Next.

11 In the next view of the same dialog box, if the first row of the imported data does *not* include column headings, clear the check box.

12 Click Finish to close the Wizard.

The Excel list appears as an Access database.

13 To view the worksheet within Excel, double-click the table.

● The Excel list appears as an Access database.

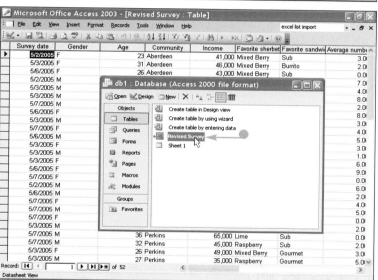

TIPS

Did You Know?

In addition to linking a list from Access, you can use a Microsoft add-in called AccessLinks to export it from Excel. You can find AccessLinks by doing a search at http://office.microsoft.com/ and install it as instructed in Task #93.

Did You Know?

On a network, conflicts can arise when more than one person tries to update the same record at the same time. Access resolves conflicts by enabling Access users to create replicas of the original database by clicking Tools, Replication, and Create Replica, and then synchronizing replicas and resolving any conflicts manually using the Access Conflict Viewer. More information is available via Microsoft Access Help by clicking F1.

Use Excel data to
CREATE LABELS IN WORD

Office applications have complementary benefits. Microsoft Word, for example, enables you to do just about anything with letters and language, while Excel provides a more structured environment for working primarily with numbers. Word includes a Mail Merge Wizard so you can *pour* the structured information from Excel into flexible Word documents of your own design. You can use mail merge to create mailing labels, form letters, printed envelopes, directories, and other useful documents.

The task has three major steps. First, create an Excel list consisting of addresses or other structured data. Second, use Word's Mail Merge Wizard to identify the features of the Word document into which you want to integrate the Excel list. Third, review and print the Word document.

You can use labels to create name badges, return addresses, CD labels, notebook tabs, business cards, and more. Choose a label option in Word, and Word automatically formats the output to fit the special-purpose labels for your printer, which you can purchase at any office-supply store.

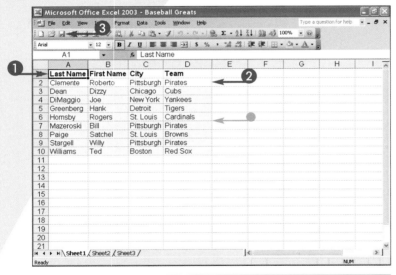

① To create an address list in Excel, type descriptive column heads for the task.

② Type in values for each column.

● Repeat steps **1** to **2** for each address, leaving no blanks.

③ Click the Save button to save your document.

④ Open a new document in Word.

⑤ Click Tools.

⑥ Click Letters and Mailings.

⑦ Click Mail Merge.

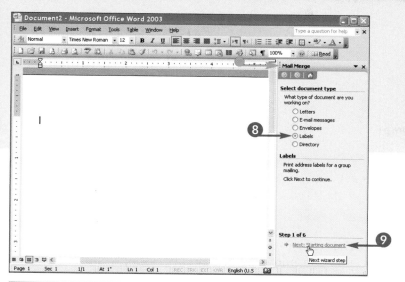

- The Mail Merge Wizard appears in the task pane.

⑧ Click Labels.

⑨ Click Next.

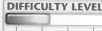

⑩ Select the type of printer you use (○ changes to ◉).

If Manual Paper Feed is not selected, you may want to select it instead of placing the labels in a tray.

⑪ Click here and select the label type.

⑫ Scroll and select a specific label.

⑬ Click OK.

⑭ Click Next.

The Word document is formatted into a grid corresponding to the label size selected in step **12**.

Caution!
Make sure to start Word in step **3** with a blank document. Otherwise, in step **11** Word attempts to overwrite the current document and use it as part of the mail-merge task.

Did You Know?
Make sure your Excel data is divided into small units such as Title. In this example, City and Team are separate columns because some cities, such as New York, have multiple teams, while others have teams whose names changed over time.

Did You Know?
In Step **2** of the Wizard, you can select a different Word document to use to hold the text for your labels by clicking Start from existing layout. When you do so, a new window appears in the task pane. Click Open to navigate to the file, and double-click the file you want to use for your labels.

Use Excel data to
CREATE LABELS IN WORD

The Mail Merge Wizard gives you many options as it steps you through the process of bringing Excel data into Word. Choices made early in the process constrain later choices, but at each step you can click the Previous link to modify earlier choices. Note that after creating the Excel list with addresses, everything else you do in this task takes place in Word.

In step 1 of the Wizard, you choose document type, such as a label or letter. In step 2, you indicate which Word document will contain your labels and you

select a label type. In step 3, you specify the Excel list with your address data. In step 4, you design your labels by dragging list elements into the Word document. In step 5, you preview labels, and in step 6, you print the results.

Special-purpose label paper costs more than plain printer paper, so you might want to run some trial printouts on regular paper. Also, some special-purpose papers require an inkjet printer and must be inserted a certain way, such as face down in the printer tray.

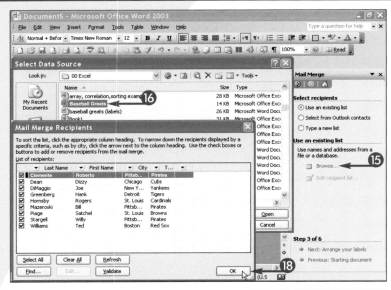

⑮ Click Browse to select your Excel list.

⑯ In the Select Data Source dialog box, locate the file and double-click it to open the Select Table Dialog.

⑰ Double-click the worksheet with your list.

The Mail Merge Recipients window enables you to filter names on the list and thus create labels for selected names. You may click the arrows to filter a column.

⑱ Click OK to continue to Step 4 of the Wizard.

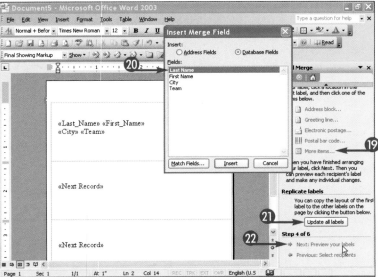

⑲ Click More items.

The Insert Merge Field dialog box appears, listing field names.

⑳ Double-click one or more field names to insert them into Word.

You may need to close the box to add a space between words or move down a line. To re-open the Insert Merge Field dialog box, repeat step **19**.

㉑ When you have selected the elements you want, click Update all labels.

㉒ Click Next to continue to Step 5 of the Wizard.

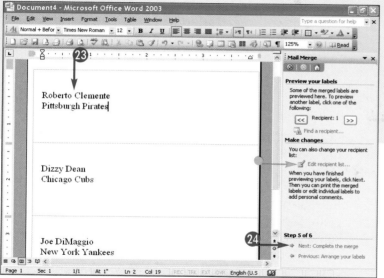

23 Preview your particular entries.

● Click here if you have a label on the list that you do not want to print.

24 Click Next to continue to the final Step 6 of the Wizard.

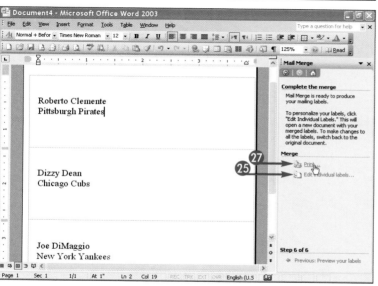

25 Click here and select individual labels to edit and include in a new document.

26 When complete, insert the label paper identified in step **12** into your printer.

You might want to do a trial run of part of the list.

27 Click Print when you are ready.

Your labels print with the information you requested.

Did You Know?

When creating an Excel list for mail-merge purposes, begin by identifying your data needs. For name badges, you may not need address information, but might need a new column called Affiliation. For shipping labels, you might need a customer ID number in addition to address information. For multiple tasks, you can use existing lists as templates to create new ones.

Did You Know?

You can download decorative label templates from the Web. Within Word, click File and then New. In the task pane, click Templates on Office Online. On the Web, click the Stationery and Labels category.

Customizing Excel

Excel, the standard graphical spreadsheet since the mid-80s, has a large number of integrated features that you can customize and adapt to suit your purposes. This chapter samples a few important ways in which you can customize Excel. For more ideas, consult the integrated help resources, which are always at your fingertips by pressing F1.

The simplest way to customize Excel is to install new features, called *add-ins*. This chapter shows how to install the add-ins included with Excel and how to find add-ins available from third-party developers.

Several tasks in this chapters focus on ways to customize workbooks. You can find out how to open Excel to a specific workbook or set of

workbooks and how to create, and switch between, multiple views of a single workbook. One view might apply special print settings; another might display, or not display, certain rows and columns; and so on. You also learn to create a workspace, so that you can control window size and positioning. Another task shows how to create custom formats for use in a workbook.

The task on macros introduces an enormous topic, which more than any other task enables you to extend and customize Excel. Then, you find out how to assign a macro to a toolbar button and create a button for it. Finally, you find out how to make Excel easier to *see* and thus easier to use.

Top 100

Add features by
INSTALLING AND USING ADD-INS

An *add-in* is software that adds one or more features to Excel. Tasks #54, #57, and #67 introduce a few of the statistical add-ins in the Analysis ToolPak, add-in software that is included with Excel but not automatically installed when you install Excel. Other Excel add-ins include the Lookup and Conditional Sum Wizards, both of which simplify complex functions. The Euro Tools add-in, also included with Excel, enables you to calculate exchange rates between the Euro and other currencies.

In addition, you can take advantage of third-party add-ins. This type of software adds functionality in support of advanced work in chemistry, risk-analysis, modeling, project management, statistics, and other fields.

You install one of the bundled add-ins using the Add-ins dialog box. The new tool, in most cases, is available right away from the Tools menu. Third-party add-ins usually have their own installation and usage procedures. Consult the developer of those programs for documentation.

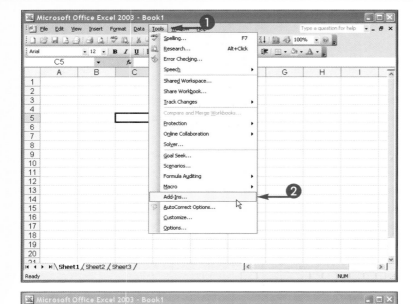

INSTALL THE ANALYSIS TOOLPAK

1️⃣ Click Tools.

2️⃣ Click Add-Ins.

The Add-Ins dialog box appears.

3️⃣ Click the Analysis ToolPak option (☐ changes to ☑).

4️⃣ Click OK.

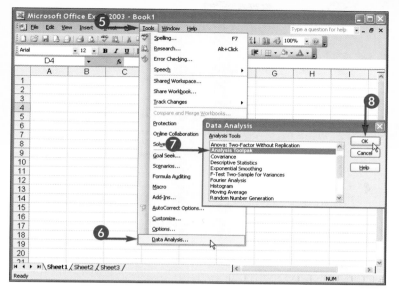

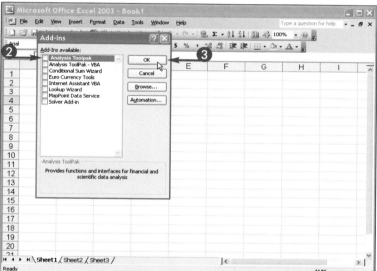

The Excel title bar may blink once during installation.

The new tools are now available.

⑤ Click Tools.

⑥ Click Data Analysis.

The Data Analysis dialog box opens and provides access to more than a dozen statistical functions.

⑦ Click a function.

⑧ Click OK.

Excel opens a dialog box for the function.

REMOVE THE ANALYSIS TOOLPAK

① Repeat steps **1** and **2** on the previous page.

② Click to uncheck the add-in (☑ changes to ☐).

③ Click OK.

Again, you might notice a brief blink in the toolbar.

The Tools menu no longer includes Data Analysis.

TIPS

Did you know?

Once you install add-ins, you can access them from the Tools menu. In order to view the entire Tools menu as well as all the commands on other menus, click Tools, and then Customize. In the Options tab of the Customize dialog box, click Always show full menus.

Did you know?

To learn about special-purpose Excel add-ins in your field, you can perform a Google search by going to www.google.com. Your search terms should include Excel, the field of knowledge, for example chemistry, and other information you might have, such as vendor name. Third-party vendors are responsible for supporting their own products.

LAUNCH A SPECIFIC WORKBOOK
when Excel opens

If you work every day on the same workbook, you might want Excel to automatically open it for you. When you launch Excel, you can have it open to one or more specific workbooks. You can make these workbooks standard workbooks with the XLS file extension, or workspaces, which have the XLW extension. A single workspace can encompass several workbooks. See Task #95 for more about workspaces.

To have Excel open to a specific workbook, you must save it in the following directory: C:/Program Files/Microsoft Office/OFFICE11/XLStart. Next time

you open Excel, the workbook opens automatically. If you keep several Excel workbooks in that folder, or a combination of workbooks and workspaces, they all open when you launch Excel.

The XLStart folder can also contain default templates containing formats, styles, and content that you want to apply to all workbooks or worksheets. For Excel to recognize a file as a default template in the XLStart directory, you must call it book.xlt, for a workbook template, or sheet.xlt, for a worksheet template. For more about templates, see Task #77.

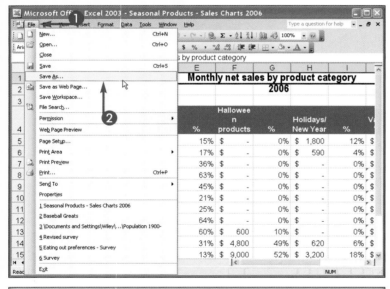

① Click File.

② Click Save As.

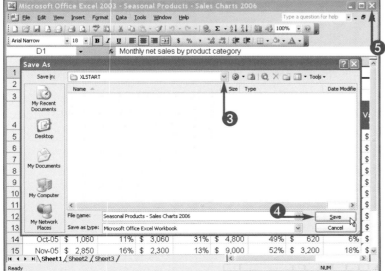

The Save As dialog box appears.

③ Click here and select XLStart.

Note: XLStart is usually located at C, Program Files, Microsoft Office, Office11, XLSTART.

④ Click Save.

⑤ Click the Close button to close Excel.

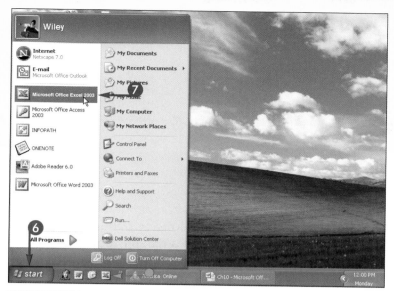

6 To re-open Excel, click Start.

7 Click Microsoft Office Excel 2003.

● Optionally, you can double-click the Excel icon on the desktop to open Excel.

94

DIFFICULTY LEVEL

All Excel files in the XLStart folder open.

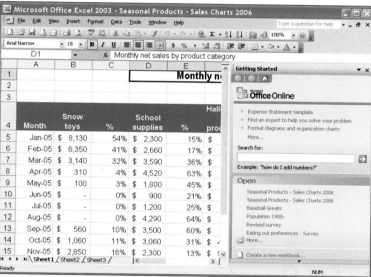

TIPS

Did you know?

When you save a workbook template, book.xlt, in the XLStart folder, it becomes your default for creating all new workbooks. A worksheet template named sheet.xlt becomes the basis of new sheets inserted into any workbook. You insert new sheets by opening a workbook and clicking Insert, Worksheet.

Did you know?

You can make another folder the startup folder instead of XLStart. In Excel, click Tools and Options. Then click the General tab. At startup, open all files in a field and type the path of your desired startup folder. Next time you start Excel, the files open.

Create a
CUSTOM WORKSPACE

95

When you use one or more workbooks, a *workspace* is the collection of all the settings that affect how each workbook *looks*. With Excel you can adjust several aspects of this look, and save the settings. The zoom settings affect how much of a workbook appears on your screen. By splitting and freezing worksheets, you can compare non-adjacent rows and columns. In addition, for any worksheet you can adjust row height and column width by clicking and dragging row/column borders. Opening a saved workspace causes all the workbooks with saved settings to open at the same time.

 TIP

DIFFICULTY LEVEL

Did you know?
By clicking Window and then Arrange, you can tile and cascade open workbooks, or have them appear as adjacent vertical or horizontal windows. After saving the workbooks as a workspace, you can restore these arrangements, along with each workbook's look, by opening the saved workspace.

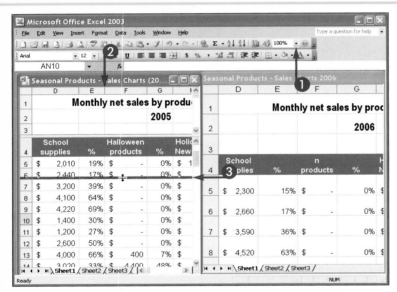

① Click a percentage to adjust cell size (Zoom).

② Click and drag column and row borders.

③ Split a worksheet by clicking and dragging the *Split box*.

Each setting applies only to the active worksheet.

④ Click File.

⑤ Click Save Workspace.

⑥ Type a name for the workspace.

Note: To automatically open the workspace, save it in XLStart. See Task #94 for more information.

⑦ Click Save.

Excel saves the workspace.

You can now open the saved workbook.

Although views and workspaces both affect the visual aspects of a workbook, *view* refers only to print settings and to the display of hidden rows, columns, and column filters. Custom views come in handy when you want to go back and forth between a workbook with frozen panes and the same workbook without frozen panes. Likewise, you can create separate views with different print settings. A view applies only to the workbook within which it was created. For more on workspaces, see Task #95. For more on frozen panes, see Task #7.

TIP

Did you know?

If you want to use repeating rows in your printouts, you can create one worksheet view that includes rows and another — for printing purposes — that does not. See Task #82 for more information.

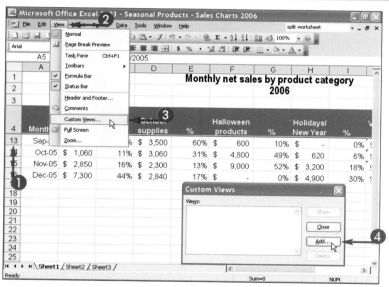

1 Hide rows in your spreadsheet.

   Note: To hide rows in a spreadsheet, see Task #8 for more information.

2 Click View.

3 Click Custom Views.

   The Custom Views dialog box appears.

4 Click Add.

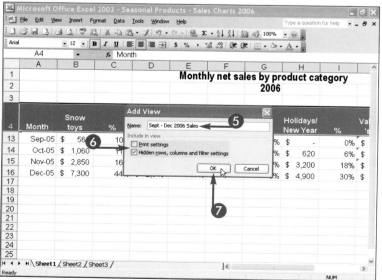

The Add View dialog box appears.

5 Type a name for the view.

6 Click an option to include print settings, hidden elements, or both (☐ changes to ☑).

7 Click OK.

   Excel adds the view.

   To use the view, open the workbook, click View and then Custom Views, and then click the name of the saved view.

Create a
CUSTOM NUMBER FORMAT

Excel provides many formats for presenting numbers, dates, times, currencies, and other types of information involving numerals. You can use these formats to create your own custom formats for specific purposes. For example, you may want to include the letters SSN before social security numbers or include an area code in parentheses before a telephone number.

Creating formats requires that you use number *codes*. Common codes include 0 or # to stand for any digit. For example, to represent a social security number, your code is *000-00-0000*. For a phone

number with area code, you type (000) 000-0000. In these examples, you just type numbers into the cell with the custom format; Excel adds the dashes and parentheses automatically. To code text, you simply place the text in quotes, for example: SSN 000-00-0000.

The best way to learn these codes is to study the ones included with Excel. Click any category in the Format Cells dialog box, and then click the Custom category to view the codes Excel uses for the built-in formats.

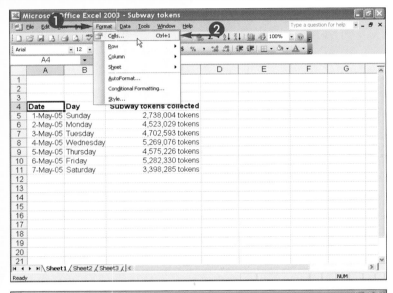

❶ Click Format.

❷ Click Cells.

The Format Cells dialog box appears.

❸ Click the Number tab.

❹ Click a category with formats similar to the one you want to create.

❺ Click a format type similar to the one you need.

❻ Click Custom.

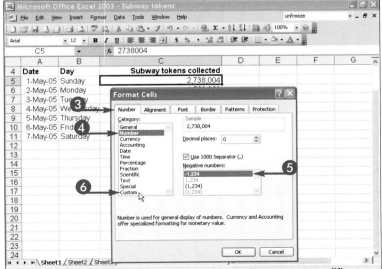

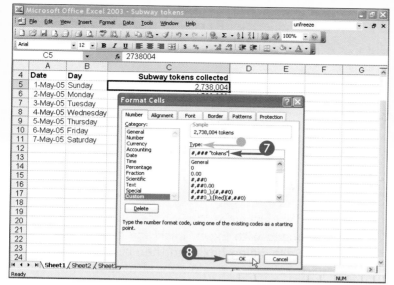

- The Type box appears in the dialog box.

7 Type the appropriate codes to represent your format.

Use a period (.) for decimal point and a comma (,) to separate thousands.

Note: See Excel Help for a complete guide to codes.

DIFFICULTY LEVEL

97

8 Click OK.

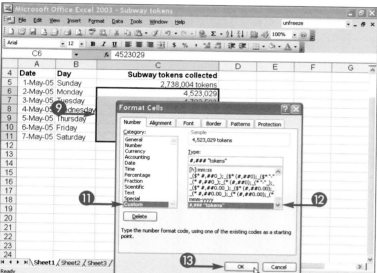

Your format now appears at the bottom of the list of Custom format types.

9 To apply the format, select one or more cells.

10 Repeat steps **1** to **2** to re-open the Format Cells dialog box.

11 Click Custom.

12 Click your custom format.

13 Click OK.

TIPS

Did you know?

To use a custom format in another workbook, copy a formatted cell from the workbook with the format and paste it into the workbook without the format. It then becomes available in the Format Cells dialog box.

Caution!

Excel correctly applies custom number formats as long as you type the correct number of digits. For example, for the format ##-##, if a user types too many digits, Excel correctly formats numbers starting from the right, but incorrectly formats the excess digits on the left. To mitigate the problem you can create an input message to guide users. With the cells selected, click Data, Validation. Click the Input Message tab, and type a message such as: **Enter numbers only. Use the ###-##-#### format. For example, type 123455555 for SSN 123-45-5555.**

Create a
MACRO TO FORMAT NUMBERS

A macro enables you to automate a common task, like entering a series of dates or formatting a column of numbers. You create a macro by recording each step of the task and then assigning all of the steps to a single keystroke. The user presses the keystroke to replay the steps.

To record a macro for a specific task, you turn on the Macro recorder, give the macro a name, assign a keystroke to it, and carry out the task. Excel records

every keystroke you make, along with every toolbar or menu command. When you are done with the task, turn the macro recorder off.

To run a macro, you select it from the Macros window. Alternatively, use the keystroke you assigned to the macro before you recorded it. Yet, another choice is to create a button to run the macro, which you can place on any toolbar. To find out how to create a button for a macro, see Task #99.

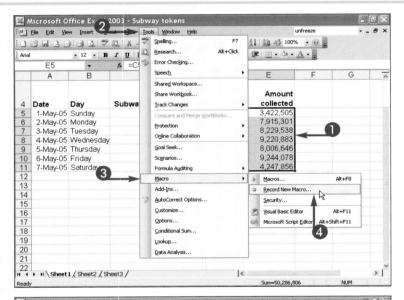

1. Click and drag to select a column of numbers.

2. Click Tools.

3. Click Macro.

4. Click Record New Macro.

The Record Macro dialog box appears.

5. Type a name for the macros.

6. Type a letter to assign a keystroke.

You can press and hold Shift and a letter to assign a capitalized keystroke.

7. Click to indicate the scope of your macro.

8. Click OK.

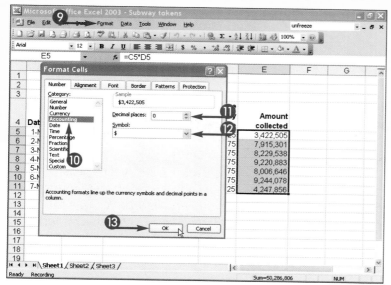

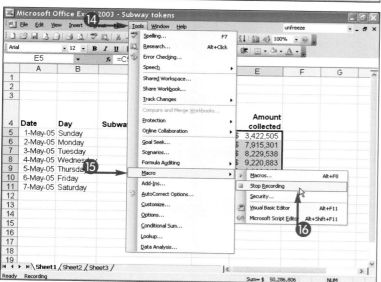

Excel starts recording every keystroke and command.

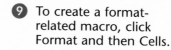
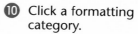

⑨ To create a format-related macro, click Format and then Cells.

⑩ Click a formatting category.

⑪ Click here and select the number of decimal places.

⑫ Click here and select the styling for negative numbers.

⑬ Click OK.

DIFFICULTY LEVEL

⑭ Click Tools.

⑮ Click Macro.

⑯ Click Stop Recording.

You can now apply the macro anywhere in the workbook by typing the keystroke from step **6**.

Did you know?

If a macro is not working, you may need to change security settings. Click Tools, Macros, Security. In the Security Level tab, click Medium or Low.

Did you know?

Macros are limited in the kinds of tasks they automate. If you have programming experience or aptitude, you can edit and enormously extend Excel macros using the Visual Basic Editor, available by clicking Tools, Macros, and Visual Basic Editor, or pressing Alt + F11.

Did you know?

A macro is available, by default, in the workbook within which you create it. To use a macro in other workbooks, select Personal Macro Workbook in step **7**.

Create a
BUTTON TO RUN A MACRO

You can create a toolbar button that you can click to run one of your macros. For a common task like applying a format, using a toolbar button can speed up your work and spare you the annoyance of repeatedly opening the same dialog box and clicking the same buttons.

To assign a macro to a button, you must first create the macro, as explained in Task #98. You must then drag an editable button to the toolbar. You finally assign a macro to a button and customize the button with a graphical design that represents the macro.

To add a button to any displayed toolbar, you must open the Customize dialog box. You click a menu in the left-hand pane of the Commands tab, click a command from the right-hand pane, and drag it to any toolbar. To edit the button, you must still have the Customize box open. Right-clicking the button opens a menu that lets you both assign a macro to a button, and to edit the button image.

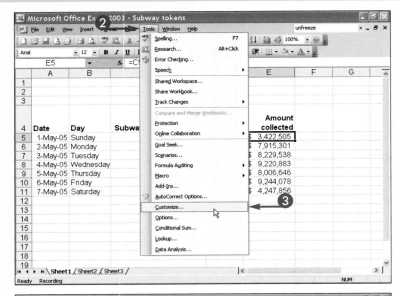

CREATE A NEW BUTTON

① Open a workbook containing a macro that you created.

Note: See Task #98 for more on creating a macro.

② Click Tools.

③ Click Customize.

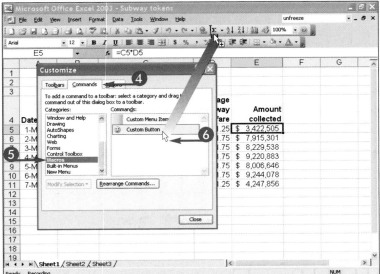

The Customize dialog box appears.

④ Click Commands.

⑤ Click Macros.

⑥ Click and drag Custom Button to the toolbar.

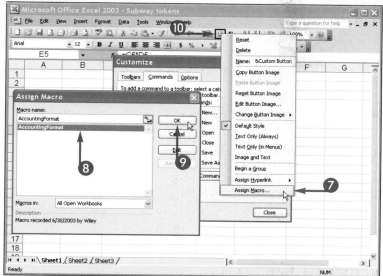

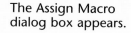

ASSIGN MACRO TO BUTTON

7 With the Customize dialog box open, right-click the button and select Assign Macro.

The Assign Macro dialog box appears.

8 Click the macro.

9 Click OK.

10 Right-click the new macro button and select Edit Button Image.

 # 99

DIFFICULTY LEVEL

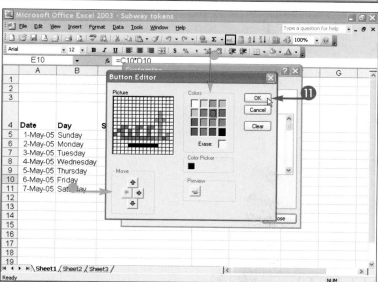

EDIT BUTTON IMAGE

The image appears in the Button Editor.

● Use the Colors section to edit individual pixels.

● Use the Move section to move the entire image.

Here, the image shows the stylized letters *acct*, short for Accounting.

11 Click OK.

Excel changes the image of the created button.

TIP

Did you know?

Using the Excel Button Editor, you can create your own button image. To do so, follow steps **1** to **11** to bring up the Button Editor. In the editor, you apply color by clicking one of the squares in the Colors section, then clicking a *pixel* — a tiny, square picture element — in the Picture section. Click the pixel again to clear it. Click the Color Picker to get a wider color range. To center the entire image, click the Move arrows in the lower left. The Preview box shows the finished button. Click OK to apply the image. The goal of making a button is usually to keep the image simple enough to represent a function clearly while also staying sharp at a small size, for example, when displayed at high screen resolutions.

Enlarge
SCREEN ELEMENTS

Like any Windows application, Excel requires eye-hand coordination. You must view menus, read dialog boxes, and then know where to click and what to do next. For visually impaired users, Excel can pose a challenge.

This task shows several ways of making Excel easier to see. First, you can increase the size of the toolbar buttons. Doing so makes it easier to see and thus to click these important buttons. Second, you can zoom in on a workbook to make cells and data appear larger. Excel makes it as easy to zoom out again as to zoom in. Finally, you can lower your screen resolution so that *everything* looks larger.

Combining these elements — enlarging buttons, zooming in, and lowering screen resolution — can all help people with visual impairments as well as those of us who get tired of squinting at the screen all day.

Chapter 1 included two additional tasks for making Excel more accessible. Task #9 shows how keyboard alternatives can take the place of the mouse in navigating workbooks, making selections, and using menus and dialog boxes. For those with a visual impairment, Task #10 shows how to enter data by voice rather than keyboard.

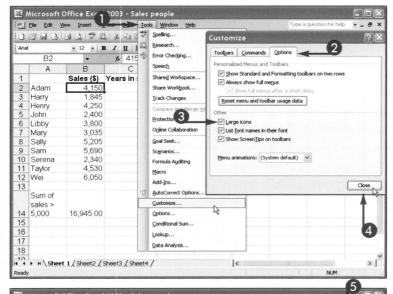

ENLARGE BUTTONS

1. Click Tools and then Customize.

2. Click Options.

3. Click Large icons (☐ changes to ☑).

4. Click Close.

The buttons appear bigger but also a little fuzzy.

5. Click here and select a percentage.

Page width fits your content to the dimensions of the Excel application window.

To use a custom percentage, type any number from 10 to 400.

Zooming occurs when you release the mouse button.

You can change the zoom percentage at any time.

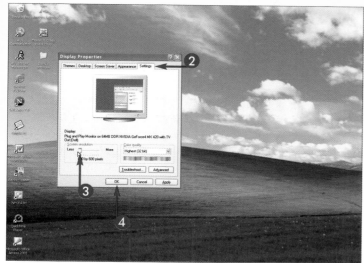

1 On the Windows desktop, right-click and select Properties.

The Display Properties dialog box appears.

2 Click Settings.

3 Click and drag the Screen resolution slider to the left.

4 Click OK.

After a moment, the new settings take effect.

● Enlarging icons makes toolbar buttons look larger.

● Zooming makes cells appear larger.

Lower resolution makes everything look larger.

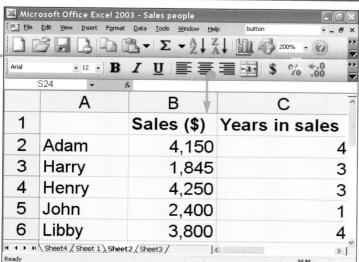

TIPS

Did you know?

To lower the screen resolution below 800 × 600, you use the Display Properties box, available by right-clicking the Windows desktop. In the Settings tab, click Advanced. In the new dialog box, click Adapter. Click List all modes. In the new window, click 640 × 480, True Color, or other setting. Click OK three times to close the open boxes and activate your selections.

Did you know?

Windows 98 and above offers accessibility features such as MouseKeys, which enable you to simulate a mouse using a numeric keypad. If your keyboard has a keypad, you can use it to click, double-click, and hold and release, as you would a mouse button. To find and use the wizard, click the Start menu, then Help and Support. Type **wizard** into the Search box.

INDEX

Symbols and Numbers

(pound signs) characters, error display, 57
(pound signs) characters, column display, 157
/ (forward slash) character, cell address separator, 154
{ and } (curly braces) characters, array functions, 49
+ (plus sign) character, addition operator, 30
< (less than) character, comparison operator, 48
= (equal sign) character, formula requirement, 30–31
= (equal to) character, comparison operator, 48
> (greater than) character, comparison operator, 48
100% stacked area, chart type, 133
100% stacked column, chart type, 132
2D area charts, error bar support, 141
2D line chart, missing data display, 139
2D pie chart, slice emphasis, 143
3D line chart, missing data display, 139
3D pie chart, slice emphasis, 143

A

AccessLinks add-in, Microsoft Access, 201
Account format, number display, 156–157
Add Scenario dialog box, cell selections, 122
Add Trendline dialog box, charts, 134–135
Add Views dialog box, 213
add-ins, 201, 206, 208–209
Add-ins dialog box, add-in installation, 208–209
addition operator, plus sign (+) character, 30
addresses. *See* cell addresses
Advanced Filter dialog box, 92–93, 96–97
Analysis ToolPak, 146–147, 208–209
area, chart type, 133
arguments
    `Correl()` function, 120
    `Countif()` function, 51
    `Date()` function, 59
    `Dcount()` function, 94
    defined, 28
    `If()` function, 48–49
    `IRR()` function, 44–45
    named constants, 40–41
    named range, 40–41
    `PMT()` function, 42–43
    `Product()` function, 55
    `Sumif()` function, 50–51
    `Vlookup()` function, 100–101
array functions, 49
arrays, defined, 47
Assign Macros dialog box, toolbar button assignment, 219
Autocomplete, described, 13
Autofill, 12–13
AutoFormat dialog box, PivotTables, 115
Autoformat, PivotTables, 115
AutoSum, calculation method, 30–31
`Average()` **function, 30**
averages, list sorts, 88–89
axes, chart element, 130–131

B

backgrounds, 117, 131, 164–165
bar chart, 129, 132, 141
bins, histogram definitions, 146–147
bitmaps, versus metafiles, 149
Black-and-White pie chart, 143
blanks (zeros), left-aligned values, 15
Blue pie chart, 143
borders, chart resize, 131
Button Editor, toolbar button creation tool, 219
buttons, 218–221

C

calculated fields, PivotTables, 112–113
calculations
    array, 47
    category subtotals, 88–89
    conditional formulas, 48–49
    conditional sums, 50–51
    constant uses, 39
    dates, 58–59
    filtered record counts, 94–95
    Function Wizard uses, 32–33
    Goal Seeking, 43
    internal rate of return, 44–45
    largest value, 46–47
    loan payments, 42–43
    net present value, 45
    PivotTable field average, 110–111
    round off values, 32–33
    serial values, 56–57
    text data type conversion, 60–61
    times, 56–57
    value methods, 30–31
calculators, 43, 52–53
Camera button, one page cell range print, 174–175
case, sort criteria, 87
cell addresses, 4, 8–9, 154, 181
cell ranges, 8–9, 124–125, 174–175
cells
    address conventions, 4
    Autocomplete entry conventions, 13
    Autofill entry conventions, 12–13
    color application, 165
    comment associations, 34–35
    constant entry conventions, 38–39
    described, 4
    Goal Seek selections, 124–125
    multiple named, 9
    name conventions, 8–9
    navigation methods, 4–5
    non-adjacent cell copy/paste operation, 72–73
    pick list value restrictions, 10–11
    PivotTable information summary, 113
    special character insertion, 14–15
    symbol insertion, 14–15
    value calculation methods, 30–31
    what-if analysis selections, 122

INDEX

INDEX

INDEX

Want more simplified tips and tricks?
Take a look at these
All designed for visual learners—just like you!

Read Less—Learn More®

Visual

0-7645-03619-2   0-7645-2580-8   0-7645-4393-8